The Teac...

in Spanish to the Bilingual Student
Second Edition

&❀☙

La Enseñanza de la Lectura
en Español Para el Estudiante Bilingüe
Segunda Edición

The Teaching of Reading in Spanish to the Bilingual Student
Second Edition

৪০ ❀ ৫୨

La Enseñanza de la Lectura en Español Para el Estudiante Bilingüe
Segunda Edición

Edited By

Angela Carrasquillo
Fordham University

Philip Segan
Long Island University

LAWRENCE ERLBAUM ASSOCIATES, PUBLISHERS

1998   Mahwah, New Jersey   London

Lawrence Erlbaum Associates, Inc., Publishers
10 Industrial Avenue
Mahwah, New Jersey 07430

Cover Design by Kathryn Houghtaling Lacey

Library of Congress Cataloging-in-Publication Data

The teaching of reading in Spanish to the bilingual
student second edition = La enseñanza de la lectura en español para
el estudiante bilingüe segunda edicion / edited by Angela Carrasquillo,
Philip Segan. -- 2nd ed.
        p. cm.
    ISBN 0-8058-2462-6 (pbk. : alk. paper)
    1. Reading (Elementary)--United States. 2. Education,
Bilingual--United States. 3. Spanish language--Study and
teaching (Elementary)-- United States. 4. Hispanic American
students--Education. I. Carrasquillo, Angela. II. Segan, Philip.
    LB1573.T365 1998
    372.41'6--dc21   97-44951
                                                            CIP

Books published by Lawrence Erlbaum Associates are
printed on acid-free paper, and their bindings are
chosen for strength and durability.

Printed in the United States of America
10 9 8 7 6 5 4 3 2 1

Contents

Preface   vii

Introduction   ix

Poem: Punto Y Coma   xv
Thelma Guerra

1   Bases Teóricas para la Enseñanza de la Lectura en Español   1
Angela Carrasquillo

2   Research Summary on the Teaching of Reading in Spanish
to Bilingual Students   17
Andres Rodríguez, Jr.

3   The Teaching of Spanish Literacy Development   43
Angela Carrasquillo

4   Teaching Reading Comprehension Skills   71
Angela Carrasquillo

5   Integrando la Fonética en el Proceso de la Lectura en Español   87
Elma Azurdia

6   Métodos Más Conocidos en la Enseñanza de Lectura
en Español   101
Angela Carrasquillo

7   Spanish Literacy Development in the Content Areas   125
Philip Segan and Jaime Aquino

8   Teaching Reading to Bilingual Students With Disabilities   145
        Frances Segan

9   Recursos a Utilizar en la Enseñanza de la Lectura en Español   163
        Grisel López-Díaz

10 Spanish Reading Assessment   185
        Philip Segan

        Appendix 1: Competencies for Teaching Reading and Language
        Arts in Spanish   199

        Apéndice 2: Vocabulario Básico Relacionado
        con la Enseñanza de la Lectura en Español   205

        Author Index   213

        Subject Index   217

        Indice de Palabras   221

Preface

The first edition of this text, published some years ago, explained the purpose of presenting such a dual-language text in the following way:

> This book came about to meet the need of a group of Spanish reading professors looking for a college textbook. This group of educators met frequently to discuss Spanish reading issues and Spanish literature. They found no adequate compendium of readings which may serve as a curricular guide as well as a reference source for staff development. This professional group undertook the project of developing a college text for the instruction of Spanish reading and language arts.

In the years since the first edition, many of these issues have continued to be discussed and addressed. To the extent that it could, the first edition served to meet some of the needs articulated by these professionals. Although it enjoyed wide circulation as a preservice and in-service text at colleges and universities, the 1984 edition was no longer available by the early 1990s. Feedback from the field indicated that there was valuable information in the original text; but conditions, issues, and concerns for Hispanic learners were changing. And, with those changes, there was a need to provide an updated text that could respond to these emerging issues—including changes in assessment; greater sophistication and care in identifying and placing at-risk, special needs students; and new views of the development of proficiency in the second language, specifically in terms of the number of years needed to attain mastery in academic uses of English by limited-English-proficient students.

Addressing these issues became a major focus of this edition. A panel of editorial reviewers and consultants from Lawrence Erlbaum Associates provided valuable suggestions to the editors. And the editors themselves—still actively involved in staff development in the teaching of reading and bilingual education—took a long, hard look at the current status of bilingual education and reading theories. Armed with this new set of information, and guided by educational and pedagogical considerations, the editors contacted some of the previous contributors as well as some new researchers and educators. These contributors were asked to revise and update this text in order to make it relevant to the needs of teachers working with the large number of second-language learners throughout the country. The topics of discussion included: considerations about students with special learning needs, current reading methodologies, the concept of reading as developmental literacy skills, reading in the content areas, and the uses of technology in the enhancement of the delivery of instruction. These concepts are evident throughout the text.

We are grateful to all the users of the previous edition who made valuable suggestions about the usefulness of the text. We are thankful also to our students who have incorporated some of the strategies that we shared with their own students over the last decade. We were gratified to learn that so many of their students benefited from these ideas. Finally, we extend our deep appreciation to our colleagues who have contributed to either or both editions of this book. Without their expertise, so willingly shared with others, none of the successes mentioned by teachers in the past would have been possible; and, certainly, any future benefits should be attributed to these committed professionals.

—Angela L. Carrasquillo
Philip E. Segan

Introduction

Teaching children to read is obviously a priority in the educational process. Having children learn to read is often one of the great difficulties faced by educators working with a diverse student population. Teachers bring a variety of backgrounds, experiences, and talents to their classrooms. At the same time, they recognize that the changing nature of the student body requires that their abilities, more than their technology, be constantly sharpened and refined. Teachers must adapt to meet emerging needs; they must respond to their students.

Adaptation and response do not mean, however, rejecting or eliminating those practices that have been accepted as successful in the past. Rather, teachers must build on those strategies and mold them—not the students—to produce the desired learning outcome (here, the ability to read with understanding and enjoyment).

Far too often, the teaching of reading has been pigeonholed or compartmentalized: It has been regarded as a subject "that anyone can teach," or as an esoteric endeavor characterized by eclectic, electric, and hectic approaches, machines, and personnel. Armies of specialists (i.e., clinicians, paraprofessionals, consultants) have been deployed with a vast array of hardware to mount an attack against the rising armies of nonreaders. But this merely treats the symptoms—often only the outward manifestations—of an inability to teach all children to read.

Most teachers have had their share of successes and failures in teaching children to read, and so they are constantly searching for new means—methods, materials, devices, or systems—to enhance progress toward universal literacy (if, indeed, such a goal is attainable). Teachers use what they know, and what they think they know, about the developmental processes of children, and then incorporate their best scientific, pedagogical know-how. And, from this potent mixture, they hope that what will emerge is a user of the language, a competent communicator, a deriver of meaning—in a word, a reader.

The dilemmas faced by educators in the past are not receding. The growing complexities of society in general and of urban environments in particular present new, more urgent challenges. Schools have become multicultural and polyglot communities. Previously used methods that were "successful" in teaching children to read may no longer be so. Those hit-and-miss activities that were unsuccessful have been abandoned entirely. And, the students now make new demands on teachers; more, perhaps, than teachers make on them. With these new demands comes a set of rightful demands. Parents expect teachers to teach their children to read as well as countless generations of youngsters were taught in the past. Colleges and universities are beginning to respond to these recognized needs. Teachers are being trained and retrained to teach in English these young learners, many of whom are non-English-speakers.

Universities, even those with bilingual programs in theory, methods, materials development, and the like (not including ESL exclusively) perpetuated the status quo by training pre- and in-service teaching using traditional, English-language, Anglo-oriented materials. Small wonder then that the teacher—monolingual or even bilingual—was faced with a seemingly impossible task in the classroom where perhaps one half or more of the students could not function in the language in which the materials were written. Yet, these very teachers were expected to teach these students to "read" only English-language texts; to pass English-language, standardized, Anglo-normed achievement tests; and to succeed in an English-language society with too little emphasis, if any, on the maintenance of their native language.

The individual who speaks more than one language possesses a cultural and linguistic advantage over those who do not have skills in a second language. Today, more and more people are going back to school to learn another language in order to be able to succeed professionally and to be able to relate to other groups in other cultures. Moreover, in the United States, advocates of bilingual education emphasize the need to not only learn English, but also to maintain the student's native language and culture. Therefore, bilingual teachers must be able to teach students to read in both languages. Qualified, prepared bilingual teachers are needed in order to adequately present the curriculum in the student's native language. Therefore, factors in the consideration of teachers for bilingual/bicultural programs would include their comprehensive knowledge of, and proficiency in, the student's native language, as well as the ability to teach content through it.

What this text presents to the reader—the pre- or in-service teacher, the university instructor, the administrator, the parent—is a new, dual-language text in theory and methodology of teaching reading in Spanish to language-minority, Hispanic youngsters who are increasing in number in schools across the nation. This is not a traditional reading text, and there are many excellent ones now available that are well-suited to the needs of many students. These texts provide thoughtful, sound pedagogical techniques for teaching English-speaking children to read better; and they may even include a section or subsection devoted to the "problems" of teaching reading to limited-English or non-English-speaking students. Some even take a sympathetic viewpoint toward these learners and devote a sensitive, well-written set of suggestions for meeting their needs.

What is offered here, rather, is a text that has at its very core the *hispano-parlantes*, the Spanish-speaking youngsters who, with their native language and cultures, bring to the schools a wealth of resources that must be tapped and to which educators have a responsibility to respond.

This text, true to the concepts of developing bilingual educators to serve bilingual students, presents chapters in English and Spanish. It does not offer a typical translation text consisting of a series of chapters written in English to be followed by a translation into Spanish. Each chapter is written in only one language, either English or Spanish, at the preference of its author. However, in order to give the reader a sense of the equal importance of both languages, a bilingual approach is offered by providing an abstract in the alternate language of each chapter. Thus, to be successful with this book, the reader must be bilingual, for much of the important information presented is unavailable to the monolingual reader of either language. Never losing sight of the goal—teaching reading in Spanish to bilingual students—a series of focusing questions and follow-up activities appropriate for Spanish-speaking students is provided. These are not merely translations of existing activities and techniques designed for monolingual English students. At all times, this text is sensitive to the nuances of both the language and cultures of its intended audience.

The overall design of this text is a presentation of theoretical and practical suggestions for teaching the Spanish/English bilingual student. It is divided into 10 chapters. The contributors have provided a rich source of theoretical research essential to the building of practical and effective instructional strategies. In all cases, sample lesson plans and/or activities are offered to provide the practitioner with a guide for developing similar, appropriate plans or activities for use with Hispanic students. Readers are free to utilize the suggested plans and activities as they are presented; it would be better, though, if they would modify or adapt them to meet the specific, identified needs of their particular students. Such changes will undoubtedly prove to be more responsive to the needs of their individual students than these more general plans.

ORGANIZATION OF THE BOOK

The 10 chapters in this text attempt to integrate theory and practice with the goal of providing the reader with practical applications of sound theory that has been the hallmark of successful practices in bilingual education in the past decade.

Chapter 1, "Bases Teóricas Para la Enseñanza de la Lectura en Español," presents an overview of the theoretical and philosophical reasons for teaching reading in Spanish in the United States. It discusses research and theory that recommends teaching reading in the students' native language. A set of recommendations is included at the end of the chapter.

Chapter 2, "Research Summary on the Teaching of Reading in Spanish to Bilingual Students," summarizes recent research and theory in the teaching of reading in Spanish in the United States. Although this research is scarce, the literature on teaching bilingual students provides meaningful information relevant to the teaching of reading to students participating in bilingual education.

Chapter 3, "The Teaching of Spanish Literacy Development," provides a rationale for the integration of the four processes of language. Theory, research, and methodological strategies are discussed throughout the chapter.

Chapter 4, "Teaching Reading Comprehension Skills," defines reading comprehension, and lists and discusses those areas of comprehension that students need to master in order to succeed in school.

Chapter 5, "Integrando la Fonética en el Proceso de la Lectura en Español," provides several methodological applications of Spanish phonics. The content of phonics and reading are intertwined, in the same way that the methodology of teaching them should be approached in the teaching/learning process.

Chapter 6, "Métodos Más Conocidos en la Enseñanza de la Lectura en Español," presents a brief overview of the historical development of reading methodology. The characteristics of each method are mentioned, recommending an eclectic approach and using those strategies that are successful in meeting the individual needs of bilingual students.

Chapter 7, "Spanish Literacy Development in the Content Areas," discusses the reading skills necessary for the successful mastery of concepts and skills in content-area classrooms by the bilingual learner. Examples of reading skills and concepts in typical mathematics texts are presented.

Chapter 8, "Teaching Reading to Bilingual Students with Disabilities," focuses on today's emphasis on teaching to the strengths, as well as meeting the needs, of bilingual learners with disabilities. Instructional strategies and examples are provided.

Chapter 9, "Recursos a Utilizar en la Enseñanza de la Lectura en Español," describes the resources available for the teaching of vocabulary in Spanish, ranging from the classroom library to the computer. The availability of many resources creates a classroom atmosphere that motivates students to read and learn.

Chapter 10, "Spanish Reading Assessment," describes traditionally used, standardized tests and criterion-referenced assessments. Difficulties associated with making accurate judgments about the actual performance levels of bilingual learners using these evaluation devices are addressed. The chapter also discusses such issues as class or grade placement decisions, presenting a series of suggestions for using such alternative evaluation procedures as portfolio assessments.

The book also includes two appendixes that serve as resources for the reader: "Competencies for Teaching Reading and Language Arts in Spanish" and "Vocabulario Basico Relacionado con la Enseñanza de la Lectura en Español."

Input and feedback from our readers is welcome. If plans or activities are tried out, offer up some feedback on how well they work (or do not work) and why. If modifications are made that improve their effectiveness in a particular setting, then share this information too. It is the intention that this text will fill a need—for teachers and students; even more, it is the fervent hope of those involved in creating this text that its responsiveness to these needs will help in the endeavor to provide effective, rich, and enriching instruction for Spanish-speaking students.

PUNTO Y COMA

En el cielo gris
de esta fría tarde,
observando las formas
de las traviesas nubes,
he visto claramente
un punto y coma.

¡Un punto y coma!
¿Qué uso tiene esto
en mi presente vida?
Quizás el que haga en mi vida
un punto y coma,
y piense un momento
en mi futuro.

¡En mi futuro! ¿Por qué en mi futuro?
¿Por qué no pensar mejor
en el futuro de tantos
niños faltos de cariño?
Niños que buscan en nosotros,
maestros y padres comprensivos
que les den calor y apoyo
para no naufragar
EN EL MAR DE LA ENSEÑANZA.

—Thelma Guerra
New York 1979

Bases Teóricas para la Enseñanza de la Lectura en Español

Angela Carrasquillo
Fordham University

Reading instruction plays an important role in the school curriculum. Teaching reading in the student's native language is highly recommended in bilingual programs. There are several psychological, linguistic, and sociocultural reasons for recommending the use of the native language in the teaching of reading. This chapter discusses research and theory that recommends teaching reading in the students' native language. It also discusses the implications of these theories and propositions on the teaching/learning process. A set of recommendations for the classroom teacher and the teacher trainer are included at the end of the chapter.

OBJETIVOS

Al terminar la lectura y estudio de este capítulo, el lector podrá:

1. Enumerar las razones por las cuales se dice que la lectura es un proceso complejo.
2. Identificar pre-requisitos necesarios a considerar en el acto de leer.
3. Establecer semejanzas y diferencias de varios tipos de estudiantes bilingües, en términos de su lengua nativa/dominante, grupo étnico y experiencia educativa.
4. Explicar por qué es necesario que el niño aprenda a leer a una edad temprana.

5. Mencionar razones psicológicas, lingüísticas y culturales por las cuales se recomienda que el niño bilingüe aprenda a leer en su lengua nativa/dominante.

PREGUNTAS GUÍAS

1. ¿Por qué se dice que leer es un proceso complejo?
2. ¿Qué competencias tiene que traer el lector al acto de leer?
3. ¿Por qué se dice que leer es algo más que descifrar símbolos escritos?
4. ¿Por qué es importante que el estudiante aprenda a leer a una edad temprana?
5. ¿Qué generalizaciones comunes se podrían considerar de los tres estudiantes bilingües presentados en el capítulo? ¿En qué son diferentes?
6. ¿Menciona tres razones psicológicas por las cuales se recomienda enseñar a leer en la lengua que el estudiante domina?
7. ¿Que relación existe entre las áreas que forman la estructura de la lengua española y el grado de dominio de éstas por un niño de habla española?
8. ¿Enumera tres razones sociológico-culturales por las cuales se recomienda aprender a leer en español a un niño que hable ese idioma.

EL PROCESO DE LEER

La lectura es vehículo primordial en el desarrollo formativo e intelectual de del estudiante. A pesar de que se han dado muchas definiciones acerca de "qué es leer" y se ha considerado la lectura en diferentes etapas filosóficas, es un consenso común que leer es un proceso complejo. Leer es un mecanismo psíquico-sensorial que envuelve una serie de procesos mentales, ambientales y psicológicos que ocurren a la vez (Carrasquillo, 1978, 1990; Cummins, 1981; Engle, 1975; Gómez del Manzano, 1986; Modiano, 1973). La mayoría de las autoridades reconocen que hay pasos/etapas a seguir en el proceso de leer y que estas etapas están íntimamente entrelazadas:

1. El lector reconoce la palabra por medio de unos mecanismos sensoriaales (visuales, auditivos y del tacto) y, haciendo uso de procesos cerebrales, le da significado a esa palabra o grupo de palabras.
2. Para darle significado a esa palabra, el lector hace uso de su memoria para relacionarla con el concepto que la misma expresa. Este concepto

se deriva de un almacén mental y de unos conocimientos previamente adquiridos.

3. El lector capta la información inmediata de ese pasaje, ya que sin comprensión no hay significado y sin significación no hay comprensión.

4. El lector utiliza esa información inmediata (comprensión) para extraer unas implicaciones o un razonamiento abstracto (interpretación).

5. El lector interpreta esa información en la medida en que sus sentimientos (actitudes, valores y características personales) se lo permitan.

6. El lector realiza una evaluación de esa información, con el propósito de determinar en qué medida es vàlida o adecuada la información provista o el intento del escritor.

Leer requiere interacción de las cuatro áreas de la comunicación: oír, hablar, leer y escribir. Esta interacción depende además, de una serie de factores que los estudiantes traen al proceso de leer. Estos factores individuaales varían de individuo a individuo. La siguiente figura menciona cuatro de estos factores.

Leer es un proceso activo y dinámico donde el lector construye el sentido del contenido a medida que avanza en el texto (Condemarín, 1989; Fabregat, 1989; Smith, 1988). La comprensión de la lectura depende de dos factores interdependientes: (a) las caraterísticas del texto, y (b) los conocimientos, habilidades y estrategias del lector. El lector tiene que traer ciertas competencias al acto de leer; entre éstas están:

1. El estudiante ha de tener un vocabulario adecuado y una buena estructura lingüística. Se dice que cuando el niño llega al primer grado debe tener un vocabulario oral mínimo de 3,728 palabras (Kaluger &

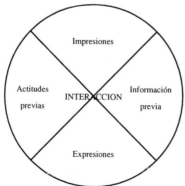

FIG. 1.1. Interacción de las Áreas de la Comunicación.

Kolson, 1969). Necesita conocer el significado de estas palabras y ser capaz de utilizarlas en sus conversaciones. El estudiante precisa entender lo que se le dice para poder hablar y ser entendido. Necesita saber que los símbolos escritos que él/ella ve, se corresponden en cierta forma, con su lengua hablada.

2. El estudiante necesita demostrar madurez perceptiva y conceptual. Debe traer una reserva de experiencias adecuadas para poder darle sentido al símbolo escrito. Necesita capacidad mental para poder trabajar con ideas y abstracciones, además de la madurez suficiente para concentrarse en el problema que se plantea. No se puede empezar a leer si el estudiante no reconoce de 40 a 100 palabras a primera vista.

3. El lector tiene que tener la suficiente habilidad para memorizar o retener las formas estructurales de las palabras en orden de secuencia. El estudiante necesita establecer semejanzas y diferencias en las formas visuales y auditivas de las palabras. Estas habilidades no se desarrollan en un año, ni en dos. El estudiante va haciendo uso del análisis estructural durante los primeros años de su niñez y va familiarizándose con el mundo escrito hasta dominar las seis etapas del proceso de leer.

Leer es más que descifrar el signifciado del texto. Leer es examinar un texto con varios propósitos, entre otros, para:

- asociar
- comparar
- identificar
- integrar
- ordenar
- organizar
- predecir
- relacionar

- clasificar
- concluir
- discriminar
- generalizar
- inferir
- interpretar
- resumir
- describir

La lectura en sí es un instrumento de aprendizaje que sirve para comprender la información, conceptos y contenido de cada una de las áreas del currículo. Se aprende a leer para conocer sobre historia, arte, ciencias y fantasías. La lectura informa, enseña, distrae y hasta permite el gozo y el placer por la lectura misma (Fabregat, 1989; Gago, 1982; Smith, 1982).

IMPORTANCIA DE DOMINAR LA LECTURA
A UNA EDAD TEMPRANA

La mayor parte del conocimiento impartido en la escuela se adquiere a través de la lectura. La sociedad en general le ha dado a la escuela la gran responsabilidad de enseñar a leer. A través de la clase de lectura, y de todo el currículo escolar, el estudiante continua desarrollando aquellas destrezas lingüísticas y gráficas que necesitará para adquirir los conceptos y las destrezas de las otras asignaturas del currículo, tales como estudios sociales, ciencias, gráficas y matemáticas (Gómez del Manzano, 1986; Smith, 1982; Weaver, 1988). Si el estudiante no sabe manejar el contenido literal y su significado, ni evaluar o predecir información, no podrá obtener resultados satisfactorios en estas áreas del currículo. Por lo tanto, la escuela deberá desarrollar buenos lectores tan pronto como le sea posible. En el año 1969, el entonces Comisionado de Educación de los Estados Unidos, James E. Allen, decía que la responsabilidad principal de la escuela era enseñar al estudiante a leer. Esa preocupación, además de comprobar que los estudiantes no estaban demostrando buenos resultados en los exámenes estandardizados, lo motivó a iniciar la campaña del *"Derecho a leer"* (*Right to Read*). Era su propósito el conseguir que todo niño terminara el primer nivel escolar como un lector independiente. Este proyecto fue financiado por el Gobierno Federal, ya que oficiales del mismo, especialmente la Oficina Federal de Educación, vieron la necesidad de promover la lectura de forma inmediata, a fin de que la escuela pudiera cumplir su función educativa. Ese programa ayudó a los niños de las minorías étnicas y lingüísticas en los Estados Unidos, especialmente a negros y a latinos (hispano-parlantes) a desarrollar destrezas básicas de lectura.

Nadie niega la importancia de la lectura. Varias organizaciones profesionales y educativas existen hoy día para fomentar la lectura y la enseñanza de la misma. Entre ellas, la Asociación Internacional de la Lectura (IRA); el Concilio Nacional de Maestros de Inglés (NCTE), y la Asociacion de Maestros de Español y Portugues (AATSP). En el área de las investigaciones, la lectura es una de las asignaturas que más se investiga. Un vistazo a las disertaciones doctorales en las escuelas de pedagogía revela que el tema sobre la lectura es el tópico primordial de investigación de los estudiantes doctorales. Instituciones y organizaciones sin fines de lucro continúan proveyendo incentivos para el estudio de la lectura, especialmente en la etapa inicial.

El leer puede considerarse también como una de las destrezas de la comunicación (Flores, K. Goodman, & Y. Goodman, 1979; Hymes, 1971).

El individuo expande conocimientos previos a través de la lectura. Leyendo, el individuo conoce el mundo a su alrededor. Es así como empieza a discernir entre lo que es correcto o no lo es; entre lo que es meramente opinión o un hecho científicamente probado. El hombre y la mujer no podrán conocer y darse a conocer si no pueden leer.

La pobreza en la lectura puede limitar el potencial del estudiante (Anderson, 1977; Dubois, 1995; Pérez & Torres-Guzmán, 1996; Smith, 1988). Se ha dicho muchas veces que la lectura es la base del conocimiento. Cuando un estudiante no puede leer al nivel de su grado, tampoco podrá hacer el trabajo que ese grado requiere que haga. Por lo tanto, no se le podrá exigir que haga el trabajo requerido en ese nivel, ya que no tiene las destrezas requeridas en la lectura. Cuando el estudiante se da cuenta de esta realidad, inmediatamente empieza a perder interés en el trabajo escolar, su asistencia a clases también se afecta, y poco a poco, su potencial mental va desapareciendo.

EL ESTUDIANTE BILINGÜE: TRES CASOS DIFERENTES

Al enseñar a leer, hay que reconocer que cada estudiante es un individuo con características y necesidades diferentes. Esta aseveración es todavía más cierta cuando se habla del "estudiante bilingüe." La siguiente ilustración muestra la dificultad que puede encontrar un maestro o el supervisor escolar cuando enseñan a estudiantes bilingües.

Imagínese por un momento que Ud. es un maestro bilingüe del nivel elemental/primario. Ud. trabaja en un programa bilingüe (inglés/español), en una comunidad que se caracteriza por tener un por ciento alto (la mayoría) de habitantes de habla española. El director de la escuela quiere pedirle asesoramiento sobre tres estudiantes que se matricularon hoy, y vendrán mañana por primera vez al salón de clases. El principal no les asignó clase específica a estos tres estudiantes, ya que quería discutir con Ud. dónde colocar a estos estudiantes, además del tipo de programa corresspondiente a cada uno. El principal lo cita a usted, a una reunión y al llegar a la reunión, usted se encuentra con un resumen del perfil descriptivo de cada uno de los estudiantes. ¿Qué programa de lectura recomendaría usted para cada uno de ellos?

Los tres estudiantes identificados indican un tipo de estudiante bilingüe diferente. Sin embargo, hay ciertas generalizaciones que se podrían aplicar a los tres casos. Los tres estudiantes han obtenido la mayor parte de su aprendizaje preescolar en español. Por tanto, el español viene a ser el mejor

Estudiante 1

Jesús es un niño de origen mejicano. Tiene 10 años. Llegó a los Estados Unidos hace cuatro años. Pertenece a un nivel socio-económico pobre. Es dominante en español pero se comunica en inglés, aunque con un poco de dificultad. Este estudiante asistía a la escuela en Méjico. Lee muy bien en español. También se comunica con un vocabulario amplio en español. En la entrevista con el principal, Jesús demostró que le gusta hablar y leer sobre su herencia hispano-indígena.

Estudiante 2

Xiomara es una estudiante que acaba de llegar a los Estados Unidos. Es oriunda de República Dominicana. A pesar de que tiene diez años, nunca había estado matriculada en la escuela. No tiene ninguna experiencia en la lectura. Su lengua nativa es el español y no tiene el más mínimo conocimiento del idioma inglés.

Estudiante 3

Alex tiene diez años. Nació en una de las grandes ciudades de los Estados Unidos. Sus padres hablan español. Él se comunica en español con los padres y en inglés con los amigos. Sus padres siempre hablan de volver a la tierra sudamericana. Su experiencia escolar incluye el haber estado en un salón de clases bilingüe, y en otro salón de clases donde toda la enseñanza era ofrecida en inglés.

FIG. 1.2. Estudiantes Bilingües.

medio para recibir instrucción. El español es para ellos, el método más espontáneo y natural de expresión.

El maestro debe recibir a los estudiantes tal cual ellos son, lingüística y culturalmente. La lengua que traen a la escuela es una parte esencial de ellos, de sus familias y de sus comunidades, y debe ser respetada y usada sin ninguna limitación. El currículo debe incluir aspectos de la cultura de estos estudiantes, ya que les servirá de motivación y estímulo para conocer otras culturas y comprender mejor el mundo en que viven (Carrasquillo, 1978; Gago, 1982; Schon, 1985, 1988; Smith, 1988).

El estudiante tiene que encontrarse cómodo en el salón de clases, sentirse que es parte del grupo, y que el grupo lo acepta. Barreras sociales, lingüísticas, culturales y educativas deben ser eliminadas por el maestro, si se quiere lograr que este estudiante lea con interés y logre desarrollar al máximo sus destrezas lingüísticas en el proceso de la enseñanza.

VENTAJAS PARA INICIAR LA LECTURA EN LA LENGUA VERNÁCULA DEL ESTUDIANTE

La lectura es un proceso complejo, pero muy necesario en el proceso de enseñanza/aprendizaje. Es recomendable que el estudiante aprenda a leer en su lengua vernácula, ya que a través de la lengua materna el ser humano aprende a formular y a expresar las ideas acerca de sí mismo, y del mundo que le rodea (Carrasquillo, 1990; Cummins, 1981; Dubois, 1995; D. Freeman & Y. Freeman, 1997).

La lectura es una de las asignaturas más importantes del currículo. Una preocupación común en los Estados Unidos ha sido, y todavía lo es, si a un estudiante que no domina el lenguaje inglés, se debe enseñar a leer inicialmente en inglés, que es el idioma de la escuela, o si se le debe enseñar a leer en la lengua que mejor domine. Este debate didáctico resulta aún más difícil de entender al revisar las investigaciones y no encontrar suficientes pruebas científicas en pro o en contra. Autoridades lingüísticas y educadores bilingües no se han podido poner de acuerdo en este debate, ya que hay una serie de factores que influyen en los resultados pedagógicos de estas dos tendencias educativas. Entre las autoridades educativas a favor de que se enseñe a leer en la lengua que el niño domina mejor, se encuentran Anderson (1977), Carrasquillo (1990), Cummins (1981), Gaarder (1977), y A. G. Ramírez y Castañeda, (1974). Es la opinión de esta autora que la evidencia en favor de enseñar a leer en la lengua vernácula del niño es más fuerte, de más peso, que la idea de iniciar la lectura en inglés, aún cuando el niño ya domina el inglés oral.

La búsqueda de identidad por parte del niño se inicia el mismo día que nace, y esta identidad comienza a hacerse realidad cuando el niño es acogido y mimado en el hogar (Anderson, 1977). Es la lengua materna, o sea la lengua que se habla en el hogar, la que en realidad lleva a cabo la gran tarea de ofrecerle seguridad y confianza a ese niño.

En los Estados Unidos se ha empezado a despertar conciencia de que no se puede cambiar drásticamente esa seguridad mental, cultural y lingüística que el niño ha adquirido durante cinco años, sólo por satisfacer una práctica mal cimentada del sistema educativo, al querer implantar la lengua oficial de la escuela a todos los niños, sin pensar en sus consecuencias educativas. Anderson (1977) ha dicho que el niño tiene, desde su nacimiento, el derecho a leer, y el niño bilingüe tiene el derecho a leer en dos idiomas.

Hay varias razones que justifican el uso de la lengua nativa en la enseñanza de la lectura. Entre estas razones se podrían mencionar aquellas de carácter psicológico, lingüístico y sociológico/cultural. A continuación se discuten cada una de estas razones.

Razones Psicológicas

Un programa efectivo de lectura debe responder a las características del estudiante en sus diferentes etapas de crecimiento, con arreglo a sus capacidades, intereses y trasfondo lingüístico y cultural. Además, la iniciación de la lectura se basa en una evaluación de la aptitud del niño para leer, determinada en gran parte por su habilidad en el uso del idioma en que va a aprender a leer (Gago, 1982; K. Goodman et al., 1979; Pérez & Torres-Guzmán, 1996). El estudiante ya tiene una base lingüística necesaria que le servirá de sostén emocional para enfrentarse a un sistema gráfico, completamente desconocido para él/ella hasta este momento. Sin embargo, el choque y el esfuerzo del estudiante no serán tan fuertes para él/ella, ya que estará aprendiendo a leer un sistema de símbolos escritos, para lo cual el estudiante ya tiene una referencia oral. Estará trabajando con una serie de sonidos con los cuales el estudiante ya está familiarizado o que puede entender con facilidad. Por tanto, las expectaciones al leer, con relación al dominio del vocabulario oral y de las estructuras lingüísticas serán reales y basadas en experiencias (Smith, 1982; Weaver, 1988).

El estudiante no tendrá que luchar con el dilema de adquirir conceptos fundamentales, a la vez que aprende una nueva lengua. El hecho de que el estudiante use en el salón de clases la lengua que domina mejor, en este caso el español, podrá eliminar sentimientos de que él/ella no puede hacer un mejor trabajo, ya que no entiende lo que se le quiere comunicar (Anderson, 1977; Carrasquillo, 1990; Condemarín, 1989). El estudiante puede seguir una secuencia apropiada en el desarrollo cognoscitivo, y ésto lo ayudará a desarrollar aquellas destrezas de lectura que necesita para poder desenvolverse en las otras áreas del currículo y progresar académicamente a la par que los demàs estudiantes de su nivel. El español será un acervo y no un entorpecimiento en su desarrollo académico.

El aprender a leer en español, le dará al estudiante motivación y seguridad en el aprendizaje, ya que tiene confianza en su habilidad mental, en su lengua y en su cultura. El estudiante disfrutará de un ambiente psicológico adecuado y agradable, aspectos indispensables para que pueda haber aprendizaje.

Investigaciones más recientes (Bennhardt, 1991; Collier, 1992; J. D. Ramírez, Yven, & Ramey, 1991) han determinado que existe un efecto psicológico dañino, cuando la identidad cultural y lingüística del estudiante no se toma en consideración en el currículo escolar. Además, se ha encontrado que los estudiantes funcionan mejor académicamente (Cummins, 1981; Gaarder, 1977; Pérez & Torres-Guzmán, 1994; A. G. Ramírez y Castañeda, 1974) cuando los maestros responden a sus características culturales usando éstas como punto de partida en el desarrollo de destrezas y conocimientos en el currículo académico.

Si el estudiante demuestra que su lengua dominante es el español, este estudiante debe aprender a leer en español. Más tarde, ese trasfondo le servirá como ayuda para leer en inglés, una vez los aspectos orales, de estructura, y suficiente vocabulario hayan sido introducidos previamente. Además, no se debe olvidar que la relativa regularidad del sistema escrito del español tiene una gran ventaja sobre el inglés para el estudiante que se inicia en la lectura.

Ya se ha dicho que el niño que procede de las minorías culturales y lingüísticas no tiene un sentido positivo de sí mismo, ya que la sociedad lo ve como un individuo diferente. El niño que viene de un ambiente cultural diferente es muchas veces visto en forma negativa por la sociedad, los maestros y los compañeros de su clase. Todas estas percepciones negativas contribuyen a sentimientos de rechazo, que muchas veces pueden llevar a una imagen negativa de sí mismo, y que afectará su trabajo académico. A. G. Ramírez y Castañeda (1974) investigaron 115 niños latinos en dos escuelas en Redwood City, California. De éstos, 58 asistieron a una escuela bilingüe; los otros niños fueron a una escuela donde sólo se les habló inglés. Los investigadores encontraron que la enseñanza bilingüe tuvo un efecto positivo en el desarrollo de sí mismo del niño y en el desarrollo de las destrezas orales del inglés. Los investigadores enfatizan que este desarrollo no se vio hasta dos años más tarde. Este descubrimiento se repite en estudios más recientes (Collier, 1992; J. D. Ramírez et al., 1991).

Razones Lingüísticas

El problema presentado en las acciones legales de *Lau vs. Nichols* en California y el Decreto por Consentimiento de *ASPIRA vs. Board of Education* en Nueva York, son dos acciones legales fundamentalmente de origen lingüístico. Estas acciones legales revelan el fracaso del sistema educativo en proveer instrucción adecuada a estudiantes que hablaban otra lengua ajena al inglés. En el caso de *Lau vs. Nichols,* esta ineptitud educativa violaba la Ley de Derechos Civiles de 1964 que prohibía la discriminación por motivos de raza, color u origen nacional en programas que estaban recibiendo ayuda federal. La Oficina de Derechos Civiles requirió que todos los distritos que recibieran ayuda federal llevaran a cabo una investigación con el propósito de identificar a los estudiantes cuya lengua materna fuera otra que el inglés. Al encontrar que había miles de estudiantes que vivían en los Estados Unidos cuya lengua vernácula no era el inglés, el aspecto lingüístico vino a convertirse en un aspecto socio-político y legal. Esta base legal fue usada más tarde en Nueva York donde, en 1975, se obligó a los distritos escolares a proveer instrucción en español a todos aquellos estudiantes que demostraran que el español era su lengua dominante. Se probó legalmente que a un niño no se le puede exigir que aprenda en un lenguaje que no domina.

Hay otras razones que determinan el que se use la lengua que el niño domina mejor, en este caso el español, para enseñar a leer a ese estudiante. Una de ellas es que el niño trae un sistema lingüístico completo. Tiene una buena base en el discernimiento visual; puede notar diferencias en la pronunciación de las palabras; un vocabulario adecuado y cierto conocimiento acerca de la estructura de las oraciones. El estudiante está más familiarizado con las áreas que componen la estructura de la lengua española, especialmente la fonología, la gramática, el vocabulario y la semántica.

El estudiante necesita demostrar que cuenta con el vocabulario suficiente para poder comenzar a leer. Si ya ha adquirido los conceptos; ahora necesita ver cuál es el sistema gráfico que se usa para escribir determinada palabra.

El estudiante está familiarizado con una serie de reglas gramaticales orales de su idioma. Este conocimiento le ayuda en la predicción del mensaje presentado. El estudiante conoce estas reglas por el uso y por inducción. Su conocimiento, aunque subconsciente, le ayuda a descifrar palabras y a reconstruir significados. Además, la habilidad para descifrar el español es más fácil que en el inglés porque las claves escritas son fonéticamente consistentes con el idioma.

Razones Sociológico-Culturales

El dominio de la lectura no sólo lleva a leer bien: Significa también la adquisición de un instrumento vinculado a la totalidad de la vida cultural del lector (Ministerio de Educación de Guatemala, 1989). La lengua española ha venido a ser el punto central de identificación entre los grupos

EL LENGUAJE			
Fonología	*Gramática*	*Vocabulario*	*Semántica*
(sonidos de la voz)	(hablar y escribir correctamente un idioma)	(significado de cada palabra)	(significado de lo que se dice, lee o escribe)
• vocales	• función de cada palabra en una oración	• concepto	• conceptos concretos
• consonantes	• etiqueta oral	• conceptos abstractos	
• sílabas	• sistema gráfico		
• diptongos			
• triptongos			
• entonación	• orden de las palabras en la oración		
• pronunciación			

FIG. 1.3. Areas del Lenguaje.

de habla española en los Estados Unidos. Sirve no sólo como medio de comunicación sino también como un símbolo actual de una herencia cultural única. Cuando la escuela no acepta que el estudiante use la lengua española como vehículo de comunicación, demuestra su intolerancia hacia el concepto de pluralismo cultural.

Se dice que el salón de clases debe ser una extensión del hogar. Y por eso, tanto a la lengua que el estudiante trae como a las características de su cultura, debe dárseles cierto reconocimiento en el salón de clases. Así se motiva al niño para desarrollar ciertas actitudes positivas de participación y responsabilidad comunal. Al comprobar el estudiante que el maestro también habla la lengua española, se afianza más su comunicación con él/ella, llegando a ser la misma, una comunicación más directa porque el maestro usará un medio verbal para comunicarse con ese estudiante. De esta manera, no sólo aprovechará mejor la experiencia de enseñanza-aprendizaje, sino que también será un puente para disminuir la barrera lingüística. Por lo tanto, las actitudes de los maestros deberán ser más positivas hacia la aceptación de la cultura del niño.

Al usar el español en el salón de clases, se le estarán dando uso a las experiencias culturales previamente adquiridas. Estas experiencias culturales se utilizarán en el desarrollo y refuerzo de conceptos. Así es que, el currículo a ofrecérsele a ese niño estará basado en realidades, ya que estas destrezas siguen el patrón lógico de las áreas de comunicación: o sea oir, hablar, leer y escribir. Además, los conceptos que han de ser aprendidos, tendrán su base en unas experiencias familiares para el estudiante.

El uso del español en el salón de clases y en la escuela le ofrece al estudiante la oportunidad de tener un sentido más completo de su propia identidad como un miembro más de su grupo cultural étnico, y de esforzarse en contribuir para conseguir una determinación cultural propia (Carrrasquillo, 1990; Gaarder, 1977). El estudiante comprobará que su lengua se respeta y se acepta en el salón de clases y en la escuela.

Allá para el 1975 el Instituto Nacional de Educación (NIE) en la Conferencia de Estudios de Lectura, enfatizó lo siguiente: "Schools have not generally been responsive to the unique psychodynamics of students from different cultural and linguistic groups and have usually attempted to force these students to conform to the mainstream sociocultural system. These attempts have resulted in value conflicts, anxiety, and frequent failure for these students" (p. 2).

Muchas veces, el estilo de aprendizaje del estudiante y el método de enseñanza del maestro no coinciden, creando barreras para el mejor desa-rrollo de destrezas cognoscitivas. El contenido del currículo usado para leer en la lengua nativa está basado en un enfoque multicultural donde se pretende que el estudiante desarrolle: (a) orgullo de su identidad cultural y racial, (b) valores positivos hacia las personas y culturas que le rodean, y (c) desarrollo de destrezas lingüísticas. Este currículo toma en consideración tanto el contenido como el proceso de la lectura para que el estudiante desarrolle destrezas de lectura y que, a la vez, mantenga sus raíces culturales.

CONCLUSIÓN

En este capítulo se le dio énfasis a los postulados teóricos que ven la enseñanza de la lectura en español como una necesidad lingüística, social y cultural. La lectura es un proceso complejo que envuelve una serie de mecanismos sensoriales, experiencias cognoscitivas y lingüísticas. El maestro no puede esperar que el estudiante lea de un día para otro. El proceso de leer toma su tiempo y exige paciencia por parte del maestro. Para poder leer, el estudiante tiene que tener un vocabulario adecuado, madurez perceptiva-conceptual y retención. Es responsabilidad de la escuela el determinar que el niño traiga estas competencias al acto de leer. Si este bagaje mental y lingüístico se posee en una lengua que no es la lengua de la escuela, ciertamente significa que el estudiante está mejor preparado para empezar a leer en esa otra lengua. La escuela debe investigar en qué idioma se comunica el estudiante con más frecuencia y mejor; en qué lengua es su vocabulario más rico y variado para así ofrecerle un programa de lectura en la lengua que el estudiante conoce y domina mejor.

El maestro debe aprovechar el trasfondo lingüístico y las experiencias que el estudiante trae al salón de clases. Es esta la razón primordial por la cual se recomienda que el niño debe aprender a leer en su lengua materna. No se debe ni se puede esperar hasta que el estudiante haya dominado todo un sistema lingüístico nuevo, especialmente el oral, para entonces enseñarle a leer a ese estudiante. La actitud del maestro y de los supervisores hacia la lengua materna del estudiante es sumamente importante y decisiva. En la escuela debe permear una actitud positiva, de respeto y de apoyo y no todos los estudiantes bilingües tienen las mismas necesidades educativas. Hay que proveerles un programa diagnóstico-prescriptivo al niño bilingüe para determinar su lengua vernácula, su experiencia escolar previa, su nivel de lectura, su dominio de la lengua oral y sus actitudes hacia la lengua española y la lengua inglesa.

EJERCICIOS DE APLICACIÓN

1. Explique si está o no de acuerdo con las siguientes aseveraciones identificando autoridades que están de acuerdo con su contestación.
   - La lectura es un proceso totalmente lingüístico.
   - Es a través de la lengua materna que el individuo aprende a formular y a expresar sus ideas sobre él/ella y sobre el mundo que le rodea.
   - Si un estudiante aprende a leer en español, cuando aprenda a leer en inglés, tendrá que volver a aprender a leer.
   - El currículo del programa de lectura debe estar basado en un enfoque multicultural.
   - Todo estudiante latino que reside en los Estados Unidos tiene que aprender a leer en español.
2. Imagínese que usted es un maestro bilingüe en un distrito escolar y tiene una presentación oral de cinco minutos la próxima semana en que debe presentar una posición teórica/filosófica del porqué hay la necesidad de enseñar a leer en español a muchos de los estudiantes latinos que asisten a escuelas en los Estados Unidos. Llene la siguiente tabla, como preparación para la presentación.

Razones psicológicas	Razones lingüísticas	Razones culturales
1.............................	1.............................	1.............................
2.............................	2.............................	2.............................
3.............................	3.............................	3.............................

3. ¿Como se podría explicar el hecho de que, a pesar de que los Estados Unidos han ha progresado muchísimo en áreas como las ciencias, la medicina y la tecnología, una gran cantidad de sus ciudadanos son analfabetos?

REFERENCIAS

Anderson, T. (1977). *A guide to family reading in two languages: The preschool years.* Los Angeles, CA: California State University, Evaluation, Dissemination, and Assessment Center.

Bennhardt, E. B. (1991). *Reading development in a second language: Theoretical, empirical and classroom perspectives.* Norwood, NJ: Ablex.

Carrasquillo, A. (1978). *La enseñanza de la lectura en la escuela elemental.* España: Anaya.

Carrasquillo, A. (1990). The role of native language instruction in bilingual education programs. *Language Association Bulletin of the New York Association of Foreign Languages, 42*(2), 10–12.

Collier, V. (1992). A synthesis of studies examining long-term language minority student data on academic achievement. *Bilingual Research Journal, 16,* 187–212.

Condemarín, M. (1989). *Lectura temprana.* Chile: Editorial Andres Bello.

Cummins, J. (1981). The role of primary language development in promoting educational success for language minority students. In California State Department of Education, *Schooling and language minority students: A theoretical framework* (pp. 3–49). Los Angeles, CA: Evaluation, Dissemination and Assessment Center, California State University.

Dubois, M. E. (1995). Lectura, escritura y formación docente. *Lectura y Vida, 16*(2), 5–11.

Engle, P. L. (1975). *The use of the vernacular language in education.* Rosslyn, VA: Center for Applied Linguistics.

Fabregat, A. M. (1989). *El encuentro gozoso con los libros.* Argentina: Editorial Cincel.

Freeman, Y., & Freeman, D. (1997). *Teaching reading and writing in Spanish in the bilingual classroom.* Portsmouth, NH: Heinemann.

Gaarder, B (1977). *Bilingual schooling and the survival of Spanish in the United States.* Rowley, MA: Newbury House.

Gago, R. (1982). *Literatura infantil.* Madrid, España: Acción Educativa.

Gómez del Manzano, M. (1986). *Cómo hacer a un niño lector.* Madrid, España: Narcea.

Goodman, K., Goodman, Y., & Flores, B. (1979). *Reading in the bilingual classroom: Literacy and biliteracy.* Rosslyn, VA: National Clearinghouse for Bilingual Education.

Hymes, D. (1971). *Language acquisition: Models and methods.* New York: Academic Press.

Kaluger, G., & Kolson, C. J. (1969). *Reading and learning disabilities.* Columbus, OH: Merrill.

Ministerio de Educación de Guatemala. (1989). *El desarrollo de la lectura.* Guatemala: Autor.

Modiano, N. (1973). *Indian education in the Chiapas highlands.* New York: Holt, Rinehart & Winston.

National Institute of Education. (1975). *Reading strategies for different cultural and linguistic groups.* Washington, DC: U.S. Department of Health, Education, and Welfare.

Pérez, B., & Torres-Guzmán, M. (1996). *Learning in two worlds: An integrated Spanish/English biliteracy approach.* White Plains, NY: Longman.

Ramírez, A. G., & Castañeda, A. (1974). *Cultural democracy, bicognitive development and education.* New York: Academic Press.

Ramírez, J. D., Yven, S. D., & Ramey, D. R. (1991). *Longitudinal study of structured English immersion strategy, early-exit and late-exit transitional bilingual education programs for language-minority children.* San Mateo, CA: Aguirre International.

Schon, I. (1985). Remarkable books in Spanish for young readers. *The Reading Teacher, 39*(3), 668–670.

Schon, I. (1988). Recent children's books in Spanish: The best of the best. *Hispania, 71*(2), 418–422.

Smith, F. (1982). *Understanding reading.* Hillsdale, NJ: Lawrence Erlbaum Associates.

Smith, F. (1988). *Joining the literacy club.* Portsmouth, NH: Heinemann.

Weaver, C. (1988). *Reading processes and practice.* Portsmouth, NH: Heinemann.

2

Research Summary on the Teaching of Reading in Spanish to Bilingual Students

Andres Rodríguez, Jr.
Office of Bilingual Education, Brooklyn, NY

El propósito de este capítulo es resumir las investigaciones recientes sobre la enseñanza de la lectura en español, a estudiantes bilingües de los Estados Unidos. Similaridades entre investigaciones tienden a enfocar los factores lingüísticos y culturales, y cómo éstos se interrelacionan con factores relacionados con la metodología de la enseñanza de la lectura en español. Por consecuencia, las diferencias entre investigaciones limitan los datos para el investigador que estudia el aprendizaje de leer en español en los Estados Unidos con otras variables de la escuela y la comunidad. Además, es difícil generalizar sobre las aplicaciones de la enseñanza de la lectura en español de una región a otra en los Estados Unidos. Este capítulo menciona investigaciones bilingües o relacionadas sobre la enseñanza de la lectura en español. Hasta el presente, los esfuerzos de los educadores han sido en la ejecución efectiva de los programas bilingües. Hoy día, se necesita más que nunca establecer una base teórica de investigaciones en todas las áreas de la educación bilingüe que traten de interrelacionar las variables del estuiante bilingüe, el hogar, y la comunidad. El capítulo termina mencionando algunas áreas relacionadas con la lectura donde se necesitan más estudios de investigación.

OBJECTIVES

The reader of this chapter will be able to:

1. List those cultural and linguistic factors found to be of great importance in developing literacy skills in Spanish.
2. Identify the advantages of employing the native literacy approach for
   enhancing bilingual students' reading and writing skills.
3. Identify two research issues related to the teaching of reading in
   Spanish to bilingual students.
4. Summarize the existing research/literature on the teaching of reading
   in Spanish to bilingual students.
5. Evaluate research methodologies, discussions, designs, results, and
   conclusions mentioned throughout this chapter.

GUIDE QUESTIONS

1. What common elements of research can be identified that support the
   importance of teaching reading in the students' native language?
2. What strategies and methodologies have been employed for the teaching of reading in Spanish to monolingual or bilingual students?
3. How important is the teacher's knowledge of the Spanish-speaking
   students' native literacy to the successful acquisition of literacy skills
   in the second language?
4. What recommendations can be made for conducting future research
   in the area of reading and bilingual education?

INTRODUCTION

Literacy for all students is a national goal of education as declared in the
Educate America Act: Goals 2000 (Brown & Santos, 1987; Crawford, 1992;
U.S. Department of Education, 1994) and by the Commission on Reading
(1985). Being literate is a vital skill that enables individuals to function in
society. Participants in a society must understand and express concern for
those policies or decisions that affect their daily existence; and literacy helps
citizens achieve these goals. Literacy involves not only reading and writing
skills but also oral and listening comprehension. Proficiency in listening
and speaking a language cannot be separated from the process of learning

decoding and written communication skills in a native or second language (Anderson & Joels, 1986; Muniz-Swicegood, 1994). Communication skills are interdependent, especially when teaching reading and writing to students who are learning with and living in two languages and two cultures. Hispanic students, especially those who initially are not proficient in English, must become literate in both languages if they are to function effectively in schools and society. Biliteracy is important because bilingual children who achieve literacy first in the native language demonstrate a faster transference of skills development in reading and writing to a second language (Engle, 1975; Jiménez, García, & Pearson, 1996; Rivers, 1986).

This chapter examines research issues on the teaching of reading in Spanish to bilingual students enrolled in U.S. public schools. To examine these issues, researchers in the areas of linguistics, psycholinguistics, cognitive psychology, anthropology, and sociology, among others, have generated various theories and hypotheses. Two of the most significant theories are Cummins (1981, 1990) "interdependent language" and "common underlying proficiency theories." Cummins postulated that the more proficient students are in their native language, the higher the proficiency they can attain in a second language. Thus, the interdependence of learning two language systems is evident in the acquisition of vocabulary and concepts first learned in a native language and then easily transferred to a second language. Thus, native-language proficiency underlies development of similar proficiency in a second language.

Speaking proficiency has been linked to reading achievement in bilingual children. Past research has emphasized these two language communication skills (Carrasquillo & Segan, 1984; Hakuta & Gould, 1987; Ovando & Collier, 1985). Moreover, current research support (Jiménez et al., 1996) has been cited for positive transfer of reading skills from a student s native language to English, and strengthens such classic transfer studies as those by Cohen (1974), Cummins (1981), Hudelson (1986), and Modiano (1968). Current researchers, however, take a broader view of issues of literacy in bilingual children and have integrated perspectives from a combination of past research studies into a multidisciplinary research framework delineating the interactive processes affecting literacy development in a native and second language. Based on a "holistic approach" to teaching and learning in bilingual education and English as a Second Language (ESL) programs, researchers have continued to examine the relationship of reading to writing in bilingual students (Barnitz, 1985; Esling & Downing, 1987; Rigg & Scott Enright, 1986; Rodriguez, 1988). In a similar fashion, comprehension-

based teaching strategies have been examined in linguistically and culturally different school settings (Anderson & Joels, 1986; Kolers, 1968, 1976;
Langer, Bartolome, & Vazquez, 1990; Muniz-Swicegood, 1994). If instruction is to be appropriate to promote literacy or biliteracy in bilingual
students, bilingual and ESL teachers need to integrate the four communication skills (listening, speaking, reading, and writing) and to structure
content and instructional materials, because positive results are not
achieved by discrete, fragmented, and discontinuous skill teaching (Cummins, 1990; Krashen, 1984; Krashen & Terrel, 1983). It is especially
important that teachers not isolate teaching of the reading process from
writing, listening, or speaking. Thus, instruction that integrates communication skills in the classroom facilitates meaningful learning. These theories
have been addressed in the literature providing discussion and interpretation
of research findings. Questions that have been addressed include the following: Should initial literacy be taught in the first language? How and
when is reading introduced to limited-English-proficient (LEP) Spanish-
speaking students? In what language(s)? Is there transfer of reading skills
from the native language (Spanish) to English? What is the best way to
introduce literacy skills to children who speak languages but who lack a
formal education?

CULTURE AND BILITERACY

Major research studies have examined the levels of literacy that are important in teaching and the role of literacy in schools and society (Brown &
Santos, 1987; Cummins, 1990; Franklin, 1986; Nieto, 1994; Ovando &
Collier, 1985; Wells, 1987). Some researchers posit that acquisition of
literacy skills is culturally based (Franklin, 1986; McLeod, 1986). Cultures
differ in establishing priorities for the teaching of reading and writing
(Freire, 1985). It is essential that LEP students participate effectively in a
culture and comprehend and interpret the goals of such institutions as
schools and government. The development of biliteracy skills is essential
for these purposes. Freire (1985) maintained that biliterate individuals have
the ability to interpret the events, institutions, and power structures that
determine their existence; they can read the world first before the word.

Wells (1987) referred to four literacy levels, all culturally bound: performative, functional, informational, and epistemic. The *performative* focuses
on speech or the written code for communication, such as answering
questions or writing a home address; the *functional* emphasizes interper-

sonal communication, such as reading a newspaper or writing a job application; the *informational* assumes that reading and writing are for informational purposes, such as for accessing the accumulated knowledge that schools transmit; and the *epistemic* level relates to literacy as a mode of communication and provides ways for literate persons to act on and transform knowledge and experiences unavailable to illiterates. The attitudes encouraged by the epistemic level of literacy are those of creativity, exploration, and critical evaluation.

According to McLeod (1986), literacy for thinking and social decision making will empower language-minority children to view society in an analytical way. This view allows them to claim control of society and counteract present educational emphasis on tests, skills, and external controls that are antidemocratic in their effects. For example, Franklin (1986) argued that literacy instruction is culturally based. Teachers hold tacit expectations of how literacy skills should be taught, the use of materials and methods, and the organization of classroom literacy events. These expectations determine the literacy success and failure of children. To examine these findings, she presented excerpts of first-grade classroom transcripts and teacher interviews in her study of literacy in bilingual classrooms. She concluded that most first-grade teachers expect students to have metalinguistic knowledge of sounds, letters, and words before the reading and writing of texts takes place. Franklin explained that when Hispanic LEP children had difficulty with these skills, it was their cultural and language background that was blamed, rather than methods, materials or teacher assumptions (p. 51).

Like Franklin, other researchers conclude that an emphasis on skill instruction at the expense of the reading and writing of texts impedes the natural literacy development process (Anderson & Joels, 1986; Barnitz, 1985; Edelsky, 1986; Rigg & Scott Enright, 1986). Moreover, in the case of bilingual students, language differences are not to be construed as language deficits. Limited English proficiency does not mean the student is limited in the capacity to develop language and thinking skills. For this reason, biliteracy instruction is important for the bilingual student's involvement in a variety of purposes and a variety of settings. Children's bilingual literacy can be studied and measured as communication skills in listening, speaking, reading, and writing in two languages for school purposes—that is, for placement, promotion, and grouping.

Four dependent and universal language functions are interrelated to the process of reading (and writing) in a native and second language: the social or pragmatic, semantic, syntactic, and orthographic/graphophonic. The *pragmatic* function concerns students' self-perceptions within a social and cultural context. The *semantic* dimension considers the content of printed material, as well as the learner's background knowledge that interacts with literacy tasks. In order to read and write in a native and second language, some mastery of the grammar of both languages—functions, structure, and *syntactic* knowledge—is required. And a familiarity with the written language—the *orthographic* (writing) and the *graphophonic* (sound-symbol) systems—is necessary before reading or writing skills are learned.

Current research studies emphasize the learning of reading and writing as interactive processes. A conceptual framework derived from K. S. Goodman and Y. M. Goodman's (1977) psycholinguistic research has been applied to the reading process. Learning to read reinforces the writing process and vice versa. The universal meaning-making processes of reading and writing are necessary in school learning tasks and for participation in social activities (Ambert & Melendez, 1985; Barnitz, 1985; Latino Commission on Educational Reform, 1992). In the process of composing a written text, or in the act of reading a text, the student's linguistic and cultural background knowledge interacts with meaning-making processes. To elicit meaning from textual information presented, there is a sharing of purpose, intention (content), and audience between the student and the author who interact within a social setting. As students derive meaning from printed text, there is an interplay between their mind and body (i.e., visual, perceptual, linguistic, neurological, memory, affective) and with the text's structure and content (i.e., its schemata). The levels of printed language that cue meaning are the *graphophonic* (sound-symbol), the *syntactic* (grammar and word order), and the *semantic* (vocabulary and lexicon). For reading comprehension to occur, the reader's private meaning integrates with the author's public meaning (Langero, Bartolome, & Vasquez, 1990; Lessow-Hurley, 1991; Padron, 1990, 1992; Rigg & Scott Enright, 1986). The reader's interest, motivation, self-concept, and attitudes, as well as teacher expectations, significantly affect student biliteracy outcomes (Rigg & Scott Enright, 1986). As in the reading process, writing (the creation of an original work or piece) is a psycholinguistic, personal, social, and culturally based meaning-making process (Fuentes, 1987; Rigg & Scott Enright, 1986). In light of this perspective, writing as an interactive process is not a classroom dictation or form-filling task, an information report exercise, or any other classroom copying exercise (Connor & Kaplan, 1987). Teachers must focus on the purpose, the intention (content and topics), the audience, or who is responding to the written work, in addition to the final sharing and editing of student products.

Reyes (1974) asserted that schools have a moral obligation to provide Spanish instruction because this society is committed to providing equal educational opportunity to all people. Several decades later, Amercican schools now have a moral obligation to provide equity and access to technology-based classroom instruction to LEP students and staff. Apart from the cognitive aspects of bilingual programs, there are psychological factors to consider. Rejecting students' language is rejecting them, their family, community, and everything with which they identify. Denying LEP students the technological and human resources available to most students in American public education impacts on the civic and social life of all Americans into the 21st century. Latino LEP students cannot be expected to develop a sense of belonging and identity with the school or even with American society if they see that their language is ignored and learning tools are not provided in the school or home environments. These observations create negative attitudes; and negative attitudes influence learning. There can be no positive learning if there are no positive attitudes. Instruction in Spanish gives official recognition to a student's language and culture, and to the identification with Spanish-speaking society (Jiménez et al., 1996; McEvedy, 1987; McInnes, 1986; Reyes, 1974).

Children from linguistically and culturally different environments share learning, communication, and motivational styles that are at variance with those of the mainstream culture. Language and culture of children appear to play an important role in the ways children communicate with and relate to others and in their methods of perceiving, thinking, and problem solving. Individual differences in cognitive functioning are due not to differences in intelligence, but, rather, to personality manifestations inherent in the sociocultural system.

Ramirez and Castañeda (1974) identified two culturally significant modes of learning: field sensitive and field independent. Ramirez asserted that *field-sensitive* students perform better when authority figures express confidence in their ability. Students respond better when educational material has human content and is characterized by fantasy, humor, and cooperativeness. *Field-independent* students learn better when material is abstract and impersonal and is not significantly affected by the opinions of authority figures. Ramirez concluded that because of the language, culture, and socialization experiences of Mexican-American children, many of them share a field-sensitive style of learning. However, many of them also exhibit cognitive flexibility, or the ability to function in either mode. Research emphasizes that teachers and program planners must take into account the different characteristics of diverse groups of Hispanic students. Becoming aware of and sensitive to the students' learning styles should be the determining factor in choosing an appropriate teaching strategy. Competencies identified under the category of cognitive styles are designed to provide a base from which specific instructional strategies can be developed consonant with the learning styles of bilingual students.

Current bilingual education teaching and learning strategies derive from a holistic approach for biliteracy instruction (Rigg & Scott Enright, 1986; Rivers, 1986). Such an approach values the bilingual students' background knowledge and strengths in developing discovery and inquiry learning modes. Thus, teaching is reactive rather than structured instruction. Holistic teaching integrates multilevels of communication skills—listening, speaking, reading, and writing—simultaneously in the learning process. The whole, rather than its parts, is important (Freeman & Freeman, 1993; Goodman & Goodman, 1977). From a holistic teaching approach, reading and writing are related processes. Reading can generate writing and writing generates reading. It should be noted that an approach derives from a theoretical perspective, whereas a method or technique is a practical application based on an approach. Holistic teaching approaches utilize the four communication skills in every learning situation. Students learn not only through formal instruction, but through the avenues of discovery and inquiry. Learners, furthermore, are surrounded by meaningful language contexts in which they can initiate and respond in the discovery and inquiry process and creatively seek to learn in a reactive, spontaneous manner, rather than in passive, structured learning settings. The holistic teaching methods and strategies most recognized in recent research for bilingual children developing literacy skills in two languages are the *language experience approach*, *dialogue journal writing*, the *conference-centered approach*, and *ethnographic teaching methods*. These approaches focus on the communicative functions of bilingual development supporting researchers who recommend the native literacy approach as a method to allow Latino children to develop proficiency in their native language so that they can begin to read in that language (Gamez, 1979; Hall, 1970; Kaminsky, 1976; Millen, 1987; Modiano, 1968; Pacheco, 1977; Ramirez, 1979). This approach has the added advantage of demonstrating to children that their native language is recognized as valuable and worthy.

The native literacy approach is based on the premise that the most effective means for teaching the national language of a country to nonspeakers of the language is to teach literacy first in the native language, then teach the second language orally, and then teach reading in the second language. For Spanish-speaking children, using this approach means reading would be taught first in Spanish, English would be taught orally, and then reading would be taught in English. There are three advantages of this native literacy approach: Teaching reading can begin at an earlier stage than if the standard language has to be taught first; the student's cultural heritage is recognized and valued; and learning to read is undertaken in the language with which the student is most comfortable and familiar.

Before Spanish-speaking students can learn to read English, they must first be able to understand and speak it effectively. Reading ability is negatively influenced by backgrounds lacking in experience, concepts, and general information; words may be meaningless to students because they cannot understand the concepts behind the words. Speech sounds are different in Spanish and English; and students must first be familiar with speech sounds before they can master the symbols used to represent them in reading. Finally, Spanish-speaking students may have a restricted vocabulary in English and might use different expressions in their native language that cannot be translated meaningfully into English. Thus, it is necessary to acquaint students with English vocabulary so that they will be able to understand printed English words and acquaint themselves with the syntax unique to the English language.

One of the methodologies most often mentioned in the literature is the *language experience approach.* The language experience approach develops native- and second-language literacy. Typically, students describe their own knowledge and experiences as the teacher records their statements in writing. The teacher reads the story aloud to students while pointing to the words. Then students read the story aloud, in group or individual exercises. As a follow-up, students receive the typed or printed story to practice sight words and study new vocabulary. In ESL classes, students say what they know, but learn added vocabulary and reading skills in the process. Initial literacy in ESL is built faster for LEP students with this approach than by using basal or phonics programs. Students exhibit more control and interest in a learning situation where the language experience approach is employed.

Another recommended method is dialogue journal writing, which is a written conversation between a teacher and student or between students themselves. Daily entries into a personal writing book are made; then the teacher or a peer reads, comments, praises, adds information, responds with remarks or requests, and so forth. Bilingual teachers, in particular, may have an opportunity to teach new vocabulary, punctuation, spelling, language complexity, or rhetorical development, with a focus on content and what is important to the reading development of students. Positive interaction is developed between students and teacher and between peers in a reading and writing class.

The aforementioned information points to the variety of topics in the area of culture and biliteracy. However, most authorities agree that there exists a relation between the acceptance of students' backgrounds and cultures and students' desire to learn in one or two languages. The next section expands on the previous topics by identifying issues in the teaching of Spanish reading.

ISSUES RELATED TO THE TEACHING OF SPANISH READING IN BILINGUAL EDUCATION

Research issues in the teaching of Spanish reading in bilingual instruction, with regard to such variables as student, text, and culture(s), have been raised. The interaction and integration of these variables help educators to fully understand the challenges students face in the process of learning to read. Research has acknowledged the needs of Latino bilingual readers in the context of pupil background knowledge, written text variables, availability of resources, and social and cultural aspects related to the literacy process. Some of the identified issues can be summarized in the following questions:

> To what extent do orthographic similarities and differences between the Spanish and English languages affect learning to read a first and second language for LEP students?
>
> Should initial literacy be taught in the first or second language?
>
> Does a transfer of reading skills take place from Spanish to English as a second language?
>
> What are the comprehension-based teaching and learning strategies in reading in the native and second languages?
>
> What is the difference between reading in bilingual education and reading in ESL programs?
>
> How can teachers help facilitate LEP students' literacy growth?

These questions/issues have been raised as they relate to literacy and proficiency in reading and writing in Spanish and English and their variety across language groups and diverse ethnic student populations within a group in the United States. For example, cultural and linguistic differences exist among Hispanics such as Cubans, Dominicans, Mexicans, and Puerto Ricans. In addition, reading tasks and reader readiness and preparation may require different levels of processing skills and strategies for the native- and second-language reader. In the past, teachers and researchers have assumed that Latino LEP children must first be orally proficient in English before reading and writing can be taught in Spanish (Hudelson, 1986). Current research, however, supports the teaching of reading skills in the native and second languages simultaneously with speaking, listening, and writing in both languages (Barnitz, 1985; D. E. Freeman & Y. S. Freeman, 1993; Padron, 1992; Rigg & Scott Enright, 1986). Hispanic LEP children should not be perceived as limited in expressing their needs, interests, and ideas in reading or written instruction when using their native and English language. Ambert (1988) wrote that teachers of bilingual Hispanic learners need not think that instruction in the student's native language will impede academic progress in learning English as a second language.

Another issue presented is the role of teachers in the teaching/learning process. For example, Monteiro (1986) reported that teachers of Latino students enrolled in bilingual education public school programs asked less demanding types of questions in reading and writing, practiced teacher-directed rather than student-centered instruction, and did most of the talking in classrooms studied across the nation. The implications of these studies is that teachers must adjust types of classroom teaching and learning practices and instructional methods and techniques, such as questioning and response strategies, to the proficiency levels of LEP pupils in their native and second languages, and need to ask more questions on higher cognitive levels of instruction (Jiménez et al., 1996; Padron, 1992; Prado-Olmos, Szyanski, & Smith, 1993).

Another issue is the use of technology in bilingual classrooms. Roberts (1987) documented the restricted use of technology and computer education in Title I programs serving the needs of LEP youngsters throughout U.S. public school systems. Sayers and Cummins (1995) and Sayers (1991; 1995) have indicated that there is a lack of research in bilingual education employing technology-based approaches and their benefits to developing literacy and biliteracy in this information age and superhighway cultural society. Cummins and Sayers (1995) reported the need to conduct native-language and ESL instruction by employing instructional hardware and recommended software programs, and for conducting staff development activities. Such instructional technology materials, activities, and curricular uses are focused on three areas: the teaching of classroom curriculum (e.g., employing word processing/graphics software programs such as "Clarisworks" developed by Macintosh-Apple Computers) integrated with technology software and computer-assisted instruction; the use of e-mail, telecommunications, and internet to communicate with other bilingual learners across the United States and internationally; and the use of teacher-made and commercially produced multimedia instructional software encompassing the use of videotaping, CD-ROMs, and sound and music on most current state-of-the-art computers.

Ironically, in the 1990s, bilingual education has been underfunded by local, state, and federal departments of education. Although educators agree that to be valuable and marketable a student does well to learn a second language (other than English), many opponents of bilingual education demonized it as a mechanism created by bilingual educators and ethnic intellectual elites to disenfranchise their own school communities by denying them opportunities to learn English and thus participate fully in an English-speaking society. However, there are many documented successes of authentic learning experiences in many bilingual education and dual-language programs in which LEP children's needs are being served in a real and meaningful way.

But the literature has drawn attention to the fact that some Latino children/youth who have been exposed to both languages in an unsystematic way prior to school or have little or no formal schooling in their native countries, come to school with less than nativelike command of the vocabulary and syntactic structures of both their native (L1) and second (L2) languages (Cummins, 1979; Kaminsky, 1976; Marsh, 1995; Ramirez, 1979; Romero, 1980). Other researchers also suggest that, under these conditions, bilingual children may switch codes because they do not know the label for a particular concept in the language they are speaking but have it readily available in the other language (Zentella, 1980). Although reading is not a universally learned phenomenon across cultures, research reveals the universal aspects of the reading process (Ambert & Melendez, 1985; Barnitz, 1985; Jiménez et al., 1996; Rigg & Scott Enright, 1986). However, biliteracy is independent of the languages in which the bilingual student learns to read. For native Spanish-speaking literate students, the similarities in the discourse printed languages in Spanish and English in both form (grammar, vocabulary, orthographies, mechanics) and function (demands, questions, commands, requests, declarations) facilitate rapid transference of reading skills from the native to the second language (Cohen, 1987).

Some authorities have investigated the issues discussed and have come up with some findings and conclusions.

Padrón Studies

Padrón (1985, 1992) utilized the cognitive reading strategies of her bilingual students in Spanish and English to improve English reading comprehension. Her purpose was to investigate whether the cognitive strategies bilingual students used during the reading process differed by grade, gender, or ability level in reading and to what extent instruction enhanced reading comprehension in English as a second language. Cognitive strategies were identified by interview form and categorized by number and type, such as recalling, summarizing, remembering, locating information, analyzing, generalizing, interpreting or concluding, and evaluating by use of contextual clues.

Padrón's method employed randomly selected control groups with a pre/posttest design. Ninety-two Hispanic bilingual students in Texas, age 8 to 12, were stratified by ability levels to form four groups (two control, two experimental). Experimental group 1 was taught English reading by using the reciprocal teaching approach. Teachers asked students to answer and form their own questions on the content of the reading task and to predict the meaning of the assignments. Experimental group 2 was instructed on how to locate information in reading tasks. Control group 1 was instructed to read stories independently and answer comprehension questions. Control group 2 did not receive any additional information. Students participated in the experiment for periods of 30 minutes, twice a week, for 1 month.

Experimental and control findings showed that bilingual children used similar reading comprehension strategies as those used by monolingual students. Padrón identified 12 strategies employed by bilingual experimental groups (i.e., text sampling, predicting, confirming, rejecting, correcting, altering, making inferences, interpreting, inserting information, deleting, adding, and omitting). Differences between genders were inconclusive. Students in the upper grades who were higher achievers used a greater number of strategies and higher level cognitive strategies than their peers in the lower grades. Finally, once students were proficient readers in their native language, instruction in cognitive strategies in English as a second language did not improve their comprehension. Reading instruction, then, must be differentiated for bilingual students by using appropriate teaching strategies. Moreover, learning styles of bilingual students and proficiency in the native language significantly affect learners reading achievement in English.

Rivera Viera's Studies

In studying Spanish-speaking readers who experience difficulty in learning to read, Rivera Viera (1986) supported the case study approach. Like Rigg and Scott Enright (1986), Rivera Viera employed a miscue-analysis profile for a Puerto Rican, middle-class, 7-year-old boy, who had serious reversal problems in decoding in his native Spanish. The subject received remedial reading instruction for 1 hour, twice a week during 1 academic year. The language experience approach was used in teaching and the researcher found this method particularly appropriate to the boy's strengths because he enjoyed storytelling. Cloze type exercises were used to teach word attack skills and comprehension. Rivera Viera concluded that the subject's problems originated from ineffectual use of native-language reading strategies. ESL and bilingual teachers may gain substantial information on a bilingual student's linguistic strengths employing a comprehensive assessment in a case study format.

Studies in Question Asking and Reading Comprehension Issues

Question asking and reading comprehension have been related to reading ability and question-asking ability in bilingual Spanish/English students (Henry, 1985; Hewlett-Gomez, 1985; Monteiro, 1986; Muniz-Swicegood, 1994; Nagy, García, & Durgonoglu, 1993). Question-asking research models and studies are comprehension based in teaching second-language learners. Prereading adjunct questions affect students' selective attention and selective rehearsal strategies for important materials and cause the reader to activate relevant background knowledge schemata that can help encode and organize new information (Monteiro, 1986). For example, awareness of cognates between Spanish and English can prompt bilingual students to better comprehend native and ESL reading materials across grade levels and content areas (Nagy, García, & Durgonoglu, 1993). Hewlett-Gomez (1985) completed 24 classroom observations and collected tape-recorded discourse from the classrooms of four bilingual teachers over a 6-week period. Five bilingual students from each classroom, grades two through five, verbally interacted with the bilingual teachers during second-language instruction in reading. Types of questions and responses elicited by both teachers and students were coded. Findings revealed that teachers asked more lower level cognitive questions than did their bilingual students. It was also found that teachers talked too much. Students initiated more questions in their second language when teachers talked less. Students mimicked teacher questioning patterns such as question–response and evaluation response. Hewlett-Gomez concluded that teacher talking and questioning patterns affect positive achievement in second-language reading comprehension. Teacher talk and questions and use of other response forms can, therefore, create an environment that stimulates students' curiosity, fostering motivation and enabling expansion of student language.

Jiménez et al. (1996) and Monteiro (1986) studied students who were already English proficient. According to these researchers, bilingual Latino students who generated questions in Spanish or English reading tasks are compelled to actively process information referred to as an *active processing hypothesis*. Also, Hispanic students' awareness of their cognitive processes and products (Muniz-Swicegood, 1994) improves reading comprehension known as the *metacognitive hypothesis*. In addition, question-asking tasks activate prior knowledge, referred to as *schema theory*. Therefore, enhancing bilingual students' questioning abilities in their native and second languages enhances reading comprehension. Types of questions asked by teachers in bilingual/ESL literacy programs merit future research attention.

Studies on Successful Literacy Programs

In an effort to identify the characteristics of effective bilingual and ESL literacy programs for bilingual learners, Soler-Galiano and Prince (1987) conducted a longitudinal research study from 1983 to 1985. They analyzed bilingual reading and writing instruction in three elementary public schools in Connecticut. The purpose of the study was to identify and describe the administrative, curricular, and instructional practices that contribute to program success and biliteracy achievement of Spanish-speaking children. Eleven first- and second-grade Spanish/English bilingual classrooms were visited twice a month. Classroom observation techniques, teacher interviews, student and staff interviews, examination of curricular materials, and collected student writing samples provided qualitative measures linked to student test scores. Successful program characteristics reported included: strong academic curriculum in bilingual instruction, well-defined instructional plans to teach reading and writing, strong administrative support, strong support for native-language instruction as a bridge to learning English, and integration into and acceptance of the school's mainstream culture.

Comparable bilingual student performance measures in English and Spanish, writing samples, and standardized reading achievement results in Spanish and English were correlated to program and curricular characteristics. In linking process information to bilingual student literacy outcomes, evaluations in bilingual education can begin to employ such a model to meaningfully improve literacy instruction and program designs for second-language learners (Hakuta, 1986; Soler-Galiano & Prince, 1987). Results of this study indicate that reading instruction reinforces writing skills acquisition and writing skills reinforce reading.

Bernhardt et al. (1995) and Feldman (1987) argued that areas of content knowledge are shared across cultures. Feldman presented three case studies of successful reading comprehension-based programs developed by school districts to meet the needs of culturally diverse student populations. The Structured Teaching in the Areas of Reading and Writing (STAR) was implemented in School District 4 in New York City, grades three through nine. STAR was developed with the assistance of researchers and university consultants. Feldman (1987) concluded that there is a need for basing reading instruction for any student, in particular second-language learners, on current theory and research. District and building administrators should support such efforts, and consultant experts from research institutions can make contributions in the areas of theory and program development, implementation, and evaluation.

TRANSFERENCE OF READING SKILLS

Current research continues to support the theory that the Spanish-speaking bilingual learner transfers native literacy skills in reading to English as a second language in an interactive, reciprocal process (Barnitz, 1985; Cohen, 1987; Garcia & Padilla, 1985; Jiménez et al., 1996). Although past studies reflected linguistic interference in transferring reading skills from a first to a second language (Segan, 1984), current investigations raise the issues of the nature of orthographic differences between a first and second language and how these influence the transfer of literacy from one language to another, known as "cross-linguistic" transfer (Barnitz, 1985; Centurion, 1986; Jiménez et al., 1986). At present, other topics in the transfer of reading skills in bilingual education focus on metacognitive strategies for reading (Brown-Azarowitz, 1987; Muniz-Swicegood, 1994; Prado-Olmos et al., 1993), such as the use of rhythmical patterns in silent and oral reading by second-language learners in relation to reading comprehension. The English language structures (nouns, pronouns, punctuation marks, connectives, verbs, adverbs, adjectives, and prepositions) that affect reading comprehension for Latino second-language learners are also being addressed, considering whether or not these language structures appear in the literate student's native language. For example, Spanish and English consonants are similar in graphophoneme correspondence and hence easier to learn and transfer across the two languages; vowel combinations and sounds are very different and need to be learned and identified in a variety of reading experiences for Latino children.

Additional current concerns deal with levels of literacy and biliteracy, the special circumstances of students who are literate in a native language with a Roman alphabet, Hispanic students from a language background and culture with no formal educational experiences, and the language proficiency skills that will support literacy learning in a second language (Marsh, 1995). It is said that teaching in the mother tongue is the most effective method because it eliminates the problem of dealing with linguistic and cultural differences and the literacy needs of bilingual students who lack a formal education. Using Spanish as a teaching medium will lessen or eliminate academic retardation, strengthen the bonds between home and school, avoid the alienation from family and lingustic community, and develop strong literacy in the native language so that it can be a strong asset in the student's adult life. Studies previously mentioned indicated that Spanish-speaking students could name pictures more readily in their more fluent language and could recall them significantly more often in that language, regardless of the language used for learning. Studies supported the view that early reading instruction depends on a student's ability to speak the language. Children learn to read a language much better after having learned to speak it. Other studies supported the native literacy approach. These studies showed positive transfer of learning from instruction in reading skills in Spanish of Spanish-speaking students to reading ability in English (Crawford, 1990; Ramírez, 1991).

Pacheco (1977) asserted that the native literacy approach recognizes the learner's primary language and culture as educational assets to the student's entire education. Reading instruction in the Spanish language would enable students to develop proficiency in their native language. Native-language fluency is also important to the Spanish-speaking student because it includes listening comprehension, speaking, reading, and writing skills. A bilingual-bicultural program recognizes that the needs of Spanish-speaking students are both linguistic and cultural. The development of comprehensive programs would offer children opportunities to gain an understanding and appreciation of the Anglo culture as well as their native language and culture.

Children coming to school speaking Spanish already have a communication skill that should be capitalized on rather than minimized or eliminated. The Spanish-speaking student who is not literate in Spanish should be given the chance to develop and maintain the native language. The student should also be allowed to progress academically in the native language while simultaneously receiving systematic, sequential, and regular instruction in English. A bilingual-bicultural program would include the native literacy approach to reading so that all these factors are taken into consideration (Nieves-Falcón, 1981; Ramírez, 1979; Romero, 1980).

There are many advocates of programs that enable children to be taught first in their native language because, these educators believe, linguistic and cultural differences could be minimized in such a program. There are, however, opponents who believe that automatically teaching Spanish-speaking students in a native literacy program might not be to their advantage. Instead, these skeptics believe that the student's language dominance and proficiency should be assessed in the community's dominant language. Anderson and Joels (1986), among others, pointed to the lexical or vocabulary differences across languages and how these affect reading comprehension, in particular, when transferring lexical meanings and concepts from a first to a second language. The vocabulary-concept knowledge construct developed by Cummins (1981) interrelated the context of the written word, the schemata (text structure and content), and the student's language proficiency in reading comprehension. For example, the English word dormitory is different in meaning from the Spanish and Italian word *dormitorio*. It is important, thus, in analyzing the transfer of reading skills phenomenon to consider first- and second-language lexical differences, such as the use of figurative language, metaphors, idioms, similes, and affective meanings in words that impact on reading comprehension (Dubin, Eshey, & Grabe, 1986; Garcia & Padilla, 1985; Jiménez et al., 1996).

Cohen (1987) developed two transferability models in teaching reading to Spanish-speaking children in the United States. Factors such as student placement in a bilingual education program, ESL instruction, types of instructional materials, and strategies employed affect the transferability process. These factors, in turn, relate to philosophical and practical considerations in a school and culture. Some important factors are the teacher's view of teaching literacy to bilingual children and program alternatives, such as individualized native-language reading instruction coupled with reinforcement of comparable skills taught in the native language in the ESL class. The Transferring Individual Skills (TIS) model from Spanish to English, on a skill-by-skill basis as they are acquired in English, focuses on a fragmented, skill-dependent process; whereas the preferred Transferring Organized Clusters (TOC) model promotes the transference of similar skills clustered, by degree of difficulty and format, at the comprehension level (Cohen, 1987, p. 11). Remembering sequence, rearranging for correct sequence, and cause–effect relations comprise a cluster. Cohen (1987) distinguished between reading as a language process and language as a communication process. The bilingual teacher working on transferability must understand reading as a visual and cognitive task; as thinking; and as personal, emotional, and social communication (p. 13). If there are reading transferability problems, bilingual and ESL teachers who have knowledge of reading as a psycholinguistic and interactive process can determine whether these problems are language related or based on reading circumstances. ESL reading instruction of LEP pupils should be compatible with native-language instruction in reading if transfer of reading skills is to enhance the process of students' reading comprehension.

RESEARCH IMPLICATIONS FOR CLASSROOM INSTRUCTION

To conclude the discussion on reading research in bilingual education instruction, three major areas point to general and specific teaching implications in terms of strategies or approaches. First, educators must possess linguistic knowledge and cultural sensitivity to the LEP student's home language and community. Second, teachers must understand the cognitive processes related to learning to read and write in bilingual programs, know the Spanish language, and help meet the needs of LEP pupils. Third, the content of a curriculum for Hispanic LEP children must be relevant and interesting. These three components need to be integrated into the learning/teaching process. For example, the process of teaching reading in English to LEP students is similar to teaching reading in the native language. Thus, teachers must first look at the language area, that is, the goals and objectives for promoting biliteracy in bilingual children, the teaching strategies, and teacher input. Teacher talk, questioning techniques, teaching methods, and curricular materials should be examined in terms of focusing reading instruction for effective comprehension. It is important to relate linguistic knowledge to other major categories of teacher and student knowledge. Cultural, pragmatic, functional, and the basic interpersonal communications skills (BICS), posited by Cummins (1981), are all important. Language discourse text forms and purposes—narrative, expository, and descriptive—should also be analyzed. Teaching approaches can then be employed to offer a balance between similar literacy goals in bilingual and ESL classes. In bilingual education reading programs, however, research suggests compatible teaching reading approaches in both the native and second languages (Cohen, 1987; Dubin et al., 1986; Muniz-Swicegood, 1994; Prado-Olmos et al., 1993; Tchaconas, 1985).

In the cognitive area, teachers should examine the pupils' different levels of thinking and interaction (peer, student, adult, etc.) in acquiring literacy skills in a second language. Thematic teaching approaches with student hands-on activities (e.g., sequencing stories in pictures and written exercises) can promote comprehension thinking skills and active participation in a natural setting that is affectively based. Low-anxiety learning tasks promote bicognitive flexibility as suggested in the research (Prado-Olmos et al., 1993; Tchaconas & Spiridakis, 1986).

Finally, the third area deals with content in the curriculum. Bilingual education teachers aim to teach content in two languages, whereas ESL teachers teach language and literacy skills in the second language. School academic language proficiency, referred to as Cognitive Academic Language Proficiency (CALP) by Cummins (1981), distinguishes between a bilingual learner's language proficiencies in the first and second language in school-related tasks. The teacher who integrates curriculum content for teaching reading and writing skills in a native and second language, in addition to listening and speaking communication skills, utilizes a whole-language approach in the development of reading and writing materials for the bilingual student. In this case, teachers do not select the learning content. Rather, content is based on what the students know, and teaching materials promote and expand on the students' knowledge. Thus, reading programs for bilingual students should balance the need for language development in first and second languages and content development in curriculum for promoting biliterate reading achievement.

CONCLUSION

The effectiveness of classroom instruction for bilingual students, especially in reading and writing, will be enhanced by the teachers' understanding of the differences that exist (cultural, lexical, in discourse forms) between the students' native and second languages. Such differences require development of multiliteracies on the part of LEP students. Native-language proficiency facilitates rapid literacy in a second language that enhances the transference of reading and writing skills to that second language. Nevertheless, transference and biliteracy may not be possible for LEP children who are illiterate in their native language. Contrastive analysis teaching strategies (e.g., the use of cognates) in written and oral language structures will aid in transferring oral and reading proficiencies from a native language to learning literacy skills in a second language (Barnitz, 1985; Jiménez et al., 1996). A holistic approach that interrelates the four communication skills may help to meet bilingual students' particular educational needs. Not only are reading and writing proficiencies dependent on language proficiency in a first language, but cognitive development in the native language also facilitates academic and linguistic proficiency in the second language. These proficiencies underlie and affect literacy teaching skills and content. There is a need to develop first the functional, communicative dimension of biliteracy in bilingual children in order to promote academic achievement in other school areas. Moreover, teachers influence the degree of expressiveness in students, suggesting that instruction be affectively based. In addition to basing reading and writing instruction for Latino bilingual students on a comprehension-based, interactive teaching approach, teachers need to show bilingual students how reading and writing interrelate in areas such as spelling, punctuation, syntax, lexicon, and orthography, as well as how they reinforce each other in both of the student's languages as meaning-making communication modes. The value of any approach depends on the teacher's creativity and ability to adapt materials or methods for teaching bilingual students.

Future research in biliteracy development in bilingual students should connect reading and writing methodologies and show how each affects the other in the learning process of bilingual students and how cross-cultural differences in orthography, rhetorical, and discourse language factors influence bilingual students' development and transfer of literacy skills to a second language. Further research is needed to assess the impact of teacher questioning abilities on reading comprehension in bilingual students acquiring biliteracy skills.

FOLLOW-UP ACTIVITIES

1. Imagine the following situation: You are a bilingual reading teacher in an elementary school. There is a group of children who have been identified as "Spanish dominant," for whom you have been asked to design a reading program. You propose the use of the native literacy approach. Write a memo to the principal outlining your reasons for advocating this approach.

2. Select three (3) of the researchers listed here. For each one, write one or two sentences describing the key aspect(s) of his/her research with implications for the bilingual student:

a. Muniz-Swicegood   d. Padron

b. Sayers   e. Cummi ns

c. Modiano   f. Rivera-Viera

What other researchers would you add to this list?

3. A university researcher is about to conduct a study comparing the reading achievement of monolingual English speakers and bilingual students. You are a member of a school committee that will provide information about the sample groups to be studied. You wish to help the researcher avoid many design errors. Make specific recommendations on each of the following aspects:
   • Methods to select the population.
   • Elimination of other factors not related to reading that might incorrectly affect the results.
   • Provisions for conducting the study over a period of time.

ACKNOWLEDGMENT

The author is especially indebted to Carmen Gloria Burgos from the Office of Bilingual Education of the City of New York Board of Education. She gave much of her time to make searches for the review of this research.

REFERENCES

Ambert, A. N. (1988). *Bilingual education and English as a second language: A research Handbook, 1986–1987.* New York: Garland.

Ambert, A. N., & Melendez, S. E. (1985). *Bilingual education: A sourcebook.* New York: Teacher's College Press.

Anderson, B., & Joels, R. W. (1986). *Teaching reading to students with limited English proficiencies.* Springfield, IL: Thomas.

Barnitz, J. G. (1985). *Reading development of non-native speakers of English: Research and instruction* (Monograph of the Center for Applied Linguistics). Washington, DC: (ERIC Clearinghouse ED No. 256182).

Bernhardt, E., et al. (1995). *Assessing science knowledge in an English/Spanish bilingual elementary school.* Columbus, OH: National Center for Science Teaching and Learning.

Brown, D. L., & Santos, S. L. (1987). Promoting literacy in the classroom. In R. Rodriguez (Ed.), *Teaching reading to minority language students* (pp. 28–58). Rosslyn, VA: National Clearinghouse for Bilingual Education.

Brown-Azarowitz, M. (1987). Oral interpretation: A metacognitive strategy for reading. In R. Rodriguez (Ed.), *Teaching reading to minority language students* (pp. 1–34). Rosslyn, VA: National Clearinghouse for Bilingual Education.

Carrasquillo, A., & Segan, P. (Eds.). (1984). *The teaching of reading in Spanish to bilingual students.* New York: Ediciones Puerto Rico de Autores Nuevos.

Centurion, C. E. (1986). *The use of the informal reading inventory to evaluate oral reading, reading comprehension, and language interference/transfer in English as a second language students.* Unpublished doctoral dissertation, Texas University, Ann Arbor, MI.

Cohen, A. D. (1974). The Culver City Spanish immersion programs: The first two years. *Modern Language Journal, 58,* 95–102.

Cohen, B. (1987, April). *Issues related to transferring reading skills from Spanish to English.* Paper presented at the annual conference of the National Association for Bilingual Education, Denver, CO.

Commission on Reading. (1985). *Becoming a nation of readers.* Washington, DC: National Institute of Education.

Conner, U., & Kaplan, R. B. (1987). *Writing across languages: Analysis of L2 text.* Reading, MA: Addison-Wesley.

Crawford, J. (1990). Bilingual education: The effectiveness debate. *Equity and Choice, 6*(2), 37–45.

Crawford, J. (1992). *History, politics, theory and practice.* Trenton, NJ: Crane.

Cummins, J. (1979). Linguistic inter-dependence and the educational development of bilingual children. *Review of Educational Research, 49,* 45–56.

Cummins, J. (1981). The role of primary language development in promoting educational success for language minority students. In California State Department of Education, *Schooling and language minority students: A theoretical framework* (pp. 3–49). Los Angeles, CA: California State Department of Education.

Cummins, J. (1990). *Empowering minority students.* Sacramento, CA: California Association for Bilingual Education.

Cummins, J., & Sayers, D. (1995). *Brave new schools: Challenging cultural illiteracy through global learning networks.* New York: St. Martin's Press.

Dubin, F., Eshey, D. E., & Grabe, W. (Eds.). (1986). *Teaching second language reading for academic purposes.* Reading, MA: Addison-Wesley.

Edelsky, C. (1986). *Writing in a bilingual program.* Norwood, NJ: Ablex.

Engle, P. L. (1975). Language medium in early school years for minority language groups. *Review of Educational Research, 45,* 283–325.

Esling, J., & Downing, J. (1987). What do ESL students need to learn about reading? *TESL Canada Journal, 1,* 55–68.

Feldman, D. (1987). Research based reading instruction for LEP students. *Journal of the New York State Association for Bilingual Education, 2*(2), 25–39.

Franklin, E. A. (1986). Literacy instruction for LES children. *Language Arts, 63*(1), 51–60.

Freeman, D. E., & Freeman, Y. S. (1993). Strategies for promoting the primary languages of all students. *The Reading Teacher, 46*(7), 552–558.

Freire, P. (1985). Reading the world and reading the word. *Language Arts, 62*(1), 15–22.

Fuentes, J. (1987). From theory to practice: Writing as process with bilingual children. *NABE News, 10*(3), 9–16.

Gamez, G. I. (1979). Reading in a second language: Native language approach vs. direct method. *The Reading Teacher, 32,* 665–670.

Garcia, E. E., & Padilla, R. V. (1985). Effects of language transfer on bilingual proficiency. In E. E. Garcia & R. V. Padilla (Eds.), *Advances in bilingual education research* (pp. 34–51). Tucson, AZ: University of Arizona Press.

Goodman, K. S., & Goodman, Y. M. (1977). Learning about psycholinguistic processes by analyzing oral reading. *Harvard Educational Review, 47*(3), 317–333.

Hakuta, K. (1986). *Mirror of language: The debate on bilingualism.* New York: Basic Books.

Hakuta, K., & Gould, L. J. (1987). Synthesis of research in bilingual education. *Educational Leadership, 33*(6), 38–45.

Hall, R. (1972). *Learning to read in two languages.* Albany, NY: The State Education Department.

Henry, R. (1985). Reader-generated questions: A tool for improving reading comprehension. *NABE News, 8*(3), 4–9.

Hewlett-Gomez, M. R., & Solis, A. (1995). Dual language instructional design for educating recent immigrant secondary students on the Texas-Mexican border. *Bilingual Research Journal, 19*(3/4), 429–452.

Hudelson, S. (1986). ESL children's writing: What we've learned; what we're learning. In P. Rigg & D. Scott Enright (Eds.), *Children and ESL: Integrating perspectives* (pp. 23–54). Washington, DC: TESOL.

Jiménez, R. T., Garcia, G. E., & Pearson, P. D. (1996). The reading strategies of bilingual Latino/a students who successfully read English readers: Opportunities and obstacles. *Reading Research Quarterly, 31*(1), 90–112.

Kaminsky, S. (1976). Bilingualism and learning to read. In A. Simoes (Ed.), *The bilingual child* (pp. 155–171). New York: Academic Press.

Kolers, P. A. (1968). Bilingualism and information processing. *Scientific American, 1*–9.

Kolers, P. A. (1976). Three stages of reading. In F. Smith (Ed.), *Psycholinguistics and reading* (pp. 28–50). New York: Holt, Rinehart & Winston.

Krashen, S. D. (1984). *Writing: Research, theory, and applications.* Elmsford, NY: Pergamon.

Krashen, S. D., & Terrel, T. D. (1983). *The natural approach: Language acquisition in the classroom.* Hayward, CA: Alemany.

Langero, J. A., Bartolome, L., & Vasquez, O. A. (1990). Meaning construction in school literacy tasks: A study of bilingual students. *American Educational Research Journal, 27,* 427–471.

Latino Commission on Educational Reform. (1992). *Toward a vision for the education of Latino students: Community voices, student voices.* Interim Report of the Latino commission on Educational Reform. New York: NYC Board of Education.

Lessow-Hurley, J. (1991). *A commonsense guide to bilingual education.* Alexandria, VA: Association for Supervision and Curriculum Development.

Marsh, L. (1995). A Spanish dual literacy program: Teaching to the whole student. *Bilingual Research Journal, 19*(3 & 4), 409–428.

McEvedy, R. (1987). Some social, cultural, and linguistic issues in teaching reading to children who speak English as a second language. *Australian Journal of Reading, 9*(3), 139–152.

McInnes, M. M. (1986, April). *A preliminary report on an investigation using a Piagetian model to teach reading to Spanish-speaking secondary students.* Paper presented at the annual international Bilingual/Bicultural Education Conference, Chicago, IL.

McLeod, A. (1986). Critical literacy: Taking control of our own lives. *Language Arts, 63*(1), 37–49.

Miller, C. H. (1987). Ready, set, write! A teacher taps the talent of bilingual third graders. *Equity and Choice, 3*(2), 3–9.

Modiano, N. (1968). National or mother tongue in beginning reading: A comparative study. *Research in the Teaching of English, 1,* 324–343.

Monteiro, R. P. (1986, April). *Question asking and reading comprehension: The relationship between reading ability and question-asking ability.* Paper presented at the annual conference of the American Educational Research Association, San Francisco, California.

Muniz-Swicegood, M. (1994). The effects of metacognitive reading strategy training on the reading performance and student reading analysis strategies of third grade bilingual students. *Bilingual Research Journal, 16*(3 & 4), 83–97.

Nagy, W. E., Garcia, G. E., & Durgonoglu, A. Y. (1993). Spanish-English bilingual students use of cognates in English reading. *Journal of Reading Behavior, 25*(3), 241–252.

Nieto, S. (1994). *Multicultural education: Affirming diversity.* New York: Longman.

Nieves-Falcón, L. (1981, March). *Bilingual education: Ideological change and institutionalization.* Fourth annual bilingual conference Keynote Presentation, State Association for Bilingual Education, New York.

Ovando, C. J., & Collier, P. (1985). *Bilingual and ESL classrooms: Teaching in multicultural contexts.* New York: McGraw-Hill.

Pacheco, L. C. (1977). Educational renewal: A bilingual-bicultural imperative. *Educational Horizons, 55,* 168–176.

Padron, Y. N. (1985). *Utilizing cognitive reading strategies to improve English reading comprehension of Spanish-speaking bilingual students.* Unpublished doctoral dissertation, University of Houston.

Padron, Y. N. (1990). Examining the cognitive reading strategies used by Hispanic elementary students while reading Spanish. In L. M. Malve (Ed.), *NABE 1988–89: Annual Conference Journal* (pp. 138–150). Washington, DC: National Association for Bilingual Education.

Padron, Y. N. (1992). The effect of strategy instruction on bilingual students' cognitive strategy use in reading. *Bilingual Research Journal, 16*(3 & 4), 35–51.

Prado-Olmos, P., Szymanski, M., & Smith, M. E. (1993). Students' "do" process: Bilingual students' interactions in a small cooperative learning reading group. *Bilingual Research Journal, 19*(3 & 4), 41–69.

Ramirez, A. (1979). Teaching reading in Spanish: A study of teacher effectiveness. *Reading Improvement, 16,* 304–313.

Ramirez, D. (1991). *The condition of bilingual education in the nation: A report to the congress and the president.* Washington, DC: U.S. Department of Education, Office of Educational Research and Improvement.

Ramirez, M., & Castañeda, A. (1974). *Cultural democracy bicognitive development, and education.* New York: Academic Press.

Reyes, D. J. (1974). Spanish language teaching and teaching the Spanish language. *Contemporary Education, 45,* 147–148.

Rigg, P., & Scott Enright, D. (Eds.). (1986). *Children and ESL: Integrating perspectives.* Washington, DC: Teachers of English as a Second Language.

Rivera Viera, D. (1986). Remediating reading problems in a Hispanic learning disabled student from a psycholinguistic perspective. *Journal of Reading, Writing, and Learning Disabilities International, 2*(1), 85–97.

Rivers, J. (1986, March). *Whole language in the elementary classroom.* Paper presented at the annual meeting of the Teachers of English to Speakers of Other Languages, Anaheim, CA.

Roberts, J. (1987). *Title I Services to LEP students: Technology, reading and math.* Washington, DC: U.S. Department of Education, Congressional Records Publications.

Romero, M. (1980, February). *Error analysis and miscue analysis: Reading diagnostic assessment for teaching bilingual students in CSD 3's reading clinic.* Paper presented at Teachers College, Columbia University, New York.

Sayers, D. (1991). Cross-cultural exchanges between students from the same culture: A portrait of an emerging relationship mediated by technology. *Canadian Modern Language Review, 47*(4), 678–696.

Sayers, D. (1995). Educational equity issues in an information age. *Teachers College Record, 96*(4), 767–774.

Segan, F. (1984). Teorías sobre la adquisición y la transferencia de destrezas de lectura. In A. L. Carrasquillo & P. Segan (Eds.), *The teaching of reading in Spanish to bilingual students* (pp. 212–237). New York: Ediciones Puerto Rico de Autores Nuevos.

Soler-Galiano, A., & Prince, C. D. (1987). *Reading and writing instruction in three bilingual education programs in Connecticut.* Hartford, CT: Connecticut State Department of Education.

Tchaconas, T. N. (1985). *Oral reading strategies in Greek and English of second grade bilingual children and their relationship to field dependence and field independence.* Unpublished doctoral dissertation, Columbia University, Teachers College, New York.

Tchaconas, T. N., & Spiridakis, J. N. (1986). Reading and cognitive styles of Greek bilingual children. *Journal of the New York State Association for Bilingual Education, 2*(1), 21–31.

U.S. Department of Education. (1994). *Improving America's school act of 1994: Public law 103-382.* Washington, DC: U.S. Department of Education.

Wells, G. (1987). Apprenticeship in literacy. *Interchange, 18*(12), 109–123.

Zentella, A. C. (1980). *Discourse processes and code-switching in the bilingual child.* Unpublished doctoral dissertation, SUNY, Albany, NY.

3

The Teaching
of Spanish Literacy Development

Angela Carrasquillo
Fordham University

Este capítulo presenta una visión general de los cuatro procesos lingüísticos: escuchar, hablar, leer y escribir. Teorías, principios filosóficos y estrategias educativas con relación a estos cuatro procesos se describen en la medida que éston están relacionados con la enseñanza y aprendizaje de la lengua española. Además, se enumeran y explican estrategias instruccionales integrando las cuatro áreas de la comunicación en el proceso de leer.

OBJECTIVES

The reader of this chapter will be able to:

1. Identify the relation between the processes of listening, speaking, reading, and writing.
2. Define Spanish literacy.
3. Identify teaching strategies to teach Spanish listening, oral production, reading, and writing skills.
4. Describe the process of constructing meaning through the reading process.
5. List and discuss writing approaches to develop cognitive and social relations through writing.

GUIDE QUESTIONS

1. What are the theoretical foundations for perceiving language as the integration of the four linguistic systems?
2. What are the disadvantages Spanish-language learners may have in developing literacy in Spanish?
3. In developing Spanish literacy, what type of curriculum characteristics/changes do you foresee as being needed in schools in the United States?
4. What Spanish literature texts would you recommend for a particular grade/level to develop a whole-language classroom using the Spanish language as the medium of teaching and learning?
5. What may be some of the disadvantages in using thematic units in a Spanish-language classroom? Discuss its advantages.
6. What "social situations" would you create in an urban classroom to promote pragmatic Spanish writing?
7. How can the teacher use media/technology in journal writing as an educational strategy?
8. Do you think it is possible to develop Spanish literacy in schools in the United States? If so, how? If not, why?

INTRODUCTION

Language is an integration of the four processes of listening, speaking, reading, and writing. Language is a complex human mental and physical process, and yet most individuals use it without any awareness of the myriad of processes that take place in producing and interpreting language. Human beings write and read for the purpose of knowing other's responses, and to connect themselves more fully with the human world. As students and adults speak, read, and write, they focus on accomplishing things with language. Language learners learn from their literacy experiences when they explain (orally or in writing) those experiences to someone, or hear or read someone else telling of other experiences. Usually, successful Spanish-language speakers come to school with a broad repertoire of language skills, including the grammatical structures of the language, the various functions of the language, the meaning of what language is, and the reasons that the language is used. This Spanish-language preparation provides the foundation for students' successful school language experiences, especially in oral language.

The four linguistic processes, although independent, are interrelated and work in conjunction with the cognitive process of learning. The language processes share a variety of characteristics, making them interdependent on each other. For example, the abilities used for oral language are the same ones necessary for developing writing abilities. Dickinson (1987) identified four types of relations between oral language, reading, and writing:

A dependence on language-processing capabilities. The same abilities that are necessary for acquiring oral language are necessary for literacy development.

Interdependence of knowledge structures. Oral language is interdependent on the control of knowledge structures necessary for reading and writing.

Support of acquisition of literacy with speech. There is a strong relationship between reading and writing development and the ways individuals project themselves orally.

Interdependence of different modalities. With proper experiences, students will be able to develop their own spelling and punctuation systems once they have learned some modality-specific information, such as letters of the alphabet.

Because there is a strong connection between oral language development, reading, and writing, teachers develop lessons, activities, and environments that encourage students to increase their Spanish vocabularies, extend their manipulation of Spanish-language structures, and develop new concepts. They make these opportunities meaningful by linking them to the students' past experiences, verbally modeling, labeling the processes and concepts being addressed, and making it necessary for students to create or apply the oral language to the written language. Students learn new words and new concepts in the Spanish language through guided experiences that teachers demonstrate and describe. Students use new vocabulary words as labels, and in context, as they relate these words to the progression of the cognitive task. The students, as part of their experiences, are expected to interact with the teacher, the materials, and their peers in an effort to explore, clarify, practice, extend, and apply new variations of language in familiar or related contexts. Thus, the development of students' Spanish oral and written language depend on and support each other. Whether at school or at home, students need many opportunities to explore and use the Spanish language.

The four language processes have an inseparable relationship, so the teaching of language should be approached from an integrated point of view. Listening, speaking (oral development), reading, and writing in the Spanish-language classroom should be taught and used together, each fostering and supporting the other. The quicker and better students start using the Spanish language, the more successful they will be at reading and writing the Spanish language. In the same manner, ability to read facilitates learning in all content areas. It also contributes to the development of writing proficiency. Research in the areas of language learning has proven that language skills are strengthened as students are encouraged to respond to literature both orally and in writing. The following actions may contribute to students' Spanish-language development: the ability to read words in print; the ability to speak with clarity, conciseness, and cogency; the ability to write easily and comfortably; the ability to communicate essential ideas via the written word; the ability to understand oral messages, attending both to the stated meaning of utterances and the implied meanings reflected in word choice, sentence structure, and the stress and juncture patterns of speech; and the ability to find satisfaction, purpose, and achievement through the various aspects of language.

Students' Spanish-language proficiency and development need to be evaluated in each of the four language processes. For example, Hispanics who appear to be proficient in Spanish may have only conversational proficiency rather than the cognitive/academic proficiency required for successful academic schoolwork. Students with a conversational proficiency may use Spanish in situations at home, in church, on the playground, and in the classroom where there are situational clues (context embedded) that they may rely on to provide meaning to the situation. However, in situations requiring higher order language skills (context reduced) —whether they be textbook work, teacher lectures, or other classroom activities—the student who is only conversationally proficient is at a disadvantage. Because the language modes are so inextricably bound up with one another, it is almost impossible to teach one in isolation from the others. Oral and written language develop simultaneously, each facilitating and supporting learners' understanding of the other (Y. Freeman & D. Freeman, 1997). Students learn written language by interacting with other learners and users in reading and writing situations and by exploring print in their communicative processes.

LISTENING COMPREHENSION

Listening is the central process in daily language use. Much of the emphasis for the teaching of Spanish in the United States has been on Spanish grammar, the primary focus on teaching to grammatically decode the Spanish grammar rules. Most of the time spent in the classroom is on analyzing the Spanish language instead of comprehending, reading, and writing it. Educators truly believe that if Spanish-language learners are able to grammatically understand the Spanish language, listening comprehension will occur simultaneously. However, research on the relationship between listening and speaking tends to suggest that only if language learners comprehend what they listen to as they read it, will the four areas of the language develop as a natural process. On the other hand, good listeners, whether native or nonnative speakers, use four basic steps plus an array of cognitive strategies to obtain meaning from what they hear. These mental steps are not always carried out in order; listeners may carry them out at the same time, or jump forward and backward as they see fit. These mental steps can be summarized as follows:

1. Listeners sort out why they are listening, and what they want or need to know. Language is to be understood in the same way on similar occasions because listeners or readers must have a pretty good idea about the meaning that was intended in the first place. There must be a reason for listening. (Often in the language classroom, the reason for listening is to pass a quiz on information heard.)
2. Listeners predict some of the information expected to be included in the utterance and assess how much of the incoming information will be new and how much will be familiar. Good listeners connect experiences and information to the language-related situation. Meaning is brought to language through prediction, which may be defined as the logical elimination of unlikely alternatives.
3. Referring to the initial reason for listening, listeners decide how much of the message is going to be relevant to the purpose of the task, or the initial reason for first listening. This check tells listeners what information in the conversation to ignore and what to select, because the first interpretation that comes to listeners is the one that makes the most sense at that particular time.
4. Listeners then check understanding of the message in a variety of ways. Some examples are: by asking or answering questions, by

making appropriate nonverbal gestures, and by acting accordingly. Listeners often receive feedback from the speaker in a real communication situation, or from a teacher in a classroom situation.

Teachers should provide Spanish-language learners with listening experiences on a regular basis. In addition, teachers should guide listeners through each experience, assisting them to proceed through the four steps and to apply cognitive strategies aimed at uncovering the speaker's message (Condemarín, 1989; Dunkel, 1993). The following poem (Freire de Matos, 1958, pp. 36–37) is effectively used to motivate students to listen to determine the author's knowledge of the arrival of the Spaniards to America, predict who the characters mentioned in the poem are, and provide different interpretations to the message being conveyed by the author.

AMERICA

Cristóbal Colón
por la mar venía
con tres velas blancas
llenas de alegría:
la Pinta, la Niña,
la Santa María.
En olas y olas
su sueño latía
de hallar una tierra
en la lejanía.
Las aves volando
mensajes traían,
de la tierra virgen,
hermosa y bravía
que el 12 de octubre
Colón descubría.
¡Y se llama América
esta tierra mía!

ORAL PRODUCTION

The main purpose of speaking is communication. The development of oral language is the foundation for students' literacy development. Speaking allows individuals to express themselves concisely, coherently, and in a manner that suits all audiences and occasions. One of the most important observations about language acquisition is that students are not taught how to talk. Students learn to talk by interacting with adults in a language-rich environment. Adults model language for students by speaking to them in natural kinds of language patterns. Language is used in naturalistic, real-life contexts in which language has a series of functions and purposes. Communication takes place when there is sharing of experience, expression of social solidarity, decision making, and planning. This principle is the same for the development of the Spanish language, especially oral language in the classroom setting. The spoken Spanish language is an important part of the identities of all participants, and it plays an active role in speaking the language to communicate. Thus, context and opportunity play a critical role in how much and how often Spanish-language learners use the Spanish language. Students who have many and varied opportunities to talk about what they have read or written become capable of expressing their high-level thinking about texts or any other related cognitive tasks. Talking about what students read and write allows them to interpret the printed word, making their academic and personal world more relevant. Meaningful communication is important and necessary for students' mastery of the Spanish language, and they need to become effective language users to help them not just to survive, but to succeed in an English-language environment. The elements of meaningful communication are illustrated in Fig. 3.1.

Students' oral language development needs instructional contexts that emphasize the following aspects:

Content is based on students' communicative needs.

Instruction makes use of extensive contextual clues.

Teachers modify their English speech to students' level and confirm students' comprehension.

The focus is on language functions or content rather than grammatical form.

Grammatical accuracy is promoted not by correcting errors overtly, but by providing more comprehensible instruction.

Students are encouraged to respond spontaneously and creatively.

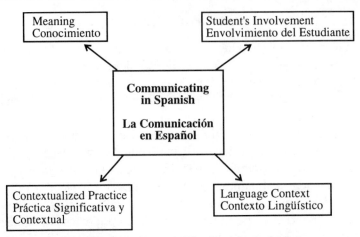

FIG. 3.1. Students' Spanish oral development: What does it involve? (¿Qué componentes envuelve el desarrollo oral del estudiante?)

- ¿Tuvieron ustedes algún inconveniente para llegar a la escuela hoy? (relevant to students' needs)

- ¿Cuáles son los factores/cosas que pueden hacer que Uds. lleguen tarde a la escuela? (contextual clues).

- ¿Podrías relatar cómo tu experiencia es diferente a la de María? ¿Cómo es similar?

- ¿Cómo podríamos mejorar la asistencia a la escuela?

FIG. 3.2. Temas sugeridos para el desarrollo del lenguaje oral.

To provide experiences for students' oral language development, teachers may ask students to react to questions/topics such as those presented in Fig. 3.2.

When students are allowed to discuss with others in class what they interpret from readings or their own writing and when they listen to others' interpretations of the same story or piece, they evolve in their thinking and are able to structure and restructure their knowledge. Teachers must identify the kinds of situations that require effective communication and the kinds of speaking skills required by those situations.

READING: THE DOOR TO KNOWLEDGE

Reading is one of the most important communication areas for students to conquer because reading is the door to most of the knowledge needed in society. Reading is a process of constructing meaning, and the sooner students can read in Spanish, the wider their door to the world. As mentioned throughout this chapter, reading is the process of constructing meaning through the dynamic interaction (transaction) among the reader's existing knowledge, the information suggested by the written language, and the context of the reading situation (Alonso & Mateo, 1985; Río, 1985; Weaver, 1988). Constructing meaning includes understanding the information in the text and incorporating the knowledge used to understand the text in the first place. Readers need to be actively involved in the act of reading and interested in the content being read. Whether it is presented through experience charts, basal readers, literature, or trade books, the printed word surrounds students in every classroom.

Students develop reading comprehension of printed language by having experiences that interpret the print, just as oral experience helps students to interpret spoken language. As students begin to read the print themselves, they use additional systems to assist their efforts in knowing which letter patterns or relations represent which spoken words. This system of relating sounds to printed symbols in making units of meaning is called decoding. As readers look at the words in a text, they engage in an intentional activity; they have a reason for reading. Their purpose for reading will significantly influence the strategies they use and how much they will remember of what they read. Kucer (1987) identified four universals that undergird the processes of reading and writing.

1. Readers and writers construct text–world meanings through utilizing the prior knowledge that they bring to the literacy event.
2. The written language system operates by feeding into a common data pool from which the language user draws when constructing the text world.
3. Readers and writers utilize common procedures for transforming prior knowledge into a text world.
4. Readers and writers display common processing patterns or abilities when constructing text worlds.

These universals can also be explained as functional tasks developed through the reading process. Carrasquillo (1994) and Carrasquillo and Rodríguez (1996) identified the following functions of reading:

1. Readers must construct purposes for reading. Why are ESL readers reading a given selection? Only by developing purposes will readers be able to gain the appropriate kind of information and enjoyment from reading.
2. Readers must activate relevant background/prior knowledge. The knowledge a reader brings to the printed page affects the comprehension of the text.
3. Readers must allocate attention in order to focus on major content and not on less important content. Given the purposes for reading, some information will be important, and other information will not be important, depending on the purpose of the reader.
4. Readers must critically evaluate the content of the text. They must determine if the information presented is internally consistent. They must also check to see if the text information is consistent with their own prior knowledge and with general knowledge.
5. Readers must monitor ongoing activities to see if they are actually comprehending the text. Students' own evaluation of their reading progress and understanding have a tremendous influence in the way they change their learning strategies to become more productive learners.
6. Readers must make and test inferences of many kinds. Readers are constantly filling in gaps and making assumptions while they read. Interpreting, predicting, and arriving at conclusions are all part of the process of reading for meaning.
7. Readers must select reading strategies that help them to understand what they read. Strategies are essential in the comprehension of texts. Students need to develop strategies to know when to skim to look for more points, when to scan for particular information, when to read quickly or slowly, carefully or curiously, silently or aloud.

Teachers often underestimate the importance that culture plays in reading comprehension. Students must have knowledge and understanding of the world around them as they interact with text or attempt to write about a topic. Comprehension will take place only when the information in the text triggers a response from readers or writers whose background knowledge has been activated (Carrell, 1989). The classroom teacher must actively deal with the cultural components of a text when teaching reading to students. The student needs to understand the basic assumptions about the world in order to interpret the new information correctly. Students who lack cultural knowledge about the content presented will only be able to make superficial predictions or inferences about what they learn. For example, the following Spanish reading verse (Asenjo, 1958, p. 198–199). needs to be related to the Puerto Rican experience:

> Mamey, zapote, algarrobo,
> toronja, uva y limón,
> guanábana, guava y jobo
> y el sabroso corazón.
> China, caimito y melón,
> almendra, lima, cereza,
> y la muy abundate fresa
> y el escasísimo anón.

THE DEVELOPMENT OF SPANISH WRITING

Writing is a complex human activity linked with cognitive and social relations. Writing influences students' oral and reading development. Routman (1988) indicated that people write to discover meaning and to figure out what they want to say. Students write about what they know and have experienced in their lives. Such writing may evolve into nonfiction accounts about personal experiences. Students develop Spanish writing skills through interaction with peers and teachers, as well as through the content, purpose, and structure of oral and written tasks. In order to communicate through writing, students need to learn grammar, vocabulary, and the functions of written Spanish.

Students can become proficient Spanish writers if teachers create writing environments that are interactive and meaningful to all the students in the classroom. In such interactive environments, teachers spend less time telling the students what to do and more time helping them realize options to pursue through writing. Studies support the idea that students, who are given choices of what to write and read, feel a greater sense of ownership and purpose (Fernández de la Torriente, 1984; Fernández & Gairín, 1985; Graves, 1983; Metz, 1985; Routman, 1988). One goal of the teacher should be to make reading and writing functional and purposeful to the student. Current research has shown that literacy learning is not a set of skills, but the result of conditions that allow students to be part of a literate community doing the things that literate people do. Writing letters, dialogue writing, keeping diaries, and reading books to obtain information on a topic that interests them are learning tasks that have a purpose for students and motivate them to do more and better writing. Teachers should be involved in the process of writing to provide students with the opportunity to see how the process of writing is developed. Teachers' modeling can be especially beneficial for students who are trying to expand their Spanish language knowledge. Cassany (1989) presented the following model that the teacher may use in presenting students with ideas on how the process of writing is developed. Cassany (1989) presented a list (Fig. 3.3) of ideas for teachers to help students in developing writing as a process and as a product. The list is divided into three areas: *pre-drafting, drafting*, and *revising*.

Escribir el Primer Borrador

Pre-Escribir

1. Saber recoger, clasificar, sintetizar, interpretar y adaptar información procedente de un curso de una materia determinada (explicaciones y discusiones en clase, apuntes, lecturas complementarias, manuales, etc.). *Son útiles para hacer exámenes, trabajos, recensiones, etc.*
2. Saber aprovechar la experiencia y los conocimientos personales: seleccionar la información sugerente, relacionarla con otras ideas, etc. *Para escritos personales, redacción libre y creativa, etc.*
3. Saber relacionar los conceptos procedentes de lecturas y clases con la experiencia personal.
4. Saber realizar un estudio de campo (experimentos, observaciones, encuestas, etc.): definir el problema y las hipótesis de trabajo, recoger datos suficientes y apropiados con métodos adecuados y saber analizarlos e interpretarlos correctamente. *Para informes y recensiones de estudios empíricos.*

---

5. Saber leer críticamente un texto (literario, periodístico, etc.): identificar los problemas de interpretación, caracterizar el estilo lingüístico, la estructura, etc. *Para comentarios de texto, críticas, etc.*

6. Saber obtener y organizar información a partir de otros textos: escoger y delimitar un tema de investigación, localizar referencias bibliográficas, valorar su interés y utilidad, *skimming* (lectura rápida de vistazo) y *scanning* (lectura atenta de fragmentos), tomar apuntes, etc. *Para trabajos basados en bibliografía.*

7. Saber refundir datos e ideas recogidas de otros textos o de investigaciones de campo: hacer esquemas, clasificaciones, comparaciones y análisis, etc.

---

1. Aplicar un proceso de composición eficiente y productivo: estar dispuesto a escribir más de un borrador, a alterar los planes iniciales, etc.

2. Controlar los pasos del proceso: primero generar ideas, dejar la corrección gramatical para el final, etc.

3. Tener conocimientos léxicos y semánticos y fluidez: construir frases bien formadas, cohesionarlas, etc.

4. Tener conocimientos morfosintáctios y fluidez: construir frases bien formadas, cohesionarlas, etc.

5. Conocer las convenciones del discurso: variedad y registro, coherencia, estructura, disposición, etc.

6. Conocer las convenciones mecánicas: ortografía, mayúsculas, puntuación, tipografía, etc.

Revisar

---

1. Evaluar y revisar el contenido: qué dice el texto y qué quisiera el autor que dijera, cómo reaccionará el lector y cómo quisiera el autor que éste reaccionara, etc.

2. Evaluar y revisar la estructura: adaptarse a la audiencia, buscar prosa de lector, etc.

3. Corregir la gramática: aplicar las reglas de gramática aprendidas conscientemente.

4. Corregir el vocabulario y el estilo: utilizar los conocimientos léxicos y las obras de consulta (diccionarios, *thesaurus*, etc.).

> 5. Corregir los aspectos más mecánicos: ortografía, separación de palabras, abreviaturas, mayúsculas, puntuación, etc.
>
> En este último apartado los puntos anteriores se agrupan en dos bloques:
> - La revisión interna o revisión de las intenciones, que afecta al contenido y a la organización.
> - La revisión externa o revisión de las convenciones, que afecta a la forma: la gramática, los aspectos mecánicos, etc.
>
> Teachers need to encourage students to take risks and to make personal

FIG 3.3. Proceso de Composición. From Cassany (1989, pp. 125–127).

written responses when interpreting what they have read or heard. Teachers should use questions such as: What did you notice in the story?, How did the story make you feel?, What does the story remind you of in your own life? Answers to these questions do not demand correct responses. Students are given the freedom to explore meaning and to express their own understanding of the text. However, in some basal readers, short precise answers do not encourage students to draw on personal experiences, nor do they encourage students to explore their thinking as they write. Open-ended questions about stories and different interpretations about text will be part of the classroom that values students' perceptions. But students need to be guided in writing answers to open-ended questions. They may be intimidated by the lack of Spanish vocabulary and language structures to express their thoughts.

RECOMMENDED STRATEGIES

Instructional approaches and strategies that promote students' oral, reading, and written Spanish-language development are mentioned in this section. These strategies provide an atmosphere for learning that is positive, meaningful, and sensitive to students' linguistic and cultural needs, ensuring that each of the processes of language literacy are developed. For example, vocabulary acquisition and development are most effective when words are appropriately contextualized, and taught in contexts that are natural, functional, and of immediate interest and use. This means that the most effective vocabulary development takes place in lessons in content areas (e.g., social studies, science, or mathematics), rather than within a discrete reading period. The linguistic and conceptual contexts of the content areas are most likely to be effective when they contain diverse areas of interest and relevant purposes. In addition, students need to become familiar with the functional use of resources available for vocabulary acquisition, such as encyclopedias, dictionaries, thesauruses, card catalogs, maps, globes, microcomputers, and other electronic tools such as e-mail and the internet.

Semantic Mapping

One useful strategy for providing structure to this process is semantic mapping. Knowledge is retrieved from long-term memory, is shared with other students, is discussed in terms of needed vocabulary and concepts, and is recorded in a graphic format that promotes organizing schemata so that relationships become more clear. For example, if students are studying about trees and their importance in society, vocabulary and context knowledge can be developed through semantic mapping. First, students should study about trees through literature or social studies/science readings. The following verses, taken from the poem *"No Hagas Daño al Árbol"* (Ramírez de Arellano, 1958, p. 194), are a good way of introducing the topic of the importance of trees.

> Tú no hagas daño al árbol. Sus altas ramas tiende
> para albergar los nidos del pájaro cantor.
> Cuando la primavera los rosales enciende
> adorna los caminos, como una inmensa flor.
> Dorados frutos tiemblan en los verdes ramajes
> y su sombra te brindan los espesos follajes.
> La copa, verde y alta, te sirve de sombrilla.
> ¿Quieres tú caridad más humana y sencilla?

A semantic mapping example may look as follows:

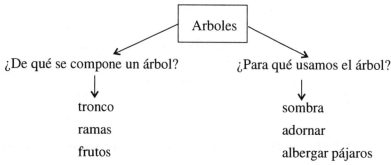

Semantic mapping, or *webbing,* is widely espoused as an effective technique for teaching vocabulary as well as for improving reading comprehension. The semantic map, like a story map, has many attractions. It graphically shows relationships in ways that appeal to and make sense to visual learners. Also, as the map or web grows and interrelates, students can see the conceptual relationships, and they can develop a fuller understanding of word families (or categories) and how they function as guides to information and meaning. In addition, the process of semantic mapping provides excellent opportunities for activating students' prior background knowledge, or for building new backgrounds of students during the prereading phase of the lesson. Many of the strategies recommended for the activation or development of background knowledge constitute direct approaches to vocabulary instruction.

Guided Reading Strategies

Guided reading may take the mode of oral or silent reading to provide students with the opportunity to read and get meaning from the printed text. Guided reading provides students with the opportunity to read at their own pace for recreational or learning purposes. Planned, whole group, and silent reading periods are the foundation of guided reading. Teachers direct this process by introducing the students to this reading routine in short time increments and gradually increasing time as students learn to focus their attention on their reading material for longer periods. After selecting a book to read, students are encouraged to attend to the text. An important component of guided reading is the wise and judicious use of questions, primarily through oral language in a discussion format, to orchestrate learning in the classroom environment and to guide individual learning in the most productive direction. For second-language learners of Spanish, especially, teachers need to include *instructional* (to teach some aspects of reading) and *monitoring* (to find out whether students understand what has been read) questions. Students need to be asked questions preceding or during the reading to help them get meaning from the reading. Most of the questions should focus on hypothesizing or predicting: What do you think this story will be about? What do you think will happen next? After asking an inferential question that requires students to project, or make predictions about coming events, teachers should follow up with specific data acquisition questions to help students to focus on the detailed information in the text. Also, it is important to include appropriate recapitulation or summary questions at the end of the text. When working with longer texts, these questions should be included in the middle of the text to pressure students to mentally review the concepts or ideas of what has been read.

When students themselves begin to read, they may benefit from having their teacher read to them. In fact, the teacher may find that presenting the entire selection as a read-aloud is helpful. The first reading of beginning readers may take the form of group echoic reading with a teacher or lead reader, probably following a read-aloud by the teacher. As the lead reader reads, students try to follow along, reading orally as a group. Also, the teacher's read-aloud lesson provides the teacher with the opportunity to model predicting, thinking about context, and other strategies by talking through some of the metacognitive processes used during the teacher's oral reading. Certainly middle- and upper-grade students need to be reading silently on an extensive basis, for it is through more rapid silent reading that students can read for the most practice and also be exposed to the most background knowledge and contextualized vocabulary. But it is more difficult for teachers to provide extra support to students learning Spanish as a second language because their need for it may be less obvious during the largely independent activity of reading silently. One strategy for providing this support during the silent reading lesson is to guide or structure the reading with questions. Guided silent reading provides an opportunity for students to work at high cognitive levels by identifying cause-and-effect relationships, making inferences and predictions, and applying other critical thinking skills to support their comprehension of the reading material. Guiding students' reading with questions can provide helpful support through bringing key story concepts to the attention of students as they read, thereby helping them maintain comprehension, and equally important, providing moral support, interest, and motivation.

The Language Experience Approach as a Postreading Activity

The purpose of the *language experience approach* is to allow students to read things that are familiar to them and within their range of experiences and capability. This strategy is recommended for use after students have read a written text. Van Allen and Allen (1970) mentioned different language experiences that can be used to develop students' interests in reading and writing experiences. These are:

- Sharing experiences
- Discussing experiences
- Expanding vocabulary
- Developing awareness of common vocabulary

- Improving writing style and form
- Dictating words, sentences, and stories
- Telling stories
- Reading whole stories and books
- Using a variety of resources
- Comprehending what is read
- Organizing ideas and information
- Writing independent books

- Listening to stories
- Studying words
- Writing independently
- Writing individual books
- Reading a variety of symbols
- Summarizing
- Integrating and assimilating ideas
- Reading critically

This strategy integrates the four communication areas. It uses students' words to create a text that becomes the material for a reading lesson. In the language experience approach, individualized reading and expressive writing reveal the intimate needs, interests, and concerns of the students. Visual materials are essential to this method. For example, in the verses presented earlier about trees, teachers may ask the students to read the verses orally to find out the following: *¿Por qué el autor le dice a los lectores que no hagan daño al árbol?*

The first step in introducing the lesson is a teacher-initiated discussion about the topic (trees). During the discussion, the teacher reviews vocabulary and structures (through semantic mapping) found in the reading. Emphasis will vary according to the level of the group. The teacher asks questions but does not force anyone to respond. Members of the group can listen to and build on each other's responses based on the content of the reading and the applications derived from the reading. Then, the teacher invites students to read the verses to answer a particular question or a series of questions.

Developing Literacy Through Literature

Mainstream classroom teachers must work to create a genuine integrated classroom literacy community, a place where the experiences, capacities, interests, and goals of every classroom member are simultaneously utilized for students' learning benefit. Literature capitalizes on opportunities to play with language, to experiment with it, and, at the same time, contributes to literacy development. Literature is viewed by many researchers and teachers as the best material for reading (Mayo, 1984; Routman, 1988). Literature not only contributes to the development of students' reading, it promotes oral and written growth. Vocabulary development and syntactic maturity have been found to be influenced positively by reading short stories, poems, and novels. Through literature, students are exposed to a diversity of ideas, oral and written, which typically demand high levels of background knowledge, vocabulary, and language structures that are challenging to students. Studies have revealed that students who did well in writing tended to do well in reading, and vice versa. Exposure to literature helps students to:

Develop sophisticated language structures: "Hace no mucho tiempo en el país de los animales, vivía una cucarachita muy trabajadora."

Accumulate background knowledge useful in learning to read: "Un día barriendo la puerta de su casa, se encontró un centavo."

Increase interest in learning to read: "¿Qué me compraré? ¿Qué me compraré?"

Build a sense of story structure: "Me compraré una caja de polvos."

Form a natural setting for the foundation of comprehension skills: "Y la cucarachita se compró una caja de polvos y muy enpolvadita, se sentó a la puerta de su casa."

Exposure to literature enhances listening skills, vocabulary, and grammatical and syntactical knowledge of the English language. The learner is introduced to new words; these words are learned within a context of a story, not in isolation. Literature, when it is read to students, also promotes listening skills. Students learn pronunciation of new words and develop skills in interpreting or telling stories. These skills are especially important for language learners, because they can hear language being modeled. This modeling can also be done by the students as they read in groups or by echoing. Thus, literature provides excellent models for students as they learn to read or write. Regardless of age or culture, when individuals relate stories they have read or heard, their retelling follows a set of patterns. For example, narrative retelling of stories develops a sense of setting, climax, and ending. Retelling stories also gives the learner a sense of grammar and structure. This sense of syntax enhances the reader's understanding of a story read, even when the reader is a second-language learner, who may be unable to decode each word.

One of the primary goals in using a literature approach to improve Spanish-language skills among students is that these students learn to enjoy reading and voluntarily choose to read in Spanish, both as a recreational and learning activity. Teachers play an important role in achieving this goal, especially when the students being introduced to Spanish reading are students who may not have achieved proficiency in the English language. When introducing students to Spanish literature, the following instructional practices or principles need to be considered:

1. Initial instructional emphasis is on shared reading that contains traditional, easy stories that many students already know by heart. Usually, there is no attempt to isolate or break down any of the words or sentence elements in this initial reading; rather, the focus is on the rhythm and pattern of the story. ¿Qué me compraré? ¿Qué me compraré?

2. The content of the literature should be used to emphasize aspects of the structure of the language that need to be pointed out, such as phonics and sight-word vocabulary. ¿Te quieres casar conmigo? A ver, ¿qué haces de noche? ¡Muuu, Muuuu! ¡Ay no, no, no; qué me asustarás!

3. The content of the literature material serves to engage students in writing activities using the literature as models for the instruction. The students' stories are reviewed by the teacher for improving the mechanics, and these stories are then shared with other classmates. ¿Estás de acuerdo con la actitud de la cucarachita? ¿Por qué? ¿Harías tú lo mismo que hizo la cucarachita?

It is recommended that teachers ask students to keep a journal of their thoughts and ideas as they read literature. The teacher, or other students, may react to this journal writing by responding in writing with their ideas to the students.

A story map may be used to sequence the story and serve as a framework for organizing the elements. A sequenced story map (Fig. 3.4) may include the discussion of an outline.

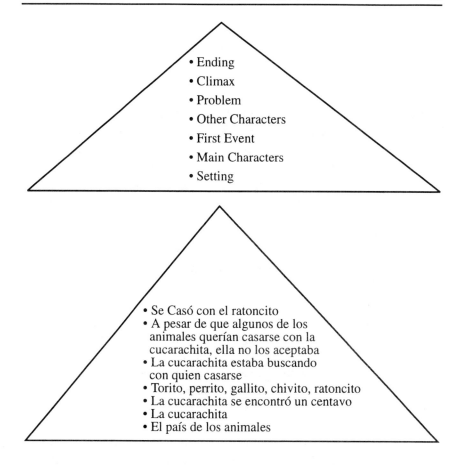

* Ending
* Climax
* Problem
* Other Characters
* First Event
* Main Characters
* Setting

* Se Casó con el ratoncito
* A pesar de que algunos de los animales querían casarse con la cucarachita, ella no los aceptaba
* La cucarachita estaba buscando con quien casarse
* Torito, perrito, gallito, chivito, ratoncito
* La cucarachita se encontró un centavo
* La cucarachita
* El país de los animales

La Cucarachita

FIG. 3.4. A story map.

As shown in the previous examples, classroom strategies need to be integrated in the language classroom to expose students to reading literature for different purposes.

Whole-language Approach to the Teaching of Reading

The whole-language philosophy embraces the definition that whole-language instruction is the simultaneous, integrated teaching of listening, speaking, reading, and writing within a meaningful context, based on students' strengths, backgrounds, and the experiences they bring to the classroom. Many educators support a whole language approach to the teaching of reading that includes the development of word identification skills. In many ways, this approach is closely related to the language experience and the literature-based approaches to reading instruction. Oral language, reading, and writing are seen as interrelated as a means for enriching the whole experience of the students' language. The language of the students is the critical foundation for all reading instruction. Thus, reading instruction is most effective when it focuses on the students' language rather than a contrived language with controlled vocabulary. Benefits of the whole-language approach include: Curriculum is learner centered; language is learned from whole to part; listening, speaking, reading, and writing are used from the beginning; curriculum is meaningful and functional; students' interaction is enhanced; and students learn at their own pace.

The whole-language approach is rich in the resources that students should be using in the classroom to learn listening, speaking, reading, and writing skills. Whole-language classes, because they are characterized by meaning-focused, learner-centered experiences, look different from traditional classes, which provide more skills-focused, teacher-centered instruction. For example, in whole-language classrooms, there are no isolated spelling, phonics, handwriting, or guided writing activities. Instead, teachers use integrated language, where all of the aforementioned skills are taught interchangeably.

Another advantage of the whole-language approach for students is the significant feature of the emphasis on collaborative learning strategies that encourage group work. The collaborative environment of the classroom is central to developing both oral proficiency and academic literacy. Students in groups become more responsible for one another's success or failure. Spanish-proficient students can help students finish the task by collaborating with them in those related areas where second-language learners may not have an adequate Spanish-language foundation to accomplish the task by themselves. Work groups offer opportunities to make meaningful connections with others who are willing to interact in speech as well as in writing. Students become communities of readers, writers, speakers, and listeners. Teachers interact with these communities and serve as models of language behaviors in how to use the four modes of language appropriately.

Journal Writing

Journals are booklets of blank paper that the students use for recording their thoughts and ideas. Used on a daily basis, the students go from learning the skills of writing, to the habit of using writing as a tool for organizing and thinking about their experiences. Teachers may select one or more of the following instructional uses of students' journals.

Recording.　Students record in the journal what is on their minds. This writing is private. Only the selections the students choose are read by the teacher or by other students. Some students may elect to read their writing to other individuals or to the group. The main teaching role is to motivate the writing and to support it by giving students words, commenting appropriately when asked, and consistently respecting the approximations of the beginning writer.

Interactive Writing.　Students and teachers use the journal for communicating with each other. The student writes and the teacher responds to the writing with thoughts, ideas, and related experiences. Teacher comments do not reflect evaluation of the writing skill, the content, or the quality of the students' thinking. It is a written, nonjudgmental discussion. In later grades, this is referred to as "journal dialoguing," with the teacher carrying on a written dialogue with students via the journal.

Instructive Writing.　As an outcome of instruction, the students use the journal as a collection of their guided and independent practice responses. (*Escribe lo que aprendiste al leer el cuento "La cucarachita."*) Teachers may assign work to be completed, or may actively use the students' writing as a source for teaching one of the writing processes, such as revision.

Students benefit when teachers provide opportunities for journal writing in the classroom. Not only do they write more on a regular basis, but they also begin to experience the varied functions and modes of writing.

Pragmatic Writing

Writing is a social action, carried out with the purpose of accomplishing a particular social function, such as writing a letter to the leader of a Hispanic church expressing a particular personal concern. Spanish-language learners need to see writing as a social tool. Unfortunately, in U.S. schools, students do not have the opportunity to use Spanish socially too often. Thus, the teacher needs to create the social situations for the student to react to in writing: to write to get information, to express an opinion or desire, and to introduce themselves to a particular audience. Pragmatic writing is reactive rather than structured instruction. Teachers need to motivate students to see the need to write, to help them identify the information, and to use the most appropriate type of writing. The teacher's role is very important because students' writings need to be guided and monitored, especially when students do not have the language mastery (grammar, spelling, syntax, functions) and may not feel motivated to write. Table 3.1 illustrates ideas of how pragmatic writing may be addressed in the Spanish-language classroom.

TABLE 3.1.
La escritura como función social.

A quién	Qué Comunicarle
1. A un amigo.	1. Cuéntale el contenido de la última película que viste.
2. A la maestra.	2. Dile que aprecias lo mucho que el/ella te enseña.
3. En una tienda por departamentos.	3. Para buscar un trabajo para los sábados.
4. Dentista.	4. Para buscar el precio de una limpieza de la boca.
5. Principal.	5. Pidiéndole una carta de recomendación.
6. Oficina de Admisiones de una Universidad.	6. Solicitud de admisión.
7. Madre/Padre.	7. Comunicándoles cuánto los quieres.

Thematic Units

To insure an integrated curriculum in the classroom that is sensitive to students' needs, the most common recommendation for teachers is to develop a theme approach. Classroom instruction should be organized around thematic projects that are initiated by either teachers or students. The theme approach to learning promotes a mode of teaching and learning that is a meaningful enterprise, with projects that are used to facilitate students' learning and usually follow a problem-solving format. For students, themes that integrate the content of the different subject areas are the most often recommended. Benefits of this approach are listed in Fig. 3.5.

Students select a project such as "Don Quijote's Voyage Through Spain." Teachers act as process monitors, coordinators, and facilitators in the students' progress toward their project's goals. With this process, teachers

Matemáticas:	¿Cuántos animales querían casarse con la cucarachita? ¿Qué hizo la cucarachita al encontrarse un centavo?
Ciencia:	¿En qué se parecen los animales del cuento? ¿ En qué se diferencian?
Estudios Sociales:	Describe el país de los animales. ¿Qué otros animales podrían encontrase en este país? ¿Por qué?
Writing:	¿Estás de acuerdo con la selección de marido que hizo la cucarachita? ¿ Por qué?

FIG. 3.5. Cuento: La cucarachita.

TABLE 3.2

Academic benefits of thematic units.

Academic Benefit	Instructional Strategy
1. Easier for students to understand why they are doing a particular task in the classroom.	1. The teacher introduces same concept using different content areas, mediums, and activities. By providing different learning opportunities to accomplish a particular task, it increases understanding in the classroom.
2. Creates more flexible problem solvers that can transfer information across content areas.	2. Students are not as afraid to try something new or different, because it is acceptable to make educated guesses.
3. Promotes metacognitive awareness.	3. Students can practice different types of study skills that will facilitate a more extensive variety of ways to learn one concept.
4. Everyone is engaged in learning.	4. Promotes positive attitudes toward reading and writing.

create and implement ways for students to experience mathematics, reading, writing, science, and social studies content in an integrated way.

CONCLUSION

Oral language, reading, and writing development should be guided by the notion that language is a social activity. The classroom environment, where authentic and motivating reading and writing experiences as well as meaningful input from peers and teachers are emphasized, promotes students' Spanish-language growth. Oral language, reading, and writing go together and must be taught to students using meaningful and enjoyable experiences. Educators need to recognize the strengths and needs of students in order to work strategically with these students to help them become independent problem solvers. Teaching students to learn how to learn and to find ways to learn more effectively are skills that all teachers should emphasize in the classroom. It is important that schools employ comprehension support strategies to help students succeed in school. These strategies should include such components as guided reading instruction, group instruction, and self-teaching. For students, learning how to use these strategies is very important, because it is possible that they may not have been exposed to such strategy use before. Teachers encourage and contribute to students' academic success by providing learning experiences and assignments that enable students to feel productive, challenged, and successful. Emphasis on collaborative learning and activities that combine reading, writing, listening, and speaking are those most recommended by authorities.

FOLLOW-UP ACTIVITIES

1. Prepare a 10-minute talk to a group of school principals, who oppose the teaching of Spanish in their schools, on the academic and cognitive benefits of developing bilingual literacy to their school's students.
2. Based on your own personal experience as a teacher and using the knowledge gained through this chapter, prepare a thematic unit in which you plan for the development of the four language areas.
3. Make a list of 10 Spanish books you would recommend to another teacher to use. Be ready to provide a brief description of each book as well as the reasons for recommending each of them.

Grade Level	Books	Reason for Recommendation
Grades 4–6	1. 2. 3.	1. 2. 3.
Grades 7–9	1. 2. 3.	1. 2. 3.
Grades 10–12	1. 2. 3.	1. 2. 3.

4. Complete a chart of activities you would include in the classroom to develop students' pragmatic writing. The chart should be divided as follows:

Grade Level	Type of Activity	Brief description of the Activity
	1. 2. 3.	1. 2. 3.

REFERENCES

Alonso, J., & Mateos, M. (1985). Comprensión lectora, modelos, entrenamiento y evaluación. *Infancia y Aprendizaje, 32–33,* 5–19.

Asenjo, C. (1958). Las frutas borinqueñas. In Departamento de Instrucción Pública (Eds.), *Poesía puertorriqueña para la escuela elemental* (pp. 198–199). San Juan, PR: Departamento de Instrucción Pública.

Carrasquillo, A. (1994). *Teaching English to speakers of other languages: A resource book.* New York: Garland.

Carrasquillo, A., & Rodríguez, V. (1996). *Language minority students in the mainstream classroom.* Clevedon, England: Multilingual Matters.

Carrell, P. (1989). Metacognitive awareness and second language reading. *Modern Language Reading,* *73*(2), 121–134.

Cassany, D. (1988). *Describir el escribir: Cómo se aprende a escribir.* Barcelona, España: Ediciones Paidós.

Cassany, D. (1989). *Describir el escribir.* Barcelona, España: Ediciones Paidós Ibérica.

Condemarín, M. (1989). *Lectura temprana.* Chile: Editorial Andrés Bello.

Departamento de Instrucción Publica. (1958). *Poesía puertorriqueña para la escuela elemental.* San Juan, PR: Author.

Dickinson, D. C. (1987). Oral language, literacy skills and response to literature. In J. R. Esquire (Ed.), *The dynamics of language learning* (pp. 147–183). Urbana, IL: Clearinghouse on Reading and Communication Skills.

Dunkel, P. (1993). The assessment of an L2 listening comprehension construct: A tentative model for test specification and development. *Modern Language Journal, 77*(2), 180–191.

Fernández de la Torriente, G. (1984). *Cómo escribir correctamente.* Madrid, España: Playor.

Fernández, A., & Gairín, J. C. (1985). *Didáctica de la escritura.* Barcelona, España: Humanitas.

Freeman, Y., & Freeman, D. (1997). *Teaching reading and writing in Spanish in the bilingual classroom.* Portsmouth, NH: Heinemann.

Freire de Matas, I. (1958). América. In Departmento de Instrucción Pública (Eds.), *Poesía puertorriqueña para la escuela elemental* (pp. 36–37). San Juan, PR: Departmento de Instrucción Pública.

Graves, D. (1983). *Writing: Teachers and students at work.* Portsmouth, NH: Heinemann.

Kucer, S. B. (1987). The cognitive bases of reading and writing. In J. R. Esquire (Ed.), *The dynamics of language learning* (pp. 27–51). Urbana, IL: Clearinghouse on Reading and Communication Skills.

Mayo, W. J. (1984). *Cómo leer y memorizar rápidamente.* Madrid, España: Playor.

Metz, M. L. (1985). *Redacción y estilo.* Medico: Trillas.

Ramírez de Arellano, H. (1958). No hagas daño al árbol. In Departamento de Instrucción Pública (Eds.), *Poesía puertorriqueña para la escuela elemental* (p. 194). San Juan, PR: Departmento de Instrucción Pública.

Río, P. (1985). Investigación y práctica educativa en el desarrollo de la comprensión lectora. *Infancia y Aprendizaje,* 31–32, 21–43.

Routman, R. (1988). *Transitions from literature to literacy.* Portsmouth, NH: Heinemann.

Van Allen, R., & Allen C. (1970). *Language experience in reading.* Chicago, IL: Britanic Enciclopedic Press.

Weaver, C. (1988). *Reading process and practice.* Porthsmouth, NH: Heinemann.

4

Teaching Reading Comprehension Skills

Angela Carrasquillo
Fordham University

El objetivo principal de este capítulo es definir qué es comprensión en la lectura y enumerar aquellas áreas que son imprescindibles enfatizar en la lectura. El capítulo presenta estrategias metodológicas al desarrollar comprensión en la lectura con diferentes tipos lingüísticos de estudiantes hispanoparlantes. Comprensión es un proceso complejo que envuelve no sólo aspectos sensoriales, perceptivos, sino aún más importante, aspectos cognoscitivos. Además del trasfondo cultural y lingüístico, las experiencias físicas y mentales del estudiante son elementos que contribuyen a la comprensión en la lectura. La comprensión de tipo literal, analítica, aplicativa y evaluativa son áreas que necesitan ser enfatizadas al enseñar a leer a estudiantes bilingües ya que el estudiante necesita dominar las destrezas comprendidas en cada área, para así poder estudiar el contenido y las destrezas de otras asignaturas como ciencias y estudios sociales. La metodología y el material de lectura a usar en estas áreas dependen del tipo lingüístico de estudiante bilingüe.

OBJECTIVES

After reading this chapter, the reader will be able to:

1. Describe reading comprehension as it applies to bilingual students.

2. List specific skills and recommend activities at each of the following reading comprehension levels: literal, analytical, applicative, evaluative.
3. Identify two successful reading comprehension strategies for Spanish monolingual students.
4. Identify two successful reading comprehension strategies for Spanish-surnamed students who are dominant in English.
5. Identify two successful reading comprehension strategies for monolingual English-speaking students learning Spanish.

GUIDE QUESTIONS

1. Define reading comprehension as it applies to bilingual students. Mention in your definition the role of the bilingual students' linguistic/cultural background and experiences.
2. Identify two skills emphasized at the following reading comprehension levels: literal, analytical, applicative, evaluative.
3. How do perception and cognition require the student to apply more than the information given in the text?
4. Why do bilingual readers not always master activities that require the use of evaluative skills?
5. Why do reading strategies for developing comprehension skills vary depending on the dominant language of the student?
6. What instructional materials are best for teaching the three linguistic students groups mentioned in the chapter?

INTRODUCTION

Bilingual educators recognize that reading skills must be taught and acquired in the stronger language of students if they are to be successful readers. Most children can acquire reading skills in each of their functional languages. Bilingual students need vocabulary development, practice in structural/grammar formation, a sense of their own ability to succeed, and interest in what they read (Goldenberg, 1990; Jiménez, García, & Pearson, 1994; Williams & Capizzi-Snipper, 1990). As students move along in skill attainment, they should develop a feeling of strength and an interest in mastering the challenge presented by the written material. Thus, the reading act involves a tough process that needs to be considered on two different levels and stages. Although both the sensory and perceptual processes are necessary to the reading act, it is in the student's cognitive response that true reading comprehension is demonstrated. First, students "think" as they read or speak in response to the text. Second, thinking takes place in an involuntary fashion. Readers are continuously developing cognitive skills thinking "abilities" that work at their current level and allow them to develop more sophisticated cognitive skills. The background, experiences, and interests of the reader; the physical, intellectual, social, and emotional development of the reader; and the efficacy of the reader's past instruction all bear on the students' ability or deficiency in the comprehension of what has been read. Therefore, there are several objectives in teaching reading in Spanish to bilingual students. These objectives are related to students' needs and interests in Spanish reading. If these needs and interests are met, students will become fluent and literate in Spanish; develop admiration for and pride in Spanish as a major world language with a significant and diverse literature; recognize that the Spanish language reflects a legitimate and varied culture with a long and rich history; strengthen their self-identities as they learn about their own cultural heritage; and acquire the knowledge, skills, attitudes, and motivation to enable them to make a positive contribution to the advancement of cultural pluralism.

READING COMPREHENSION: A DEFINITION

Comprehension is the ultimate reading skill that provides the link between the known and the unknown. People come to understand what is new in the context of what is already known to them. Reading comprehension is the skill used to obtain meaning from the printed page. Some implications of this concept are that comprehension is active, not passive; comprehension involves much inference making; and comprehension is a dialogue between the writer and the reader. The teaching of reading has always required a series of comprehension skills to be mastered through the grades, including identifying main idea and details and predicting outcomes. Today, it is felt that these skills do not exist as separate, or discrete, entities. Authorities (Carrasquillo, 1978; Condemarín, 1988; Durkin, 1989; K. Goodman, G. Goodman, & Flores, 1979; Jiménez et al., 1994; Weaver, 1988) have listed some factors that affect comprehension. These factors include knowledge of word meanings, ability to see relations among ideas, and the ability to use reasoning processes. Major differences in comprehension can probably be accounted for by experiential factors in the readers' backgrounds.

If the postulate is accepted that reading is more than learning to pronounce words, that it also involves understanding and recognizing meanings that have their wellsprings in individuals' past experience, then the need of Spanish-speaking children to be able to enrich their experiences must be recognized. One of the most important sociocultural features of meaning is the "value," or connotation, people attach to words, which are usually culture specific. Reading comprehension is a developmental process in which the reader can get meaning from the written symbols through which the author is expressing a message (Durkin, 1989; Sáez, 1978; Weaver, 1988). This meaning will be associated with past experiences. Readers, of course, have two sources of information—the reading material, and their own point of reference (experiences)—within a specific cultural frame stored in their memory to which they can refer in order to derive the author's meaning. Can students integrate these experiences into a larger, meaningful whole? Students' experiences help them in deriving meaning from context and eventually understanding abstractions and categorization. Learners use their experiences to interpret contextual clues and must be alert to aids given by the writer, such as synonyms, illustrations, explanations, and word signals (*pero, sin embargo*).

There is no guarantee that bilingual students will not have some problems with comprehension. However, the degree of difficulty encountered at this level will depend on the background of experiences from which concepts have been acquired, and the speed, accuracy, and richness of meanings that they bring to the reading act (Gersten & Jiménez, 1994). Another aspect of the difficulties in reading is the nature of vocabulary, because there may be words that students do not know, simply because they have never encountered them or because they have forgotten them. The acquisition of vocabulary depends largely on the education and, to a certain extent, on the degree of sophistication and the personal experiences of the speaker, as well as differences in the nature of the lexical and grammatical systems.

Figure 4.1 summarizes factors to consider when teaching reading in Spanish to bilingual students.

AREAS OF COMPREHENSION

Reading authorities do not agree on one set of labels for the categories involved in comprehension (Weaver, 1988; Williams & Capizzi-Snipper, 1990). These categories are called "steps," "skills," "stages," or "levels." Sometimes these areas are called "modes of comprehension." But all authorities agree that comprehension involves different areas or categories, and some areas require more concentration and effort than others. These areas range from the literal repetition of facts to making inferences, to

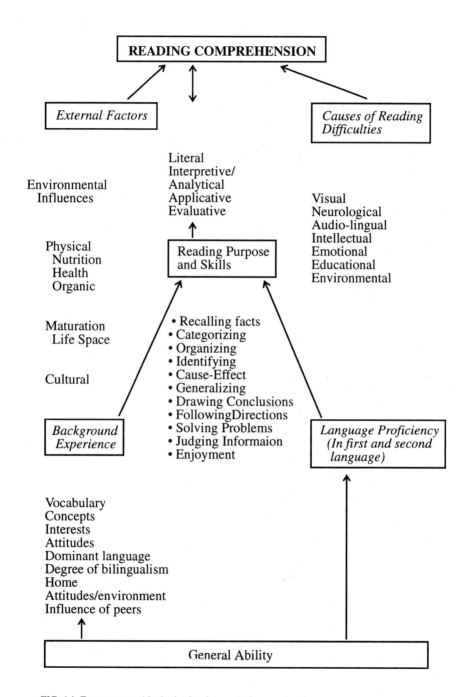

FIG. 4.1. Factors to consider in the development of comprehension

75

reaching conclusions and generalizations, to subjective thinking. Skill development in each of these areas is essential for successful instruction.

Educators teaching reading in Spanish must be aware of these areas of comprehension in order to give emphasis to all of them in their reading classes. Rather than providing an explanation of how these areas can be taught in the classroom, this chapter opts for providing visual illustration of these skills. For methodological purposes, these areas are summarized as literal, analytical/interpretive, applicative, and evaluative. Table 4.1 explains the nature of these areas and how they are presented in the classroom when teaching Spanish reading. The examples are presented in Spanish to provide readers with activities they can implement in their bilingual classes.

SUGGESTED SPANISH READING STRATEGIES
BY LANGUAGE GROUPS

Reading is an act of personal involvement that is synchronized with the students' growth and development. The need for classroom organization stems from differences among students within the classroom. Among the most significant differences are language proficiency and development, school literacy/experiences, learning deficiencies, rate of learning (aptitude and attitude), and self-image (García, 1994; Tikunoff, 1985). No one instructional approach is equally appropriate for all students in a given class. Although students may be grouped according to specific areas of interests or themes, the most important grouping for teaching Spanish reading in the bilingual classroom should be based on language dominance/mastery. Grouping can narrow the range of differences and reading problems with which a teacher has to cope during a lesson or class. The grouping that is recommended is based on language dominance. In terms of language, it is recommended that students be placed in one of three groups: Spanish-monolingual students, Hispanic students who are dominant in English, and English-speaking students with a desire to learn Spanish.

The Spanish Monolingual Student

The students grouped in this category will follow a regular reading and language arts sequence in Spanish starting in kindergarten. Listening comprehension skills in Spanish will be strengthened in kindergarten, and students will begin learning to read formally in first grade. A developmental reading program (listening, speaking, reading, writing, appreciation of

TABLE 4.1

Teaching reading comprehension skills.

Area	Mode in Which Comprehension Occurs	Examples of Skills Included	Recommended Activities
Literal	1. Ability to recall and identify stated facts and information contained in reading materials	1. Restatement or recall of facts or meanings • Enumera las cinco partes de … • Identifica las cuatro razones …	1. Ask for verbal definitions of common objects, names. (*¿Qué es un escritorio? Dos contestaciones serían: Es un sitio donde los estudiantes se sientan, o Es una clase de mueble.*) 2. Ask them to define abstract terms (*caliente, hambre, tristeza*). 3. Compare the students' definitions with those found in the reading. 4. The following paragraph is recommended for literal reading:
	READING COMPREHENSION (Sample Text)		Guadalajara es una de las ciudades más lindas de Méjico. Es una ciudad que conserva lo bonito del pasado con la vida moderna. Sus calles siempre están limpias. Está adornada con muchas flores y árboles. **Contesta:** • *¿Dónde se encuentra Guadalajara?* • *¿Qué aspectos hacen que Guadalajara sea una ciudad bonita?*
Analytical /Interpretive	1. Ability to understand causative factors, inferences and conclusions 2. Drawing meaning from figurative language	1. Categorizing and organizing content 2. Getting the main idea 3. Seeing relations among events, people and ideas 4. Recognition of characterizations 5. Differentiation of time	1. "Why" is the key question to ask for the deep meaning in this reading material: *¿Por qué la mamá de Petra estaba triste?* 2. Careful questioning and careful guidance toward correct answers can help to foster awareness of relations between cause and effect. (*¿Qué causó que el carro del cuento se desviara de la carretera?*) 3. One of the most fruitful strategies is the exploration of predictions in the plot of stories: *¿Cómo tú crees que Sancho Panza reaccionará al saber que don Quijote se está muriendo?* 4. The following paragraph is recommended for analytical/interpretive reading:
	READING COMPREHENSION (Sample Text)		*El Drama de Pinocho* Pedro se levantó muy temprano hoy. Hoy es el día en que el drama *Pinocho* se presentará a todos los niños de la escuela. La maestra le había dicho a Pedro que el haría el personaje de Pinocho. Pedro se vistió rápidamente. Apenas si probó el desayuno. Abrió la puerta y corrió a la escuela. Llegó a la escuela y saludó a sus compañeros y a su maestra. Niños—dijo la maestra: Uds. no se han olvidado de lo que van a hacer en el drama, ¿verdad? Especialmente tu, Pedro. Todos los niños rieron … **Contesta:** • *¿Por qué Pedro estaba tan ansioso?* • *¿Por qué la maestra le recalcó a Pedro que no se olvidara de lo que iba a hacer en el drama?*

Applicative	1. Ability to apply information gleaned from reading to one's own pursuits, purposes, and problems. It involves ability to transfer previously attained knowledge to new situations and ability to arrive at generalizations and draw conclusions.	1. Making generalizations 2. Drawing conclusions. 3. Following directions. 4. Solving problems.

1. After readers have abstracted the main principle or idea they will analyze the content of the second situation and will make the application. (*¿Qué aspectos de este cuento son parecidos a otra historia que ya leímos?*

2. Learning to read printed directions is a basic skill of this area (*recetas de comida*).

3. Students need to be made aware that what they learn in their reading may be applied to their own everyday lives and that, indeed, in many cases there may be specific reading material designed to aid in solving specific problems. (*¿Qué podría pasar si voy a nadar solo? ¿Qué podría pasar si hoy aprendo a bailar?*)

4. The following paragraph is recommended for applicative reading.

READING COMPREHENSION (Sample Text)

María, una muchacha de Boston, está pasando el verano en San Juan, Puerto Rico. Para mejorar el español, está tomando un curso para estudiantes de habla inglesa en la Universidad de Puerto Rico. Como parte del programa, tiene que vivir con una familia puertorriqueña. María está viviendo ahora en casa de los Rodríguez.
Generalización:

Evaluative	Ability to make value judgments about content reading.	1. Separating facts from fiction. 2. Questions of right and wrong answers. 3. Judging information.

1. Value judgments are based on experience, and sophisticated value judgments come only with maturity. However, young children can make simple judgments.

2. Help students sharpen judgmental skills by teaching the students to apply them to reading.

3. Fairy tales provide excellent opportunities for teaching young children to read evaluative material. (*¿Estuvo bien que la cenicienta no ayudara a sus hermana?*)

4. Teach students to be aware that a writer's background may be relevant to reader judgments. (*¿Está en realidad el escritor presentando un hecho científico?*)

5. The following paragraph is recommended for evaluative reading.

READING COMPREHENSION (Sample Text)

La mujer ha tratado de abusar de la liberación femenina. Nunca está en la casa, y si está, la encuentras siempre al lado del teléfono. Nunca lava los platos los fines de semana. Después de todo ha lavado los platos cinco días de la semana y si la invitas a salir, siempre quiere saber de antemano, a dónde la llevas y con cuánto dinero deberá contribuir. **Contesta:** ¿Cual es la opinión del autor sobre la liberación femenina?

literature and study skills) is recommended to at least the sixth grade, by which time students have developed a high degree of Spanish literacy. They will have a rich vocabulary, be able to read complicated grammar and syntactical structures, and be able to analyze difficult literary passages. All these reading activities will serve to foster an appreciation of and pride in the students' language and in culture. During this time, the students will be learning English as well. They will receive daily instruction in English as a second language and will study selected subjects in English. The following activities are recommended to be used with these students. Students should be familiar with all areas of reading comprehension and the emphasis should be not only on literal comprehension but in all areas, especially in analytical and evaluative skills. Table 4.2 illustrates some activities that emphasize these areas. They are presented in Spanish to familiarize readers with the Spanish terminology.

TABLE 4.2.
Desarrollando Destrezas de Comprensión

Area (Area)	Skills (Destrezas)	Reading Material (Material de lectura)
Literal	• Parear	• artículos periodísticos
	• Preguntar	• eventos
	• Identificar	• personajes
	• Localizar	• cuentos
Analítico	• Clasificar	• cuestionarios
	• Categorizar	• tablas
	• Contrastar	• tirillas cómicas
		• novelas
Aplicativo	• Construir	• diagramas
	• informar	• dramas
	• rehacer	• mapas
Evaluativo	• Juzgar	• cartas
	• Debatir	• inventarios
	• Editorializar	• artículos periodísticos
	• Discutir	

The following are recommended supplementary Spanish books to use for developing the above reading comprehension skills in Spanish.

Campanillitas Folklóricas, de Angeles Pastor, (Grade 1 and 2)

La Cucarachita Martina, de Pura Belpré, (Grade 1 and 2)

Arco Iris, de Ester Feliciano, (Grade 3)

Un mundo para ti, de Blanca Hernandez, (Grade 4)

Cuentos folklóricos de Puerto Rico, de Beatriz LaSalle, (Grade 5)

Mundo sin geografía, de Carmen Cadilla, (Grade 6)

Mi isla soñada, de Abelardo Díaz, (Grade 6)

María, de Jorge Isaac, (Grade 8)

Pepita Jiménez, de Juan Valera, (Grade 9)

Martín Fierro, de José Hernández, (Grade 10)

La carreta, de René Marqués, (Grade 11)

La amortajada, de Maria L. Bombal, (Grade 12)

The Spanish-Surnamed Student
Whose Dominant Language Is English

Students grouped here should begin a reading program in English in the first grade. Concurrently, they should receive daily instruction in Spanish. In kindergarten and first grade, Spanish language arts should emphasize the development of skills in Spanish. Opportunities will be given to develop vocabulary in Spanish and to practice grammatical structures and pronunciation. Reading in Spanish should begin in the second or third grade to give the child the opportunity to acquire the basic reading skills first in English. When students begin to read in Spanish using the basic skills they have acquired in English, this foundation will serve as an aid and shortcut in learning to read in Spanish. The oral-aural program will continue, and many opportunities will be provided to help students expand their vocabulary, increase the complexity of grammatical and syntactical structures, improve fluency in the language, and develop skills in reading comprehension. By the sixth grade, these students should be able to understand, speak, read, and write in both languages. Students should have the opportunity to learn the content of subject areas such as mathematics, science, or social studies in Spanish or in English. The following are recommended activities for this group:

1. Help them enrich their vocabulary: paraphrasing, using cognates (because the languages have similar word roots) such as antonyms, synonyms, words in the same family (*joya, joyero, joyería*).

2. Define abstract words in the students' native language (*capaz, incapaz, habilidad*—able, unable, ability).
3. Help the students arrive at the meaning of long syntactical structures by giving practical exercises. The following is an example of a long structure: *Aguadilla es conocida como "la Villa del Ojo," por haber allí un manantial que la naturaleza puso para inspiración de artistas y poetas.*

The teacher should help students to identify the ideas contained in this long sentence such as:

Aguadilla es una ciudad.

Aguadilla tiene un manantial.

Al manantial se le llama "El ojo del agua."

Muchos artistas y poetas le han cantado o escrito al manantial.

Manantial significa salida natural de agua (pozo) de debajo de la tierra.

4. Give pupils insight into the cultural allusions with the help of concrete materials (pictures, clocks, calendars).
5. Insure comprehension through questioning. Some suggestions are:

Ask different kinds of questions about the same sentence, i.e., (literal—*¿Es Maria una estudiante?*) (inferential—*¿Qué clase de estudiante es Maria?*)

Ask questions, the answers to which are directly stated details.

Ask for main idea (directly stated or inferred).

Rearrange the order of the sentences and ask students to correctly arrange them (in sequence).

Ask students to summarize the selection or paragraph.

6. Combine known words and structures and prepare a different dialogue using the same words. Students then read this newly organized material, which has all familiar elements in it.

7. Once the students have gained independence in reading, they may profit from self-selection, self-pacing, and ego-centered conferences, as monolingual students do. There should be Spanish books available

that focus on all aspects of the students' lives. The following list contains books that are popular with Hispanic bilingual students. These books are written in English. The teacher asks the students to read them in English, then develops oral language skills in Spanish. Then both the teacher and the students can develop language experience stories in Spanish based on the content of these stories.

Mexican Americans	Puerto Rican Americans
Benito	Getting to Know Puerto Rico
Citizen Pablo	Young Puerto Rico
Manuela's Birthday	The Three Wishes
A Mexican Boy's Adventure	Juan Bobo and the Queen's Necklace
Juanita	Barto Takes the Subway
Popo's Miracle	Rosa-Too-Little
And Now Miguel	City High Five
First Book of Mexico	Moncho and the Dukes
Blue Willow	Sleep in Thunder
No, No, Rosina	That Bad Carlos
Garbage Can Cat	Perez and Martina
	Feast on Sullivan Street
	When I Was Puerto Rican

Although most of these books are written in English, they have a great cultural message for Hispanic students. Many of the Latino students living in the United States can relate to the experiences described in these books.

English-Speaking Students with a Desire to Learn Spanish

The Spanish speaking and reading skills of these students are virtually nonexistent, but they are ready to learn Spanish, and they may have some degree of understanding of the spoken language. This group requires a very strong oral-aural program. Reading in Spanish will be introduced as soon as the students have enough vocabulary and language structure/understanding to make reading meaningful. The following are recommended activities in developing Spanish reading skills with this group of students:

1. Passages with a clear storyline should be chosen first because they will be easy to understand and will build up the readers' confidence in their ability to handle the comprehension tasks.
2. Initially, passages should not be lengthy, because recognizing cues is one of the main problems of foreign language readers. They should not be too short either, for the cues would be too few and there would be no challenge for the students.
3. Students need to read for comprehension. Therefore, teachers should use silent and oral reading properly. During the initial stages, it may be necessary to do more reading aloud so that the modeling of stress and intonation helps students with comprehension. If students' vocabulary and Spanish-language structures are limited, a language experience approach is recommended. The following are recommended topics through which teachers can develop reading comprehension skills using a language experience approach: *Un viaje al parque zoológico, mi programa favorito de televisión, el español se habla en la ciudad de Nueva York, Una visita a (Colombia, Santo Domingo, Puerto Rico), Es interesante viajar.*

The following is a suggested paragraph that includes short sentences, simple structures and vocabulary:

Fui a Puerto Rico en diciembre. Mi mamá y mis hermanitos también visitaron a Puerto Rico. El avión me gustó mucho. Conocí a mis abuelos. Mis abuelos me regalaron juguetes. El juego electrónico me gustó mucho.

Puerto Rico es muy bonito. Tiene muchos árboles. Las playas son muy lindas. La gente es muy amable. La gente vive en casas muy bonitas. Me gustaría volver a Puerto Rico.

CONCLUSION

The emphasis throughout this chapter has been on reading comprehension. Reading should be approached as a process and not only on the development of isolated skills. Process and skills should be emphasized in all areas of instruction, for which teachers should choose appropriate reading materials and strategies. But, reading is not an easy, smooth process; and the process that the teacher—usually a native speaker—finds trivial and uncomplicated is often difficult and complex. From the very beginning, overall comprehension should be emphasized, and passages or reading texts should be chosen with extreme care, taking grammatical structures and vocabulary into consideration. Reading materials and approaches used are extremely important when several language groups are addressed. Spanish-dominant students are challenged with complex themes and inferential questioning. English-dominant, Spanish-surnamed students need culturally relevant texts, positively portraying their experiences. English-dominant speakers may be motivated to read Spanish texts with relevant topics related to their daily lives and struggles.

FOLLOW-UP ACTIVITIES

1. The following list is written in Spanish. Prepare a reading activity to teach students the specific reading skill or process for each.

Destreza	Actividad Sugerida
1. Reconocer semejanzas y diferencias entre los personajes.	1.
2. Emitir juicios en favor o en contra de la conducta de un personaje.	2.
3. Resumir la trama de un cuento.	3.
4. Identificar el lugar donde se desarrolla la acción.	4.
5. Reproducir en secuencia los sucesos de un drama.	5.
6. Identificar la idea principal de un poema.	6.
7. Mencionar las palabras que indican estados de ánimo en un poema.	7.
8. Identificar la veracidad de una fábula.	8.
9. Nombrar las dos generalizaciones que se derivan del cuento.	9.
10. Identificar los personajes de una narracion.	10.

2. Go to the library or resource room of your school, college, or university. Identify four reading texts (not mentioned in this chapter) that you would recommend to use in the reading class for each of the following bilingual reading groups:

Spanish Monolingual Student		English-Speaking, Spanish-Surnamed Student	English-Speaking Student
1.		1.	1.
2.		2.	2.
3.		3.	3.
4.		4.	4.

3. Identify three reading reference books that discuss how to teach reading comprehension in Spanish. List two methodological strategies mentioned in each book.
4. Identify five different definitions of the concept *reading comprehension*. Prepare a 5-minute oral presentation to discuss similarities and differences among these definitions.

REFERENCES

Carrasquillo, A. (1978). *La enseñanza del español en la escuela elemental.* New York: Las Americas.
Condemarín, M. (1988). Descripción de los componentes básicos de un programa de lectura y sugerencias acerca de su implementación y evaluación. *Lectura y Vida, 9*(4), 5–9.
Durkin, D. (1989). *Teaching them to read* (5th ed.). Boston: Allyn & Bacon.
García, E. (1994). *Understanding and meeting the challenge of students cultural diversity.* Boston: Houghton Mifflin.
Gersten, R. M., & Jiménez, R. T. (1994). A delicate balance: Enhancing literacy instruction for language minority students. *The Reading Teacher, 47*(6), 438–449.
Goldenberg, C. (1990). Beginning literacy instruction for Spanish-speaking children. *Language Arts, 87*(2), 590–598.
Goodman, K., Goodman, G., & Flores, B. (1979). *Reading in the bilingual classroom: Literacy and biliteracy.* Washington, DC: National Clearinghouse for Bilingual Education.
Jiménez, R. T., García, G. E., & Pearson, P. D. (1994). *The metacognitive strategies of Latino students who read Spanish and English* (Tech. Rep.). Urbana-Champaign: University of Illinois, Center for the Study of Reading.
Sáez, A. (1978). *La lectura: Arte del lenguaje.* Río Piedras, Puerto Rico: Editorial de la Universidad de Puerto Rico.
Tikunoff, W. (1985). *Applying significant instructional features in the bilingual classroom.* Rosslyn, VA: Inter-America Research Associates.
Weaver, C. (1988). *Reading processes and practice.* Porthsmouth, NH: Heinemann.
Williams, J. D., & Capizzi-Snipper, G. (1990). *Literacy and bilingualism.* New York: Longman.

5

Integrando la Fonética en el Proceso de la Lectura en Español

Elma Azurdia
Educational Consultant

This chapter was written with the practitioner in mind, and its purpose is to present practical information and applications with regard to Spanish phonics. It was not written to give an exhaustive description of the different aspects of Spanish phonics, but rather to present instructional applications for teachers.

Phonics and reading are intertwined. Models of the uses of phonics in the context of reading are followed by examples that reflect some of its characteristics in the spoken and written language. The teaching of phonics is useless if it does not lead to the practical application and development of the reading process, where students have the opportunity to read, comprehend, analyze, and practice what they have read while applying these skills to the writing process.

When students come to school, they bring from home some useful tools such as listening skills (auditory expression) and speaking skills (oral expression) to communicate their ideas. Consequently, creative teachers can begin the phonics process in a progressive manner by tapping into these resources, which lead to the initial development of the reading/writing process.

OBJETIVOS

Al terminar la lectura y estudio de este capítulo, el lector podrá:

1. Identificar la función de la fonética en la enseñanza de la lecto-escritura.
2. Identificar estrategias progresivas para la enseñanza de la fonética en contextos significativos.
3. Describir las habilidades lingüísticas que el estudiante necesita antes de empezar con el aprendizaje de la fonética para fomentar la lectura.
4. Describir cuál es el proceso de aprendizaje del lenguaje del estudiante para la adquisición de la fonética.
5. Delinear algunos ejercicios de lectura para desarrollar la fonética.
6. Señalar algunas variaciones del español de los distintos grupos de habla española.

PREGUNTAS GUÍAS

1. Explique lo que significa fonética .
2. ¿Cuál es la función de la fonética en relación a la lectura?
3. ¿Por qué se considera la fonética como parte integral de la lectura?
4. ¿Cuál es la diferencia entre la fonética como destreza y la fonética como estrategia?
5. ¿Qué estrategias se podrían utilizar para enseñar la fonética en forma gozosa?
6. ¿Por qué se debe enseñar la fonética de una manera multisensorial y multicultural?
7. ¿Cuál es la ventaja en aceptar las variaciones de fonemas que trae el estudiante a la escuela?

¿QUÉ ES LA FONÉTICA?

Leer a nivel informativo requiere más que la fonética. Sin embargo, la fonética ocupa un lugar importante en relación al proceso de la lectura. El tema de la fonética ha sido controversial y se ha debatido en el campo pedagógico y político por muchas décadas. El objetivo primordial de este artículo no es para entrar en detalles de estas controversias, sino para señalar el valor de la fonética como un medio de enseñanza en el aprendizaje de la iniciación a la lectura en forma significativa. La fonética es la ciencia de la expresión que trata de los sonidos básicos de un idioma. En la iniciación a la lectura hay instantes en que el estudiante debe comenzar a describir los sonidos de las palabras o las letras en un contexto significativo, ya que tales sonidos pueden sufrir variaciones o modificaciones según las letras que preceden o anteceden. Según Alvarez Henao, (1977) la fonética es la ciencia de los sonidos concretos de una lengua. Indica Alvarez Henao que el Diccionario de la Real Academia tiene dos significados para este término: (a) conjunto de los sonidos de un idioma; y (b) estudio de los sonidos de uno o varios idiomas, ya sea en su fisiología y acústica, o sea en su evolución histórica.

Con respecto a la fonética fisiológica se puede decir que trata de los órganos, cavidades y funciones y del proceso respiratorio fundamental. La fonética acústica tiene que ver con la amplitud y frecuencia de las vibraciones de las cuerdas vocales así como con la intensidad y la altura, timbre, tono y voz. La fonética abarca fonemas y sonidos. Los fonemas son los aspectos significativos de los sonidos de un idioma y son unidades diferenciadoras, por lo tanto, el cambio de una de ellas implica un cambio en la significación. Según Monroy Casas (1980), es un hecho universalmente aceptado que un fonema sólo puede pronunciarse en un contexto silábico. Como tal, todos los idiomas limitan el número de sus sonidos.

El español tiene veinticuatro fonemas de los cuales diecinueve son consonánticos y cinco vocálicos. Las diecinueve consonantes son: b, c, d, f, g, j, k, l, m, n, ñ, p, q, r, s, t, y, v, z. Las grafias *ch* como en *chupar,* *ll* como en *llave,* y *rr* como en *cerrar,* se conocen como diagrafias, que es la combinación de dos letras que representan un fonema. Las cinco vocales son: a, e, i, o, u. Las vocales se caracterizan por su sonoridad ya que son las que represantan la mayor abertura de los órganos articulatorios. Tanto las vocales como las consonantes se utilizan para ir formando sílabas. Además, el español tiene letras para fonemas que no se pronuncian. Con relación a la *h* este fonema no se pronuncia en posición inicial como en *hamaca* aunque se emplea ortográficacmente. La vigésima sexta letra del abecedario español es la *w* como en Washington, que no se emplea sino en voces de procedencia extranjera. Por último el sonido de la *x* como en *expediente,* está formada por un sólo signo pero equivale a dos sonidos fusionados, las cuales son *ks.*

Es indispensable el conocimiento del alfabeto español para todos aquellos maestros que desempeñan el papel en la enseñanza de la lectura. El abecedario en español aparece a continuación con letras mayúsculas y minúsculas y con sus nombres respectivos.

En la actualidad, aún sigue el debate entre la mejor forma para enseñar a leer. Unos pedagogos se aferran a que el estudiante aprende a leer usando el método fonético, mientras que otros aseguran que el método estructuro-global es la mejor manera para la enseñanza de la lectura. El método fonético enfatiza la correspondencia que existe entre los sonidos, mientras

A, a (a)	N, n (ene)
B, b (be)	Ñ, ñ (eñe)
C, c (ce)	O, o (o)
D, d (de)	P, p (pe)
E, e (e)	Q, q (cu)
F, f (efe)	R, r (ere) rr (erre)
G, g (ge)	S, s (ese)
H, h (hache)	T, t (te)
I, i (I)	U, u (u)
J, j (jota)	V, v (ve, uve)

Fig. 5.1. El Abecedario en Español.

que el método estructuro-global propone paradigmas que apoyan el desarrollo de la lectura en forma global. Pero no importa el método preferido por el maestro, la fonética en español es fundamental en la iniciación para el desarrollo de la lectura y se puede decir que es la columna que sirve como base para encaminar al estudiante hacia la lectura. Por consiguiente, el estudiante necesita oír los sonidos, identificar las letras, discriminar entre los sonidos y las letras y visualizar cómo se forman las letras para luego traspasar estos símbolos a la lectura.

El estudiante tiene que ir descubriendo las distintas características de los escritos, identificando las letras, la sílaba y luego la palabra. El maestro deberá ir dándole al estudiante muchos ejemplos para que él o ella genere sus propias reglas. Adquirir las bases fundamentales de la lectura y el código escrito no significa solamente aprender la correspondencia entre el sonido y la grafía, sino aprender un código sustancialmente distinto del oral.

La introducción de los elementos fonéticos no se presentan al azar sino en una forma lógica según el contenido. A continuación aparecen algunos pasos progresivos que ayudarán al estudiante a convertirse en lector. Estos son:

1. Diferenciar auditivamente entre una vocal abierta o cerrada, y una consonante. Las vocales abiertas son: *a, e, o,* y las cerradas son: *i* y *u.* Por ejemplo:

   Por aqu*í* paso un coq*uí* (vocales cerradas)

chi*qui*ti*to* y acoge*dor* (consonantes)

en l*a* boca ll*e*va un c*o*librí (vocales abiertas)

y en la espalda un armador.

2. Notar que cada grafía o digrafía representa un sonido particular. Por ejemplo:

El *d*edo pulgar es el más corto.

Sale humo de la *ch*imenea.

3. Conocer los sonidos representativos del abecedario español.

4. Identificar las vocales y las consonantes en sus sonidos y variantes.

5. Entender de que el sonido de algunas consonantes dependen de la vocal que le antecede o le sigue. Por ejemplo:

La *ge*nte camina por las *ca*lles.

La *ga*ta y los gatitos están en la *ce*sta de paja.

6. Identificar correctamente la sílaba en cada palabra. Por ejemplo:

fue = una sílaba,

me-sa = dos sílabas,

es-co-ba = tres sílabas,

rec-tán-gu-lo = cuatro sílabas.

7. Unir sílabas correctamente en una palabra.

fue = una sílaba

rectángulo = cuatro sílabas.

8. Distinguir la sílaba con acentuación prosódica y su pronunciación. Por ejemplo:

El *pú*blico se paró para recibir a los concursantes.

Yo pu*bli*co la revista escolar una vez al mes.

9. Identificar diptongos, triptongos, y grupos consonánticos. Por ejemplo:

El c*ui*dado del niño es importante (diptongo).

Urug*uay* es un país de la América del Sur (triptongo).

10. Reconocer grupos consonánticos en posición inicial, medio o al final de palabras. Por ejemplo:

La *bl*usa de Marisa es roja.

El a*pl*auso del pú*bl*ico se oyó por todo el gimnasio.

El unifo*rm*e es azul y blanco.

11. Reconocer palabras de exposición rápida que inician con vocales, consonantes, diptongos, o digrafías. Por ejemplo:

*e*ntre, *d*ebajo, *ai*re, y *ch*orro.

12. Colocar en columnas palabras que empiezan con un sonido específico o con una sílaba específica. Por ejemplo:

j	ll	y
jamón	llano	yarda
jenjibre	llave	yema
jirafa	lleva	yegua
joroba	llorón	yuca
jugo	lluvia	yodo

13. Distinguir el sonido de la *r* en posición inicial, media o al final de palabra, y después de la l y n. Por ejemplo:

*r*aíz, a*r*aña, flo*r,* a*lr*ededor y so*nr*eír.

14. Distinguir entre las consonantes *c* y *g* antes de i y e. Por ejemplo:

bi*c*icleta, si*g*ue, be*c*a, y se*g*uro.

15. Distinguir entre las consonantes ortográficamente *g* / *j*; *c* / *z* / *s* cuando se usan en forma escrita.

g/j	c/z/s
gato/jardín	cama/zapato/saco
gemelo/jefe	cena/zebra/seco
gitano/jirafa	cine/zigzag/silla
goma/jota	codo/zona/sobre
gusano/juguete	cuna/zurda/sudor

La letra *b* y *v* en posición inicial tienen el mismo sonido en español. Lo mismo podría suceder con *c, z, s* en ciertas regiones del habla española.

16. Distinguir entre *que, gue,* y *güe*; *qui, gui* y *güi.* Por ejemplo:
   • El ratón se comió el *que*so.

- La *gue*rra duró un año.
- A la niña le dio ver*güe*nza entrar tarde a la clase.
- Adriana le *qui*ta la pelota a su primo.
- La *gui*tarra de Pepe tiene cuatro cuerdas.
- El músico toca el *güi*ro.

17. Descifrar palabras analizando su escritura por los elementos fonéticos y sílabas que las componen.

ESTRATEGIAS PARA INTEGRAR LA FONÉTICA

La lectura debe ser agradable. A continuación se ofrecen algunas sugerencias para integrar la fonética en la lectura.

Ejemplo 1: El Juego de las Barajas es un juego que ofrece la posibilidad que el alumno se divierta en lo que se considera la primera fase de la lectura, aún cuando no puede gozar la lectura propiamente. Una de las variaciones del juego es que cada alumno posee seis tarjetas y en cada tarjeta hay una sílaba. Un jugador puede seleccionar entre sus compañeros las tarjetas que quiera para ir formando una palabra o unas palabras. También partiendo de una información conocida como el nombre propio del estudiante, se puede ir formando nombres comunes al igual que oraciones. Por ejemplo:

Estos juegos ayudan a los estudiantes a tener dominio del idioma oral y escrito en forma divertida.

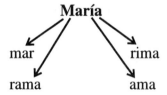

1. María ama el mar.

2. María mira la rama.

3. ¡Mira el mar María!

Ejemplo 2: El Juego de las Adivinanzas. (Para desarrollar las consonantes iniciales). Por ejemplo:

a. Se empieza el juego indicando que empieza con la letra *M,* tiene siete letras y se usa en la cara como disfraz. ¿Qué es? Es la letra m _ _ _ _ _ _. (máscara)

b. Empieza con la letra *T,* tiene cinco letras y es la sombrilla de la casa. ¿Qué es? Es la letra t _ _ _ _. (techo)

c. La palabra amor al revés nombra a una cuidad. ¿Cuál es? R _ _ _.
(Roma)

A menudo los estudiantes de primaria se plantean la pregunta ¿A qué jugamos ahora? Y sin esperar una respuesta del maestro, inmediatamente se ven involucrados en una y otra actividad. Los juegos individuales o colectivos proporcionan las primeras etapas de la adquisición a la lectura y la escritura y sirven de guía en el proceso de aprendizaje, donde el estudiante es el forjador de sus propias conquistas. Esto requiere que el estudiante pueda oír los sonidos y saber distinguir palabras debido a los diferentes sonidos. El conocimiento de los sonidos ayuda al estudiante a aprender la relación entre el sonido y la letra. Algunos estudios sugieren que fundamentalmente los fonemas ayudan al estudiante a entender la lectura.

Ejemplo 3: El Uso de Trabalenguas. Este juego es muy eficaz para practicar el mismo sonido en posición inicial o media. A continuación aparece un trabalenguas que dice así:

> El que poca capa parda compra,
> poca capa parda vende,
> yo, que poca capa parda compré,
> poca capa parda vendí.

De tal manera, a medida que vaya progresando el estudiante, el maestro puede ir introduciendo palabras con dos o tres conjuntos consonánticos.

> ¡Qué fresca es la *brisa* del mar!
> Chabelita corta un *clavel* del jardín.
> El temblor *destruye* la ciudad.
> Hay un *contraste* entre el gato y el perro.

Ejemplo 4: El Uso de las Jitanjáforas

> *Canto Negro*
> Tamba, tamba, tamba, tamba,
> ¡tamba del negro que timba!
> tumba del negro, caramba,
> caramba, que el negro tumba:
> yamba, yambó, yambá, bé.

La jitanjáfora, es cualquier elemento lingüístico o combinación de palabras, que puede o no carecer de sentido pero que posee un atractivo ya sea fonético, metafórico o de gracia poética. Creando jitanjáforas, el estudiante puede descubrir y analizar elementos fónicos que no lo rigen a reglas, más bien, consiste en jugar con el lenguaje como se puede apreciar en un verso de la poesía *Canto Negro* de Nicolás Guillén.

Ejemplo 5: Uso de las Adivinanzas

La adivinanza es otro aspecto lingüístico que sirve para despertar en el estudiante el apetito por la lectura, así aprende a leer y al mismo tiempo a amar la lectura. Las adivinanzas de las vocales por ejemplo incita al estudiante a leer, sin crearle ansiedad.

En el mar y no me mojo;
en brasas y no me abraso;
en el aire y no me caigo,
y me tienes en tus brazos. (Respuesta: la letra A)

En medio del cielo estoy
sin ser lucero ni estrella,
sin ser sol ni luna bella;
¿a ver si aciertas quién soy? (Respuesta: la letra E)

Soy un palito
muy derechito
y encima de la frente
tengo un puntito. (Respuesta: la letra I)

La última soy del cielo
y en Dios del tercer lugar,
y siempre me ves en navío
y nunca estoy en el mar. (Respuesta: la letra O)

Ejemplo 6: La Poesía Como Recurso Fonético

El lenguaje poético es imprescindible para el más profundo despertar de los sentidos (Hamilton, 1966). Por medio de la poesía, las adivinanzas u otros medios de lectura, el estudiante logra aprender, apreciar y respetar escritos de otras culturas, sus semejanzas y sus diferencias. Algunos libros de poesías que podrán ser útiles son: *Antología de la Poesía Infantil, Once*

Grandes Poetisas Americo-hispanas, Seis Poetas Latinoamericanas de Hoy, y *Coquí.* Además, para aquellos estudiantes que necesitan más tiempo para descifrar las claves de la lectura, aquellos estudiantes que están leyendo las figuritas, es conveniente tener libros bien ilustrados de presentación atractiva, con contenidos breves, sencillos y repetitivos, de letras grandes y lenguaje directo y claro. El estudiante que aún no decodifica podrá leer las ilustraciones.

Conforme el estudiante vaya desarrollando las destrezas de la fonética, el maestro puede ir creando otras actividades de acuerdo a las necesidades que se presenten.

Aunque el estudiante va desarrollando sus propias estrategias para ir identificando palabras, habrán momentos en que tendrá tropiezos y allí es cuando el maestro debe utilizar ciertas técnicas para ayudar al estudiante a descifrar palabras desconocidas. En conclusión, un alumno que desarrolla los conceptos expuestos tendrá más facilidad en el manejo de la lectura.

LIMITACIONES EN EL USO DE LA FONÉTICA

La fonética funciona como destreza cuando su única función es la de descifrar palabras, o distinguir los sonidos. Por ejemplo, se ha visto que muchos sonidos son influenciados por la letra que les sigue, y representa cierta dificultad para el principiante como se puede ver en *ca-sa,* o *se-se* en donde la *c* sufre variaciones según la vocal que le sigue. A continuación se encuentra una lista de palabras donde la *c* y la *g* sufren cambios.

ca	ce	co	ga	ge	go
camisa	ceniza	codo	gato	gemelo	gota
caña	cena	cobarde	gavilán	gelatina	goma
cabeza	ceja	cola	gallina	genio	gorra
caballo	cebolla	colgar	gallo	germen	gordo
café	cerdo	color	galleta	gentil	golpe

Otros problemas resultan cuando los estudiantes tratan de aplicar las reglas de los sonidos, resultando en (a) recarga de la memoria y (b) termina perdiendo la comprensión de la lectura. Además, el énfasis en las reglas limita la capacidad de la memoria para retener la información de la lectura. El método fonético es relativamente ineficiente porque tiene un sinnúmero de reglas que para un estudiante puede aparentar tener mucha contrariedad. Además, como dijo Smith (1971), el uso de las reglas es el método más lento para identificar palabras, limitando el proceso de información y la capacidad mental del sistema visual el cual no puede tolerar el ritmo lento de la lectura. Por lo tanto, las reglas fonéticas sólo son una parte del conjunto de conocimientos que utiliza el usuario de la lengua.

La fonética como estrategia al nivel de lectura sirve para desarrollar la comprensión en forma auténtica. Al nivel de estrategia, el estudiante no sólo decodifica el texto sino que también comprende y valora, si es bueno o no, si transmite lo que se propone y puede llegar a jugar y crear en un plano estético. Estas estrategias de lectura llenan al estudiante de nuevos e insondables matices hasta el punto que podría afirmarse que una lectura renace con cada lector. La lectura representa una forma de conocimiento del mundo y es un vehículo de comunicación pero es más que todo, una forma inagotable de entretenimiento y placer. El estudiante vivirá intensamente las historias que le causan risa, emoción y asombro, y es responsabilidad del maestro y otros adultos, estimularle esa relación con la palabra, el lenguaje y la lectura. La lectura es uno de los instrumentos de aprendizaje que ocupa un lugar muy importante en la adquisición del conocimiento.

El maestro tiene que tener ciertos conocimientos relacionados con la lectura y el estudiante. Tiene que conocer cuál es la actitud del estudiante hacia la lectura, su cultura, su medio ambiente, su salud y su experiencia previa; éstas se relacionan al lenguaje, a la salud mental, y a la madurez. Además, es de suma importancia que el maestro conozca el estilo de aprendizaje del estudiante, ya que puede ser gestual, gráfica, u oral o una combinación de éstas. Un buen maestro orienta al estudiante a la adquisición de conceptos, canalizando el proceso de aprendizaje de ellos y haciendo una buena graduación de las áreas difíciles sin prescindir de los aspectos positivos.

El lenguaje es un fenómeno social. En algunos países donde hay grandes poblaciones de aborígenes, el español tiende a ser afectado principalmente al nivel de léxico. Un ejemplo, es la oración ¿Dónde está el niño?

¿Dónde está el zipote? (en Honduras)

¿Dónde está el patojo? (en Guatemala)

¿Dónde está el chamaco? (en México)

Según Badía (1977), Seco (1977), y Quiles (1992), el léxico es siempre el más afectado, seguido por la gramática, y por último la fonología. El léxico es el más directamente afectado y es el que refleja las realidades sociales. El maestro ingenioso acepta estas realidades y le enseña al estudiante la variación normal para que logre precisar el idioma a modo de comunicarse con otros de habla española sin tacharle al estudiante el habla que ya trae. Además, el maestro debe saber que cualquier lengua presenta variaciones y todos los miembros de una comunidad lingüística no hablan ni escriben de la misma manera. Al igual, el maestro tiene que rechazar la noción de que algunos hablan español del bueno y otros hablan español del malo.

Los distintos contactos, mezclas de personas de distintas regiones, son otros factores que siempre han contribuido a la evolución lingüística en donde los estudiantes en las escuelas se ha visto influenciados por las situaciones de intercambios lingüísticos que son provocados por las múltiples vicisitudes del acontecer histórico y en el caso de Latinoamérica, de las diferentes lenguas, migraciones, colonizaciones, guerras, invasiones, ocupaciones e inmigraciones, y la relación social jerárquica. Todos estos aspectos son influyentes en la evolución del léxico.

Otros aspectos que intensifican los cambios que sufre un fonema en tiempo y espacio son muy complejos y atribuibles a múltiples causas de orden geográfico, léxico y cultural. Los cambios lingüísticos se producen por las necesidades que existen para la comunicación. El incremento de la industria, del comercio y del mundo tecnológico intensifica la renovación del léxico y a así irrumpe la terminología científica y técnica. El maestro se puede actualizar leyendo periódicos y revistas didácticas de mayor renombre.

En el Caribe al igual que en Norte, Centro y Sudamérica hay millones de personas que hablan español. En estos diferentes grupos étnicos existen variedades de vocablos. Hay que recordar que el africanismo, el tainismo, el aztequismo y el quechismo, para mencionar algunas lenguas en contacto, afectan la integridad y la estructura del idioma en cada uno de estos países en donde ha habido grandes contactos. Estos cambios enriquecen la lengua española.

Por consiguiente, es preciso que cada maestro sepa sobre estas influencias y al mismo tiempo reconozca que existen grandes ventajas en aceptar las variaciones de los fonemas que el estudiante trae al aula. El vocablo que el estudiante trae consigo a la escuela lo identifica y lo vincula al contexto social al que pertenece. Aceptando este vocablo, ayuda al estudiante a mantener una buena opinión de sí mismo y lo ayuda a aprender. Tanto el lenguaje oral como el escrito necesitan un determinado contexto cultural para desarrollarse y ser aprendidos, capacitando al estudiante con potenciales comunicativas.

CONCLUSIÓN

Dado el cúmulo de información que existe sobre los grupos minoritarios en las escuelas públicas, se sabe que el grupo más grande es el hispano-hablante. Entre estos grupos se destacan los mejicanos, puertorriqueños, cubanos, dominicanos, ecuatorianos y colombianos. Estos grupos varían de ciudad en ciudad.. Las estadísticas indican que el crecimiento de la población latina es cuatro veces mayor que la otra población estadounidense. Se estima que en el año 2.000 habrá 31 millones de hispano-hablantes. Las implicaciones para la enseñanza de estudiantes que habla español presentan condiciones urgentes en las escuelas públicas. En sí, y como nos aclara Otheguy, (1982) la influencia del inglés sobre el español de Estados Unidos es profunda. Se habla de diferentes tipos de español, por ejemplo "Spanglish" y "Tex-Mex." Estas manifestaciones lingüísticas, con variantes dialectales inevitablemente han logrado una mayor convivencia con los naturales calcos sintácticos y vocablos ingleses latinizados. Según Badía (1977) en el contacto entre dos lenguas, ambas pueden ver afectadas la integridad de su propia estructura. Estas influencias preponderantes influyen en la enseñanza de la lectura en español. Por lo tanto, los maestros deben recibir los adiestramientos adecuados ya que mucho dependerá de la preparación que estos maestros reciben para enfrentarse al reto de estas realidades educativas e incentivar al estudiante a que aprenda a leer en español en forma gozosa.

Por tanto, este capítulo hace énfasis en la enseñanza de la fonética vinculada al desarrollo de la lectura. Se comentaron las siguientes ideas:

1. La fonética y la lectura se deben enseñar complementándose una con otra.
2. El estudiante necesita el contínuo contacto con un lenguaje rico y variado y así puede ir incrementando su repertorio lingüístico a través de las varias estrategias.

EJERCICIOS DE APLICACIÓN

1. Explique por qué la fonética debe enseñarse como un complemento de la iniciación a la lectura.
2. Prepare dos jitanjáforas en verso con sentido gracioso.
3. Identifique las palabras que tengan diptongo: *poema, ciudad, mutuo, bueno, Luis, ruido, deuda, duende, maestro, piano.*

4. Mencione cuántas sílabas hay en cada una de las siguientes palabras: obstáculo, Sandra, diez, emplear, también, hermosa, griego, ilustración, urgente, Paola, Adriana.

5. Investigue qué otras palabras se usan en Latinoamérica y el Caribe para decir:

niña   autobús

chiringa   naranja

cuaderno

REFERENCIAS

Alvarez Henao, L. E. (1977). *Fonética y fonología del español.* Bogota: La Cátedra.

Badía. A. M. (1977). Lenguas en contacto: Bilinguismo, diglosia, lenguas en convivencia. En R. Lapesa (Ed.), *Comunicación y lenguaje* (pp. 105–133). Madrid, España: Editorial Kardos.

Hamilton, C. D. (1966). *Historia de la literatura hispanoamericana.* Madrid, España: Ediciones y Publicaciones Españolas, S. A.

Monroy Casas, R. (1980). *Aspectos fonéticos de las vocales españolas.* Madrid, España: Sociedad General Española de Librería, S. A.

Otheguy, R. (1982, noviembre). *Una visión comunicativa del calco lingüístico como factor explicativo de la influencia del inglés sobre el español de los Estados Unidos.* Sexto Simposio sobre el Bilingüismo y Español y Portugués, Mayagüez, Puerto Rico.

Quiles, A. (1992). *La lengua española en cuatro mundos.* Madrid, España: Editorial MAPFRE.

Seco, M. (1977). El léxico de hoy. En R. Lapesa (Ed.), *Comunicación y lenguaje* (pp. 183–201). Madrid, España: Editorial Kardos.

Smith, F. (1971). *Understanding reading.* New York: Holt, Rinehart & Winston.

6

Métodos Más Conocidos en la Enseñanza de Lectura en Español

Angela Carrasquillo
Fordham University

Reading is an individual process. Not all children learn to read following the same sequential patterns. How students learn to read depends on their background, attitudes, cultural environment, and the way reading is introduced to them. Therefore, there are different methods used to teach students how to read, and no one method is more important or better than the other. This chapter presents a brief overview of the historical development of reading methodology. It explains what constituted the most important elements of the reading process at any one time as determined by the reading method emphasized. Synthetic and eclectic methods are described. An attempt has been made to point out the characteristics of each method and to recommend those that are more effective in teaching Spanish reading. Practical/methodological strategies are also presented.

OBJETIVOS

Al finalizar la lectura de este capítulo, el lector podrá:

1. Describir el desarrollo histórico-filosófico en la metodología para enseñar a leer en español.
2. Establecer semejanzas y diferencias entre el proceso sintético y analítico al enseñar a leer.

3. Enumerar las características de los siguientes métodos: alfabético, fonético, palabras generadoras y global.
4. Enumerar razones por las cuales se dice que todos los métodos tienen ventajas y desventajas.
5. Identificar formas de combinar los métodos presentados para que respondan a las necesidades, intereses y estilos de aprendizaje del estudiante.
6. Preparar lecciones modelos, utilizando cualquiera de los métodos anteriores.

PREGUNTAS GUÍAS

1. ¿Cómo la percepción de lo que es la lectura ha contribuído al desarrollo de la metodología para enseñar a leer en español?
2. ¿Por qué el período de 1935 a 1950 es conocido como el período de conflicto internacional en la lectura?
3. ¿Por qué se dice que en la década del 1960 hay un marcado interés en la lectura como proceso?
4. ¿Qué método o métodos predominaron en el comienzo de la década del 1980?
5. ¿Cómo se prodría caracterizar la década de los noventas con relación a la enseñanza de la lectura?
6. ¿Por qué se podría concluir que todos los métodos tienen ventajas y desventajas?

INTRODUCCIÓN

Leer es un proceso individual y está determinado, no sólo por la naturaleza del proceso, sino por las características del que aprende y por su actitud frente a la lectura. Al hablar de métodos para enseñar a leer, hay que tener en cuenta el medio cultural del estudiante, sus experiencias educativas y las asociaciones que este estudiante ha ido haciendo con el propósito de que las palabras tengan significado. Leer no es sólo reconcer símbolos, sino que es interpretar estos símbolos en una perspectiva de acción, de tiempo y propósitos (Goodman, 1989; Sáez, 1978).

BREVE HISTORIA DE LA ENSEÑANZA DE LA LECTURA Y SU RELACIÓN CON LA METODOLOGÍA

La lectua se ha enseñado durante varios siglos. La enseñanza de la lectura ha sido tema de muchísimas investigaciones y discusiones. Estas investigaciones han contribuído a cambiar la forma de pensar de los educadores sobre cuál es el mejor método para enseñar a leer. Muchas veces, el método seleccionado depende de la definición de lectura en el momento, y de cómo se describe el proceso de aprender a leer. Es pues, necesario, hacer un breve recuento de cómo se enseñó la lectura en el pasado, y qué destrezas y métodos se enfatizaban. Se puede inferir que los métodos que el maestro usaba indicaban qué destrezas, él o ella, creía más importantes; cómo visualizaban el proceso por el cual un estudiante pasaba al aprender a leer y, sobre todo, cómo definían la lectura. Debido a que es muy difícil, en un sólo capítulo, hacer un recuento histórico sobre el desarrollo de la lectura en todos los países de habla española, se comentará brevemente el desarrollo histórico de la lectura en general, incluyendo los movimientos profesionales en los países de habla española, Estados Unidos y Europa.

La enseñanza de la lectura en los siglos XVII y XVIII se caracterizó por su énfasis religioso (Dolch, 1955). Para aquel tiempo, era un deber moral y religioso el aprender a leer. Era obligación de todo ciudadano aprender a leer la Biblia y otros libros religiosos y así entender mejor la vida religiosa. El método de enseñar lectura consistía en la memorización del alfabeto y pasajes escritos de la Biblia.

A partir del año 1776, el Estado estaba a cargo de la educación. Por tanto, la lectura, según el gobierno, era el instrumento de los ciudadanos para purificar y enriquecer la lengua, así como para desarrollar conductas morales. Se enfatizaba la memorización del alfabeto, y el conocimiento de los sonidos de las letras. Se le daba mucha importancia a la elocución y a la lectura oral; aspectos muy importantes bajo un gobierno representativo y democrático.

El siglo XIX fue considerado como un período evolutivo en la historia de la enseñanza de la lectura. La lectura se vio como un medio necesario para adquirir conocimientos, y se consideró en este período un molde adecuado para formar al ser humano. Pestalozi y Horace Man influyen en cómo enseñar a leer. En este período se predicaba que el éxito de la democracia dependía del desarrollo de la inteligencia del individuo. Por lo tanto, había que desarrollar los sentidos, los músculos y las habilidades mentales del hombre y la mujer. La lectura se enseñaba usando todos los recursos mentales y musculares del ser humano. Al enseñar la palabra, se presentaba el objeto, se hacía una relación semántica entre el objeto y la palabra; el estudiante escribía la palabra en el aire, y se presentaban los sonidos y las combinaciones silábicas. A fines del siglo XIX, los

silabarios fueron desapareciendo para dar cabida al énfasis en el recono-
cimento de palabras y a la fonética en general.

A principios del siglo XX, hubo un énfasis muy marcado en la mecánica
del reconocimiento de la palabra y en la fluidez en la lectura oral. Además,
se le daba mucha importancia al uso de trozos literarios como materiales
literarios para enseñar a leer. En los grados primarios se comenzaron a
desarrollar elementos elaborados del método fonético. En los grados inter-
medios, la apreciación y estilo de la literatura fueron características comunes en los salones de lectura. Entre 1910 y 1925, la aplicación de la teoría
de Froebel desarrolló un marcado interés por la lectura silenciosa. Se decía
que la lectura oral era una forma de expresión pero la lectura silenciosa
desarrollaba la atención y el pensamiento. Al enseñar la lectura silenciosa
se enfatizaba la comprensión al leer; el no mover los labios; el pensar y el
usar las experiencias anteriores para sacarle sentido a lo que se leía. La
fonética se usaba solamente como un método para iniciar al estudiante en
la lectura.

En la década de 1930, los maestros enfatizaban en sus clases de lectura
el que sus alumnos adquirieran la comprensión de lo leído y pudieran llegar
a sus propias interpretaciones. Se introdujeron las series básicas para
enseñar a leer, los carteles de experiencias, y el uso de cuentos y rimas para
atraer la atención del estudiante. La fonética quedó relegada a un segundo
plano. Se recomendó el usar la fonética para establecer similaridades y
diferencias entre palabras, elementos fonéticos comunes y establecer relaciones entre sonidos y combinaciones silábicas. La fonética se enseñaba
cuando había una necesidad individual; no era parte integrante de las
activades diarias de la clase de lectura.

Al período de 1935 a 1950 se le ha llamado "el período del conflicto
internacional." Entre las razones que existieron para llamarle época de
conflicto, están las siguientes:

1. Surgieron muchas diferencias en relación a cómo se definía qué era
   leer, cómo motivar la lectura y cuáles eran los mejores materiales para
   enseñar a leer.
2. La Segunda Guerra Mundial había revelado que muchos adultos no
   poseían las destrezas básicas de leer. Por lo tanto, la definición de qué
   es leer, se amplía; la lectura incluía una gran cantidad de destrezas, y
   éstas variaban dependiendo de la clase de material a leerse, el
   propósito de la lectura y los valores perseguidos.

3. Las actitudes del estudiante en la interpretación de la lectura, y el papel de la lectura en el desarollo de la personalidad fueron aspectos enfatizados en este período.

De 1960 en adelante, la lingüística, la psicología y la sociología contribuyeron a crear una nueva visión de la lectura. Es el período durante el cual los educadores estuvieron muy activos en investigaciones sobre el proceso de leer y la lectura en general. En esta época surgieron los estudios de Brown (1973), Durkin (1974), Chall (1967), y Gagne (1968). Es el período en que se expandieron los conocimientos y teorías anteriores y se empezó a hacer uso de la tecnología educativa. El movimiento de los derechos del ser humano despertó el interés por los valores morales y culturales de los materiales de lectura. Hubo un énfasis marcado en la lectura como proceso, más que en la evaluación de los resultados. Los programas de lectura individualizada reemplazaron en parte, las series básicas de lectura. Se introdujo la instrucción programada. La metodología le dio prioridad a las destrezas de análisis, aplicación y evaluación en la lectura. El reconocimeinto de palabras y la fonética fueron recursos que el maestro utilizó al individualizar la lectura.

En la década de 1970 y comienzos del 1980 se percibió la preferencia por una forma específica de cómo enseñar a leer. El maestro, el ambiente y el estudiante determinan qué combinación de métodos usar para conseguir los objetivos de la enseñanza. Por eso, en este período se le da importancia a cómo es que el estudiante reconoce y procesa mentalmente esa información. Se ve un marcado énfasis en el desarrollo de destrezas de comunicación oral y escrita, el uso de la lectura en otras áreas de contenido y el papel que desempeña la estructura del material escrito en el análisis y comprensión por parte del estudiante (Arnaldi de Olmeda, 1978; Ferdman, Weber, & Ramírez, 1994).

Las décadas de fines de los ochenta y la mitad de los noventa se caracterizó por un marcado énfasis en la individualidad en la selección de la metodología de la lectura. Aunque una gran mayoría de programas bilingües descubren en esta década el método global, conocido en inglés como el *whole language* method, la literatura de esa época expresa aceptación por la variedad de métodos en la enseñanza de la lectura. Se identifican ventajas y desventajas en todos los métodos. Asociaciones profesionales como la Asociación Internacional de la Lectura publican artículos en pro y en contra de los métodos global y fonético. Se dice que ambos métodos contribuyen al proceso cognoscitivo y académico del estudiante. Se le da importancia a la alfabetización (literacy development) en ambos idiomas (Ferdman, Weber, & Ramírez, 1994; Ovando & Collier, 1985; Williams & Capizzi-Snipper, 1990). Es época de reflección más que de crítica y donde la madurez instruccional del maestro, el estilo de aprender del estudiante los materiales y textos, especialmente de tipo multicultural vienen a ser factores importantes en la enseñanza de lectura.

A continación se presenta una breve descripción y características de los procesos filosóficos y sus métodos que contribuyeron a cambiar la enseñanza de la lectura.

Características del Proceso Sintético y Analítico

En 1948, Antonia Sáez expresó que la lectura es una actividad instrumental. No se lee por leer, se lee por algo y para algo. Siempre, detrás de toda lectura, ha de haber un deseo de conocer, un ansia de penetrar en la intimidad de las cosas, y un deseo de ampliar el contacto del hombre con el hombre. Por lo tanto, la base de todos los métodos para enseñar a leer ha sido siempre la de reconocer los símbolos escritos; o sea, el hacer comprender al estudiante que, entre lo signos de la lengua escrita y las palabras de la lengua hablada, existe una determinada correspondencia. Sin embargo, han habido diferents puntos de vista al visualizar este proceso. De acuerdo a Chall (1967) la metodología de la lectura se puede dividir en dos grupos: el qrupo que le da énfasis al significado o contenido de la lectura (meaning, emphasis), y el grupo que enfatiza el reconocimiento del símbolo escrito (code, emphasis). Al hablar de esos dos grupos, se hace más en términos de los pasos a seguir al introducir la lectura que en diferencias basadas en los fines óptimos de la misma. Estos procesos o pasos se conocen como sintético o analítico.

El proceso sintético está basado en la temprana introducción de las reglas de la fonética y la individualización en la enseñanza de éstas. Este procedimiento requiere que el estudiante combine elementos para construir palabras. Exige que el estudiante reconozca las letras por su nombre, por su sonido y establezca relaciones de letras y sílabas y de palabras aisladas. Siempre se empieza con una sola unidad de lenguaje como punto de partida para enseñar a leer.

El proceso analítico pone énfasis en la inmediata adquisición del significado a través de la enseñanza de palabras en conjunto, el desarrollo de un vocabulario de palabras comunes aunque puedan ser deletreadas irregularmente y la lenta introducción del alfabeto y la fonética. Los educadores que recomiendan este proceso están interesados en el proceso en sí, o sea en la manera en que la mente recibe ideas y usa éstas para reconocer palabras.

De estos dos procesos o formas de describir los pasos al enseñar a leer, han surgido varios métodos. Cada uno de ellos se afianza en uno de estos dos procesos, dependiendo de la percepción de la lectura que se tenga. Hay muchos métodos y, muchos de ellos, aunque tienen diferentes nombres; en el fondo, persiguen el mismo fin y usan los mismos procedimientos. La figura 6.1 presenta una lista de varios de estos métodos y la categoría a la cual pertenecen.

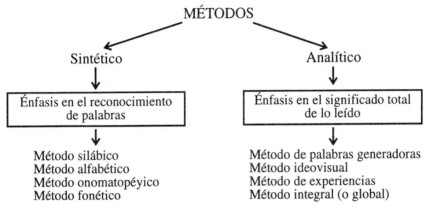

FIG. 6.1.   Métodos en la enseñanza de la lectura.

A continuación se explican algunos de estos métodos.

MÉTODOS BASADOS EN EL PROCESO SINTÉTICO

El Método Alfabético

La proposición filosófica de este método es que el estudiante aprenderá a leer al familiarizarse con las formas, nombres y sonidos de las letras. El procedimiento por el cual el estudiante aprende a leer, es el siguiente:

1. El estudiante aprende los nombres de las letras del alfabeto.
2. El estudiante aprende a pronunciar las letras del alfabeto.
3. El estudiante aprende a pronunciar combinaciones de dos letras.
4. Luego, el estudiante combina tres letras, cuatro letras, hasta que eventualmente se reconocen monosílabos y palabras de más de dos sílabas. Generalmente, las vocales se introducen primero y luego las consonantes. El maestro le explica al estudiante cómo se combinan sílabas para crear palabras.

5. El estudiante usa la combinación de palabras para ayudar al estudiante a crear oraciones. Los estudiantes tienen que conocer los nombres de las letras para poder deletrear, organizar y leer la palabra formada.

El énfasis de este método es en el reconocimiento de palabras. Supongamos que el maestro quire lograr que el estudiante lea la oración: *Mi mamá es alta.* ¿Cuáles serían los pasos? (a) Tiene que empezar por enseñar los nombres de las letras: m = eme, l = ele, t = te, etc. (b) Combinar consonates con vocales para formar sílabas: eme + i = mi, hasta formar todas las sílabas necesarias. (c) Combina sílabas para formar palabras: ma + ma = mamá, al + ta = alta. (d) Utiliza las palabras formadas para crear oraciones. *Mi mamá es alta.* En este método las vocales (a, e, i, o, u) se enseñan primero, y una vez el estudiante puede reconocer éstas, se introducen las consonantes.

El Método Fonético

Los proponentes de este método ven la lengua, en primer término, como un sistema de símbolos sonoros, como instrumento de comunicación oral. Cuando el estudiante comienza su vida escolar trae destrezas de comunicación oral que incluyen un vocabulario de miles de palabras y patrones comunes de expresión. Sobre esta base idiomática es que se apoyan los proponentes de este método para iniciar la lectura. Para ellos, la lengua esta compuesta de sonidos. Como las letras corresponden a sonidos, algunos educadores han considerado que la mejor manera de enseñar a leer es la de lograr que los estudiantes reconozcan y asocien los signos acústicos y gráficos de las letras, y que una vez éstos aparecen combinados en palabras, podrían leerlas mediante el reconocimiento sucesivo de letras y sílabas. El método fonético le da énfasis a los sonidos que las letras del alfabeto representan. Los estudiantes tienen que memorizarse todos los sonidos representados por las letras y sus combinaciones, ya que el dominio de los sonidos de las letras llevará eventualmente al dominio de los sonidos de las sílabas y las palabras. Hay variaciones de este método pero en general sigue el siguiente procedimiento:

1. Enseñar al estudiante los sonidos de las cinco vocales con todas las posibles combinaciones, incluyendo los diptongos.

    ae ao ee ei
    ai au ia eu

2. Enseñar al estudiante los sonidos de las consonantes comenzando por las más fáciles como *m, s y l.*

3. Al introducir una consonante, ésta se combina con las vocales para producir todas las sílabas posibles (m = ma, me, mi, mo, mu).

4. Enseñar oraciones derivadas de estas sílabas (Amo a mi mamá).

5. Luego se enseñan el resto de las consonantes, creando oraciones más complejas hasta que el estudiante pueda leer cualquier sílaba y palabra.

Navarro (1936) expresó que los idiomas no son meras sumas de sonidos y que la lengua española, aunque más fonética que muchos idiomas, tampoco es tan fonética como se cree. Navarro expresó que la ortografia oficial española dista mucho de reflejar convenientemente la pronunciación. Además, estos signos sonoros están sujetos a las asociaciones del que habla y la función de estos elementos fónicos varía según la unidad semántica en que se estudien. El maestro no debe enseñar combinaciones fonéticas que no tengan significación o que no existan en la lengua española; por ejemplo, combinaciones tales como "seamse" y "amsa" no se deben utilizar, ya que no tienen ninguna significación.

Método Onomatopéyico

El propósito de este método es el desarrollar sistemáticamente asociaciones auditivas de letras y sonidos basados en algo o en alguien del ambiente del estudiante. El estudiante aprende a hacer asociaciones individuales y desarrolla destrezas en descifrar la palabra impresa y reconocerla en su expresión oral. Las consonantes son generalmente repetidas en palabras y frases para crear un efecto aliterado: Por ejemplo, en la oración "El dardo de David daba duro," la consonante *d* es repetida varias veces. El maestro tiene que establecer relaciones entre las letras y aquellos sonidos que son familiares para el estudiante. Entre esta relación de sonidos y letras, se pueden mencionar:

1. El sonido de la vocal *u* es enseñado relacionándola con el sonido que hace un ratón;
2. La vocal *u* se relaciona con el sonido del tren;
3. La sílaba *gra* se estudia relacionándola con el sonido del agua pasando por el cauce del río;

4. El diptongo *au* se estudia relacionándolo con el sonido pronunciado por el gato o el perro;
5. La *m* se enseña relacionándola con el mugido de una vaca.

Después que el estudiante ha hecho estas asociaciones en una forma correcta y rápida, se le estimula a analizar las partes de la palabra e identificar las sílabas. El material de lectura se organiza para proveer el reconocimiento de los sonidos en diferentes posiciones, dentro de la palabra y de las oraciones: al principio, en el medio y al final. El siguiente ejemplo explica cómo este método funciona.

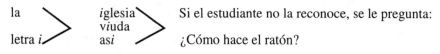

la   *i*glesia   Si el estudiante no la reconoce, se le pregunta:
               v*i*uda
letra *i*.   as*i*   ¿Cómo hace el ratón?

El identificar la letra en diferentes posiciones dentro de la palabra ayuda al estudiante a recibir práctica en descubrir la misma relación de sonido y símbolo en una variedad de situaciones: vocales precedidas por consonantes (ta, me, bi), consonantes entre vocales (ata, iba). Este método no es en realidad un método sistemático para enseñar a leer. Es un recurso adicional que el maestro puede utilizar al ayudar al estudiante a descifrar el elemento fónico de una palabra o frase.

MÉTODOS BASADOS EN EL PROCESO ANALÍTICO

Los siguientes métodos se consideran parte del proceso analítico.

Método de Palabras Generadoras

Los proponentes de este método se basan en la idea psicológica de que una palabra no es una combinación de letras, sino que tiene carácter reconocible por sí sola. Según este método, la lectura consiste de una serie de palabras indivisibles, con características y significados propios. Por tanto, se enfatiza el significado de la palabra. Al utilizar este método el maestro: (a) presenta palabras completas para que el estudiante las analice, (b) el maestro explica al estudiante el significado de la palabra o palabras, (c) el estudiante pronuncia la palabra, (d) las palabras se presentan como unidades indivisibles primero, y luego se lleva al estudiante para que identifique las sílabas y cada uno de los sonidos encontrados en cada sílaba y, finalmente, las letras que representan estos sonidos. Este método ofrece al estudiante la oportunidad de ver la relación que existe entre las letras y los sonidos y entre sílabas y palabras, (e) cuando los estudiantes han terminado el proceso de hacer el análisis de todos estos elementos, se les pide que reorganicen la palabra o que creen otras palabras nuevas, organizando sílabas ya previamente introducidas, y (f) se les pide a los estudiantes que usen las palabras conocidas para crear frases y oraciones. Visualmente, el método sería el siguiente:

Propósito: El estudiante identificará el significado y estructura de las siguientes tres palabras:
mamá, casa, alta.

Paso 1: El estudiante pronunciará las palabras mamá, casa, alta. Explica el significado de mamá, casa y alta, las pronuncia y las usa en oraciones.

Paso 2: El estudiante divide las palabras en sílabas; ma-ma, ca-sa, al-ta.

Paso 3: El estudiante identifica los sonidos de cada sílaba y de cada letra.

Paso 4: Se pide al estudiante que forme las palabras de nuevo.

Paso 5: Se presentan las siguientes sílabas para que el estudiante forme palabras nuevas y explique su significado; luego crea oraciones con estas palabras:
ma + ta = mata
ca + ma = cama
al + ma = alma
al + ta = alta

Paso 6: El estudiante crea palabras nuevas con las sílabas aprendidas. Forma oraciones con estas palabras.
mata mamá
cama casa
alma saca
alta tasa

Método Integral (o Global)

Este método nació de la actitud que ante el desarrollo integral del estudiante tuvo la psicología. Los proponentes de este método ven al estudiante como un todo, y ven la lectura como un componente de ese aspecto (Altwerger, Edelsky, & Flores, 1987). Presupone que el estudiante se interesa por aspectos generales y no se interesa mucho por los detalles. Es por este proceso de visión de conjunto que el estudiante adquiere conocimientos. Estos educadores aplican las ideas de Piaget (1974), Durkin (1974) y Gagne (1968) cuando explican que estas percepciones de conjunto permiten la adquisición de lectura y lenguaje en general. Leer es, pues, un proceso visual y no auditivo. Por tanto, la lectura silenciosa ayudará al estudiante a captar el significado de ese conjunto de palabras que forman oraciones. El material a leerse tendrá que venir de las necesidades inmediatas del estudiante. Temas como la escuela, el hogar y las experiencias diarias del estudiante tendrán que formar parte del contenido de la lectura. Este material de lectura debe estar basado en centros de interés que vengan del ambiente del estudiante. Este método, pues, sustituye el dominio de la audición por el de la visión. Como puede notarse, este método surge como una reacción en contra de los métodos que le daban más importancia al reconocimiento de palabras y al aspecto sonoro de las palabras.

El método integral (global) atiende esencialmente al contenido ideológico en la lectura, y afirma que la fonética es un medio para llegar al fin: la interpretación de ideas. El método integral (global) expresa la idea de que el significado e interés del estudiante es el factor más importante en la enseñanza de la lectura (Forgione, 1965; Goodman, 1986; 1989). Antonia Saez (1978) presenta cuatro etapas en el método integral (global):

1. **Etapa de Iniciación.** El estudiante reconoce ciertas frases y palabras de la convivencia diaria.
2. **Comprobación y Aplicación.** El estudiante reconoce el significado y relación de las palabras y frases antes enseñadas.
3. **Elaboración.** El estudiante construye nuevas frases, al combinar las frases y palabras ya aprendidas. Se inicia la escritura creativa.
4. **Descomposición.** El estudiante empieza a hacer el análisis de la estructura lingüística.

No todos los educadores que recomiendan el método integral (global) usan las etapas mencionadas anteriormente. Pero, en términos generales, la mayoría de los maestros siguen los siguientes pasos:

1. La lección se inicia estimulando al estudiante en una conversación sobre algún tema que les interese a los estudiantes y que les permita hablar sobre el tema.
2. El maestro escribe lo que el estudiante va diciendo (o ya lo tiene previamente escrito en un cartelón).
3. Cada lección tiene un tema y hay una serie de vocabulario correspondiente a la lección. Por tanto, el maestro toma todo el tiempo necesario para hablar sobre el tema y enfatizar las palabras que le dan significado al mismo.
4. El maestro usa dibujos, conversación y ejercicios escritos. Luego, invita a los estudiantes a leer todo el cuento o composición. Puede subrayar el vocabulario correspondiente, o escribirlo en tarjetas. El estudiante va notando una relación funcional entre lo que él/ella dice y cómo se ve en forma impresa.
5. El estudiante, con la ayuda del maestro, empieza a hacer el análisis estructural de las palabras: identifica la palabra, las sílabas y las letras; o sea, el estudiante descompone toda la selección escrita.
6. El maestro invita al estudiante a hacer un ejercicio, para determinar si él/ella capta el significado de la selección escrita; o si es capaz de reconstruirla visualmente, o si puede establecer ciertas comparaciones visuales.

Al estudiante se le puede invitar a: (a) escribir la selección, ya sea haciendo uso de las tarjetas o en su cuaderno de escritura, (b) darle la selección de nuevo para que complete la oración que falta, con la palabra que él ya aprendió, (c) hacer un dibujo del mensaje representado, y (d) hacer oraciones con las palabras aprendidas. En la siguiente lección se presenta una ilustración corta del método integral (global).

Tema: El tren.

Objetivos:
    Al finalizar la lección el estudiante:
1.   Identificará al tren como uno de los medios de comunicación más usados en el mundo.
2.   Identificará el significado de las siguientes palabras: vagones, motor, pasajeros, e identificará las mismas visualmente.
3.   Leerá oralmente la unidad de lectura para contestar preguntas relacionadas con el tema y contenido de la lectura.

Pasos:

1.   Conversación sobre los diferentes medios de comunicación que
     tenemos hoy en las grandes ciudades: el automóvil, el avión, el
     tren. De esta conversación surge la lectura.
2.   Mediante preguntas y respuestas se desarrolla la siguiente unidad
     de lectura que el maestro ya tiene escrita en la pizarra o en un
     cartel. El maestro puede utilizar dibujos para el desarrollo del
     tema. El maestro se asegura que en la conversación se introducen
     y se explican las palabras y frases que podrían ser desconocidas
     para el estudiante.
3.   El maestro lee la lectura (o le pide a los estudiantes que la lean
     silenciosamente) para contestar la pregunta tema: ¿Por qué el tren
     es importante en una ciudad?

EL TREN

El tren es necesario. Nos lleva de un sitio a otro. Hay trenes de pasajeros y trenes
de carga El tren tiene vagones. Camina por medio de un motor. Hay trenes con
motor que trabajan con electricidad. Otros trabajan con carbón. El tren va a
diferentes sitios dc una ciudad. También viaja de ciudad a ciudad y de país a país.

4.   A través de preguntas específicas el estudiante reconoce las
     oraciones y las frases individualmente.
a.   ¿Qué diferencias hay entre los trenes de carga y los de pasa-
     jeros?
b.   Describe un tren de pasajeros. Describe uno de carga.
c.   ¿Qué ventajas tiene el viajar en tren? ¿Qué desventajas tiene?
5.   La creacion de la unidad, ofrece oportunidades para la práctica y
     seguridad en el dominio del uso de los signos de puntuación y
     letras mayúsculas. Se presenta la unidad escrita en fajas de
     cartulina, una faja para cada oración y se realiza una actividad de
     análisis.

Conclusión:
     a. Resumen:
       • *El tren es necesario.*

• *Nos lleva de un sitio a otro.*

b. Busca la oración que tiene la palabra *necesario* y la que tiene la palabra *sitio.* Este análisis se hace siguiendo el orden en que aparecen en la unidad y más tarde se hacen independientemente del orden en que están escritas para asegurar el reconocimiento y evitar la memorización.

6. Se escribe la selección en oraciones individuales. Se colocan las fajas de cartulina en un tarjetero en el orden en que corresponden. El niño que tiene la oración la lee y la coloca en el tarjetero.

7. En la pizarra hay unas oraciones escritas con unos espacios en blanco. Se le suple al estudiante una tarjeta con la palabra que falta. El estudiante lee la palabra y luego la coloca en el espacio correspondiente.

Palabras	*Oraciones*
tren	1. El_____ es necesario.
motor	2. El tren camina por medio de un _____.
carga	3. Hay trenes de _____ y de _____.
electricidad	4. Hay trenes con motor que trabajan con _____.
pasajeros	

8. Se presentan ejercicios variados para asegurar el dominio de la lectura del material estudiado.

9. Se comprueba el reconocimiento de las palabras en cualquier situación. A continuación aparecen tres ejercicios que sirven para demostrar esta destreza.

Hay que mencionar que este método es muy útil al iniciar al estudiante en la lectura. Sin embargo, el maestro tiene que combinarlo con otros métodos y técnicas para evitar el caer en la monotonía y la repetición.

Ejercicio A	*Ejercicio B*	*Ejercicio C*
Escribe palabras que pertenezcan a la misma familia que la palabra *carbon*	Señala las palabras que en la selección tienen la sílaba *ne*	Tira una línea de la columna izquierda a la derecha que completa la oración
		1. El tren a. carga
• carboncito	• tre*ne*s	2. Hay trenes de b. a varias ciudades
• carbonera	• vago*ne*s	3. El tren va c. es necesario

FIG 6.2. Reconocimiento de palabras.

El Método Integral (o Global) de los Años 1990s

El método whole language que estuvo tan de moda en la década de los 1980s y principios de los 1990s no es necesariamente una copia del método global descrito anteriormente. Sin embargo, los principios filosóficos son los mismos. El método whole language (que yo le llamo "integral" o global en español) como se conoce hoy en día, parte de la premisa de que la lectura es algo individual y que parte de los intereses de los estudiantes. El salón de clases provee para una variedad de materiales de libros donde los estudiantes escogerán sus libros preferidos. A veces, estos libros están agrupados en centros de interés o por temas. El maestro necesita tener las destrezas necesarias para encauzar a los estudiantes a leer un libro o varios libros con un propósito determinado o meramente por placer. La idea básica de este enfoque es rodear a los estudiantes de literatura para que ellos despierten amor por la lectura y deseos de leer. No se recomienda el estudio y la memorización de vocabulario aislado. Por el contrario, se enfatiza la comprensión del texto como un todo. El vocabulario a estudiarse y definirse es aquel que es necesario para la comprensión del texto. Por tanto, el vocabulario se enseña por contexto, dándole énfasis a las palabras que son necesarias para comprender las ideas presentadas en la lectura.

No hay unos pasos específicos a seguir en este método. Sin embargo, se recomiendan las siguientes estrategias en la presentación del material:

1. El salón de clases provee variedad de materiales de lectura de diferentes temas y niveles de lectura. Se despliegan cuentos, fábulas, narraciones, biografías, poemas y novelas. Estos materiales han sido evaluados por el maestro para asegurarse de que son materiales apropiados para el estudiante.
2. El maestro decide cómo presentar el material: por centros de interés, por temas o meramente escoge uno o dos libros para la lectura de todo el grupo de estudiantes.
3. Se introduce el tema a base de una conversación general, donde, si es necesario, se introduce el vocabulario esencial de la lectura. También se introduce la pregunta o preguntas que motivarán al estudiante a leer.
4. El maestro tiene varias opciones: la lectura oral, (haciendo uso de recursos audiovisuales o preguntas guías), lectura por grupos (a base de tareas) o trabajo individual (para completar una tarea individual).

5. Al final de la lección los estudiantes tienen varias opciones (diarios individuales, compartir con la clase o con un grupo pequeño de compañeros) para demostrar la comprensión de la lectura.

EL MÉTODO ECLÉCTICO

Se ha notado que todos los métodos presentados tienen sus ventajas y desventajas dependiendo del tipo de estudiante al cual se quiere enseñar a leer, la visualización del proceso de enseñar a leer y los materiales de que se disponga. Todos los métodos anteriores requieren maestros competentes, dispuestos a usar una variedad de elementos técnicos y a cambiar el método si nota que no hay progreso en la lectura. La autora de este capítulo recomienda que los maestros de lectura utilicen un método ecléctico al enseñar a leer. Este método consiste en usar técnicas y elementos de los procesos descritos anteriormente—sintético y análitico—con el propósito de ofrecer oportunidad al maestro para trabajar con diferentes tipos de estudiantes. Se enfatiza la importancia del reconocimiento de las palabras en la lectura pero, a la vez se recalca la necesidad de leer para derivar unos conceptos, unas ideas y una significación.

En la actualidad, muchos programas de lectura recomiendan el uso del Método Eclectico. Este método propone que:

1. Deben realizarse ejercicios preparatorios para eliminar o reducir ciertas deficiencias visuales, auditivas, de retención y de expresión oral.
2. Los elementos fonéticos que el maestro ha determinado que son necesarios, se presentan en los ejercicios preparatorios (o al final de la lección) y están basados en las necesidades individuales.
3. Las destrezas de escritura también tienen su razón de ser desde el principio; por ejemplo, la destreza de formar las letras es necesaria, para más tarde usar esas letras en la escritura de palabras.
4. La formación de sílabas y la formación de palabras se utilizan sólo como medios de ofrecer práctica al estudiante. Se requiere, pues, que el estudiante haga asociaciones de sonido y símbolo para escribir dictados y crear nuevas palabras.
5. Actividades de comprensión e interpretación son elementos básicos y necesarios en toda clase de lectura.

Por su definición misma, "ecléctico" significa "que adopta entre varias opiniones o cosas la que más le conviene, formada de elementos tomados de varios sistemas." Toma, pues, elementos del proceso sintético (las asociaciones auditivas en el reconocimiento de las palabras y sus partes), y del proceso analítico (la comprensión de lo leído, el enseñar a leer palabras, frases y oraciones completas). ¿Qué pasos se siguen al usar este método? No puede hablarse de pasos específicos ya que los pasas dependerán del estudiante y del maestro. Si el estudiante demuestra habilidad auditiva, quizas podría comenzarse por el reconocimiento de los sonidos de las letras y las combinaciones de sílabas como medio de formar palabras y oraciones. Si el estudiante, por el contrario, demuestra más habilidad perceptiva y visual, el comenzar la lectura con un enfoque global, quizas sería más conveniente, o quizás el hacer uso de los dos métodos a la vez podría traer mejores resultados. La autora recomienda que cualquiera sea el orden a seguir, que el maestro en su presentación haga énfasis en los siguientes aspectos:

1. La necesidad de usar recursos variados para ayudar al estudiante en la comprensión de la lectura.
2. El maestro es un mediador de la enseñanza, por tanto, necesita preparar lecciones que motiven y reten al estudiante a leer.
3. El uso de literatura "auténtica" en la lectura.
4. El desarrollo de las cuatro areas del lenguaje: escuchar, hablar, leer y escribir.

VENTAJAS Y DESVENTAJAS DE LOS MÉTODOS PARA ENSEÑAR A LEER

La Table numero 6.1, (pp. 120–122). enumera las ventajas y desventajas de los métodos presentados anteriormente.

CONCLUSIÓN

¿Cuál de estos métodos o combinación de métodos es el mejor? Parecería lógico encontrar la contestación a esta pregunta en los resultados de las muchas investigaciones que se han llevado a cabo en los últimos años, pero no es así. Estamos de acuerdo con Chall (1967) cuando dijo que hay mucha inconsistencia en estas investigaciones. Muchas veces, esta inconsistencia surge porque no se tiene un consenso común de lo que es leer ni de cuáles son los propósitos últimos de la enseñanza de la lectura. Es por eso que todavía seguimos preguntando: ¿Cuándo comenzar, qué materiales usar, qué método emplear y qué organización establecer? A ese respecto, muchas de las investigaciones presentan diferentes resultados y la mejor respuesta está en decir que leer es un proceso individual y no todos los estudiantes responden igualmente a las mismas prácticas. Habrá estudiantes que pueden reconocer pensamientos completos sin necesidad de atender específicamente a las palabras aisladas, y mucho menos a las partes de las palabras. Habrá otros, en cambio, con los cuales el reconocimiento tendrá que ser auxiliado por el conocimiento de las partes separadamente. Por tanto, todos los métodos tienen unas ventajas sobre los otros, dependiendo del estudiante, de su nivel y de la habilidad del maestro para enseñar a través de ese método. Pero cualquiera que sea el método a usarse, debe incluir: actividades de grupo, enseñanza individualizada y actividades de enriquecimiento.

Al usar un método auditivo como el método fonético en la enseñanza de la lectura, se deben considerar las características del estudiante bilingüe, las transferencias positivas y negativas del español al inglés, las comparaciones de las estructuras de ambos idiomas en relación al léxico, a la semántica, la sintaxis y los patrones culturales.

El Método Integral (Global) se recomienda como método inicial en la enseñanza de la lectura, ya que parte del conocimiento que de la lengua tienen los estudiantes. Además, hace uso de las expresiones orales del estudiante como medio de desarrollar unidades de lectura. El estudiante que puede captar el significado de sus propias verbalizaciones y puede organizar experiencias, es un estudiante que está demostrando aprendizaje. Y este método podría ser la motivación inicial para introducir al estudiante a la lectura.

EJERCICIOS DE APLICACIÓN

- Lea tres libros o artículos que presenten un resumen sobre investigaciones en la metodología de la enseñanza de la lectura en español. De acuerdo a los autores leídos: ¿Cuál método es mejor? ¿Por qué?
- Si Ud. fuera a hacer una investigación sobre los métodos para enseñar lectura en español: ¿cuáles serían las cinco (5) preguntas que Ud. se haría antes de comenzar el estudio?
- Prepárese a debatir la siguiente aseveración: "La métodología para enseñar lectura en español es la misma que para enseñar lectura en inglés."
- La Sra. Rosario es la madre de un estudiante de la clase de tercer grado. La Sra. Rosario quiere que Ud. enseñe a leer a su hijo

TABLE 6.1.

Ventajas y desventajas de los métodos para enseñar a leer.

Método	Ventajas	Desventajas
ALFABÉTICO	• Podría usarse por aquellos maestros que tienen un plan definido y específico sobre el proceso de leer. • Es un recurso adicional para usarse con aquellos estudiantes que demuestran habilidad de percepción visual.	• Es un procedimiento mecánico, repetitivo y aburrido. • El tener que memorizar y repetir el nombre de la letra para luego formar la sílaba, tiende a complicar el proceso y muchas veces crea confusiones. Por ejemplo, en la letra *l* (elle) el estudiante podría decir *le* en vez de *elle*. • Algunas letras no se prestan para este análisis. Por ejemplo, el estudiante podría repetir la *p + o* y pronunciar otra palabra, la cual no se oye bien en español.

FONÉTICO	• Muchos creen que se abrevia el proceso de leer.
	• Se recomienda para dominar la mecánica de la lectura.
	• Recomendable para aquellos estudiantes que demuestran habilidad auditiva.
		• Algunos sonidos son difíciles de pronunciar en forma aislada (x, q), y otros sonidos son bien parecidos (b, t).
		• Los lingüistas han llegado a la conclusión de que una absoluta identidad fonética no es posible encontrarla, ni aún entre las gentes de una misma aldea o región.
		• Algunas letras tienen más de un sonido, o no tienen sonido:
		  • La letra c
		    ca ci
		    c
		    cu ce
		  • La letra g
		    ga ge
		    g
		    go gi

Método	Ventajas	Desventajas
ONOMATOPÉYICO	• Ayuda al desarrollo de asociaciones auditivas. • En el estudiante se despierta interes en la lectura. Debido a su aspecto repetitivo y musical despierta en el estudiante interés por la lectura.	• El maestro necesita conocer una representación auditiva para cada letra del alfabeto. • Carece de elementos sistemáticos de comprensión e interpretación. • Requiere el uso constante de la lectura y expresión oral. Por tanto, la lectura silenciosa no se enfatiza. • El maestro tiene que estar siempre presente para iniciar la asociación auditiva si el estudiante no reconoce la letra.
PALABRAS GENERADORAS	• El enfasis de este método recae en el significado de la palabra. • Desarrolla una actitud positiva hacia la lectura ya que hay creatividad y variedad de actividades y ejercicios. • Hace uso de una variedad de recursos (rimas, poesías, cuentos) al introducir las palabras.	• En el análisis estructural de la palabra se corre el riesgo de que sea el maestro el que haga el análisis. Si es así, el estudiante se convierte en un agente pasivo. • Hay un marcado énfasis en la organización escrita de la palabra, cuando todavía el estudiante no ha desarrollado la mayor parte de las destrezas de escritura. • No independiza al estudiante para lograr el sentido de lo leído. • La lectura silenciosa queda relegada a un segundo plano.
GLOBAL	• Trabaja con centros de interés. • Énfasis en las destrezas visuales y motoras. • Palabras, frases y oraciones son identificadas como unidades de lenguaje con sentido propio, y éstas son aprendidas por el estudiante antes de estudiar unidades más pequeñas.	• Muy poco énfasis en el aspecto auditivo. • El requerir que el estudiante escriba a menudo puede causarle ciertas dificultades a algunos estudiantes. • No hay restricción del material de lectura a presentarse. • No hay un plan lógico al enseñar a leer. • Exige mucha preparación y dedicación por parte del maestro.

utilizando el Método Fonético, y no el Método Global que Ud. usa actualmente. La Sra. Rosario indica que ella aprendió a leer a través del Método Fonético y que ella ayuda a su hijo en la casa a aprender a leer por el mismo método. ¿Cómo resolvería Ud. esta controversia para aprovechar la ayuda de la Sra. Rosario en enseñar a leer a su hijo?

*   Escriba una lección modelo donde indique los pasos que Ud. seguiría al introducir a un grupo de estudiantes una lectura desconocida para ellos. Indique el nivel, el grado y la lectura.
*   Identifique 5 programas de lectura en español que se usan actualmente en las escuelas en Estados Unidos. Identifique las ventajas y desventajas de estos libros. ¿Qué recomendaciones Ud. ofrece para mejorar las mismas?

Serie de Lectura	Ventajas	Desventajas	Recomendaciones
1.			
2.			
3.			
4.			
5.			
6.			
7.			

REFERENCIAS

Altwerger, B., Edelsky, C., & Flores, B. (1987). Whole language: What's new? *Reading Teacher, 41,* 144–154.
Arnaldi de Olmeda. (1978). *Claves de reconocimiento en la enseñanza de la lectura.* Rio Piedras, Puerto Rico: Editorial Cultural.
Brown, R. (1973). *A first language: The early stages.* Cambridge, MA: Harvard University Press.
Chall, J. S. (1967). *Learning to read: The great debate.* New York: McGraw-Hill.
Dolch, E. W. (1955). *Methods in reading.* Champaign, IL: Garvard.
Durkin, D. (1974). *Teaching them to read.* Boston: Allyn & Bacon.
Ferdman, B. M., Weber, R. M., & Ramírez, A. G. (Eds.). (1994). *Literacy across languages and cultures.* Albany, NY: State University of New York Press.
Forgione, J. D. (1965). *La lectura y la escritura por el método global.* Buenos Aires: Editorial El Ateneo.
Gagne, R. M. (1968). *The conditions of learning.* New York: Holt, Rinehart & Winston.
Goodman, K. (1986). *What's whole in whole language?* Portsmouth, NH: Heinemann.
Goodman, K. (1989). *Whole language research: Foundations and develpment* (Occasional Paper No. 1). Tucson, AZ: University of Arizona.
Navarro, T. (1936). *Manual de pronunciación española.* Madrid, España: Consejo Superior de Investigaciones Científicas.
Ovando, C. J., & Collier, V. P. (1985). *Bilingual and ESL classrooms: Teaching in multicultural contexts.* New York: McGraw-Hill.

Piaget, J. (1974). *The language and thought of a child* (M. Gabain, Trans.). New York: New American Library. (Original work published 1923)

Sáez, A. (1978). *La lectura: Arte del lenguaje.* Rio Piedras, Puerto Rico: Editorial de la Universidad de Puerto Rico.

Williams, J. D., & Capizzi-Snipper, G. (1990). *Literacy and bilingualism.* New York: Longman.

7

Spanish Literacy Development in the Content Areas

Philip Segan
Long Island University
Jaime Aquino
California State University at Stockton

Este capítulo presenta una visión general de las responsabilidades y las competencias que necesitan los maestros que enseñan las áreas de contenido en el salón de clases bilingües. Es la responsabilidad de estos educadores el de entender que se enseña lectura a través de todas las asignaturas del currículo. En este capítulo se hace énfasis en la integración de la lectura y las áreas de contenido. El área de las matemáticas se usa para ilustrar esta integración.

OBJECTIVES

After completing this chapter, readers will:

1. Identify the importance of language, culture, and background in the development of content-area concepts and knowledge in the bilingual learner.
2. Understand the importance of motivation for learning and the ways in which to present the content to capture student interest in the materials being presented.
3. Describe their role in teaching reading to all children in the content-area classroom.

4. List general and content-specific reading skills, and describe a strategy for teaching them.
5. Identify the new technology available for enriching the content-area curriculum and make the learning experience inviting to the bilingual learner.

GUIDE QUESTIONS

1. What are the traditionally held perceptions of content-area and reading teachers concerning their responsibilities for teaching students to read?
2. Why is it appropriate for all teachers to understand the concepts and vocabulary used in each of the content areas in school?
3. How do the students' previous experiences and their background have an effect on their ability to understand concepts presented in content classrooms?
4. What special responsibilities and skills do content-area teachers have for teaching reading to their students?
5. What are some of the features that teachers should look for in the texts and other learning materials that they choose to present content in their classrooms?
6. What are some of the roles that technology plays in the presentation of instruction in content-area classrooms?

INTRODUCTION

To the monolingual English teacher—whether in a self-contained elementary classroom; a departmentalized setting; a reading lab; or a specialized, subject-matter classroom in the intermediate grades—the frequently heard expression "every teacher a teacher of reading" continues to evoke certain negative responses that stem from a variety of possible sources:

1. The expression has been greatly overused and misused; to some content-area teachers, it suggests teaching "reading" instead of the content of their subject. Others regard the teaching of reading as a process that begins in the early elementary grades and continues later in a specific locale—usually the language arts/reading classroom or lab—not the specialized domain of the content-area classroom.

2. Teachers of subjects other than reading or, in many cases, language arts, are often ill-prepared to even begin to teach the reading skills necessary to master the content being presented.

3. Historically, too few materials and specific strategies have existed that provide the instruction and practice necessary to teach the reading skills appropriate to the content. Teachers, therefore, have often had to adapt or prepare a variety of materials so that they become suitable for developing reading skills. This additional work may include rewriting the content-area textbook to offer a simpler, less-complex presentation of material; preparing a study guide for chapters or sections of texts or reference books; and teaching students to apply special reading strategies and study skills, such as PQ4R and SQ3R, designed initially for English-language reading materials.

4. Finally, the requisite base of experiences that constitute the "readiness" of students to understand the concepts being presented often has not been built. Therefore, it becomes the responsibility of the teacher to construct such an experiential base for the students and to draw out from them, or to build on, those life experiences to which they can relate new learning.

Students whose language, culture, and background are different from that used to provide the examples or explanations face an additional problem. These examples are the keys to understanding the new concepts. And the linguistic and conceptual demands become competing forces for the learner who is not a native user of the language of the materials. Moreover, there is often little relation between the experiences of these learners and the examples used in the materials of instruction. One attempt to counter these problems is the growing efforts of curriculum development and bilingual/bicultural dissemination centers throughout the nation to make available culturally and experientially appropriate content materials. In recent years, publishers of commercially prepared materials have addressed the need to provide quality materials that will meet the needs of these linguistically and culturally diverse student populations.

The implications of the previous ideas provide the basis for the discussion that follows in this chapter. Current theory and practices in the presentation of techniques for teaching content-area materials are reviewed; general strategies for enhancing the learning of subject matter are presented; most importantly, however, specific examples of materials that are linguis-

tically, experientially, and culturally familiar and appropriate to bilingual
Hispanic learners are provided.

WE CAN ALL BE "CONTENT" WITH CONTENT

A review of the theory and literature related to content-area reading indi-
cates a set of general skills that are commonly developed to foster mastery
in all subjects as well as an identified group of very specific skills pertinent
and unique to each content area. Figure 7.1 summarizes these general skills.

> - vocabulary development
> - study skills strategies
> - the use of advance organizers and study guides
> - building experiential and literacy skills
> - developing the students' schema

Figure 7.1. Content-area reading skills.

Knowing these general and specific reading skills, teachers can use and
adapt teaching materials and strategies to the abilities, needs, experiences,
and interests of the students. Thelen (1976) explained developing content-
cognition as a process of "the reading and thinking skills necessary to
acquire and apply content. Depending on the focus, deductive and inductive
thinking can be thought of as equal parts of the cognitive process" (pp.
11–12). She defined content as subject matter and as the accumulation of
details, concepts, and generalizations of a particular curriculum. This
definition is recast and broadened by Cooper (1993), who defined content-
area reading from a literacy perspective as the construction of meaning. By
constructing meaning, Cooper referred to five major elements: (a) authentic
experiences; (b) writing, speaking, listening, reading, and thinking; (c)
activating prior knowledge; (d) building relationships between the old and
new (knowledge); and (e) providing scaffolded support. Content-area reading is identified in the literature as holistic/across disciplines; providing
experiences for informational reading through all levels of school; creating
strategic readers through the use of scaffolded instruction; activating learning by providing a focus before, during, and after reading; promoting
collaborative learning; and requiring changes in teacher education (Cooper,
1993). In short, the development of literacy in the content areas depends on
the successful development of experiential as well as metacognitive strategies in the learner.

Related to the discussion of experiences of the learner is the issue of motivation for reading and learning. The extent to which the teacher can draw on the student's experiential base for developing interest in new concepts will help that teacher make the new learning fall within the grasp of the student. In regard to motivation, Smith and Elliott (1979) suggested that "relating the need for reading to the realities of students' lives and the world in which they live is a powerful motivator for improving and increasing reading" (p. 22). Expanding on this definition, and placing it in the context of literacy development, Cooper (1993) explained that "motivation in the literacy program is crucial to creating authentic learning experiences that promote positive attitudes about reading and writing and sustain keen interests and enthusiasm" (p. 31). The particular motivating devices used for the Hispanic bilingual learner need to be drawn from the student's experiential base—the home, the language, the culture—and must be related to the materials used for instruction. It is hypocritical and unsound to prepare a motivation for bilingual students based on their background only to transfer the students' thinking to materials that are Anglo-Western in the concepts presented and examples used. For example, a teacher might motivate a math lesson on the process of adding dollars and cents by making reference to the student's experience shopping in a *bodega* for *arroz, carne, gandules,* and the like. How meaningless then to present problems in which a typical suburban Anglo family is buying frozen vegetables, white flour, and canned chop suey in a supermarket! Gonzalez (1992), who described motivating factors as needing students to become personally involved in their learning, supported Cooper's statement. Teachers need to include many of their cultural and linguistic characteristics in the curriculum. Literacy (reading, writing, and language arts) should be primarily organized for making sense of the world.

QUALIFICATIONS OF THE CONTENT-AREA TEACHER

Among the general areas that apply to instruction in the content classrooms, emphasis is placed on the role of the content-area teacher as the one best qualified to provide the instruction in the content to be studied, to incorporate the appropriate reading/processing skills, and to develop appropriate materials. It is difficult for monolingual content-area teachers to present culturally relevant and appropriate materials to bilingual learners in their classrooms Must these teachers all be specialists in a variety of cultures, languages, and in anthropology? The answer, obviously, is "no." What they must be, however, is aware of and sensitive to the history and culture of their students. They need to understand their students' background and experiences; and they need to incorporate the appropriate cultural components into their lessons to make the learning meaningful to their students. In this vein, Gonzalez (1992) pointed out that students feel more comfortable with lessons that contain familiar expressions and stories and other relevant experiences making the curriculum more accessible (i.e., with heroes and personalities). Similarly, asking students to compare personalities in their schoolbooks to persons central to their lives will help the students better comprehend and identify with generic stories that do not include their cultural and historical backgrounds.

Why are content-area teachers best prepared to teach the subject matter to their students?; what are their responsibilities?; and how important are culturally embedded concepts to the particular subject matter being studied? Content-area teachers need to know what reading skills are necessary for successful reading of the materials in their particular disciplines, and they need to be capable of assisting students in applying these skills as they complete their content-area assignments. Roe, Stoodt, and Burns (1991) offered seven characteristics of successful content-area teachers. Teachers need to have the following qualifications:

1. Knowledge of the reading skills that are needed by secondary students in order to read content materials in their disciplines. For example, teachers must have the ability to understand diagrams, graphs, charts, formulas, and equations in mathematics or science.
2. Knowledge of assessment measures that can help teachers identify students who cannot read assigned texts suggested by the curriculum. For example, using Informal Reading Inventories, teacher-made tests, and reading-aloud activities with comprehension checks are recommended methodological strategies.
3. Ability to identify specific reading gaps as deficits that should be referred to a specialist in order to provide appropriate help for identified students. For example, students who are appropriately diagnosed as being at-risk and in need of special education services may need a trained teacher in this area.
4. Knowledge of recommended instructional strategies to help students learn specific skills needed for understanding concepts and skills in the content area. For example, skimming and scanning, vocabulary used in different, particular, subject-specific content.

5. Knowledge of study skills strategies that can help students to be more successful in content-area reading. For example, guide questions and advance organizers are recommended.
6. Knowledge of effective ways of planning the delivery of instruction to differentiate tasks for students reading at different levels of proficiency. For example, using trade books written at lower reading levels—as opposed to upper-grade-level texts or reference books—that contain easy-to-read biographical information; allowing some students to use read-along tapes or to engage in shared reading with a partner.
7. Willingness to cooperate with other school personnel, such as the special reading teacher, in helping students be able to use reading to learn content: for example, meeting during common prep or articulation periods to coordinate activities and skills being taught to students, team teaching, or sharing groups in the same classroom.

In short, content-area teachers have both special skills and responsibilities for working with students and colleagues to foster effective reading habits among their students.

STUDENTS' NATIVE-LANGUAGE PROFICIENCY AND EXPERIENCES

The importance of students' language proficiency and cultural experiences on learning subject matter is seen in the statement by Davison and Pierce (1992) that bilingual students whose native language was not English experienced difficulty with English-language processing (pp. 148–149). Cultural conflicts may affect students, teaching concepts, and skills in the content areas. Discussing the role of cultural experiences in learning mathematics, Mather and Chiodo (1994) stated that "culture can also interfere in the learning of mathematical concepts in the classroom. One South American culture does not have a concept for such numbers as 4 and 5. Instead they have conceptualized numbers 1, 2, and many" (p. 3). This unclear concept, among others, may create difficulties for students from this culture studying mathematics in U.S. schools. Such conflicts may lead to "alienation" described by Cornell (1995) as a condition that "may result when beliefs expressed in the mainstream curriculum differ from those held by minority students. Often teachers or texts assume a common value structure for all students and the acceptance of certain sociocultural myths" (pp. 128–129). Mather and Chiodo indicated that teachers' knowledge of their students' cultural backgrounds and implications of this knowledge for their teaching are crucial in recognizing the impact of language on learning. To address the problems faced by limited-English-proficient students in mathematics, as well as in other subject areas, they recommend the following approaches:

1. Provide profound exposure to manipulative, concrete, sensory, and hands-on activities. These activities do not replace discussion, but support a variety of learning activities.
2. Use cooperative learning (small group activities) and minimize individual seatwork.
3. Emphasize multicultural references and relevancy in lessons.
4. Use second-language texts, materials, and resources as much as possible.
5. Use limited, simplified instruction (using caution to retain the essence of the original content and problems); make concentrated efforts to be aware of and to explain any culturally based terms.
6. Use basic content vocabulary in the second language for individualized instruction whenever possible.
7. Be aware of how other countries teach basic mathematical concepts. For example, Hispanic countries most commonly use equal addition methods of subtraction.

CONTENT-AREA TEXTS, INSTRUCTIONAL MATERIALS, AND APPROACHES

A large part of the success of content-area teachers in conveying concepts and information to their students is a factor of the textbooks and other instructional materials available to them for use in their classrooms. As discussed earlier, there is a dichotomy, largely false in reality, that seems to exist between "learning to read" in the early grades, and "reading to learn" in the upper elementary through secondary levels. Part of the problem that content-area teachers face is the late introduction of texts—used for "reading to learn"—in the typical elementary school. If students are to become successful learners of content, then they must be able to interact successfully with the materials of instruction. Texts must be accessible and, in the current terminology, "user-friendly." Research by Cantieni and Tremblay (in Mather & Chiodo, 1994) has shown that "the language skills needed for mathematics were 2 years ahead of the official system. They gave the example of a student working on mathematical problems in third grade who would need a fifth-grade reading ability to adequately comprehend the problems" (p. 3). Thus, even though the text may present appropriate mathematical concepts, the language and conceptual skills needed to solve the problems may be at a higher level than the student can deal with. How much further removed are the cultural and linguistic backgrounds of non-native English-speaking, Hispanic youngsters, many of whom are struggling to use these texts? And how likely are these students to be successful in deriving meaning—or learning—from these texts? Armbruster (in Cooper, 1993, pp. 500–501) proposed the following recommendations for improving students' interactions with texts and enhancing their ability to construct meaning from them:

1. Integrate reading (and all aspects of literacy) with content instruction. This integration should take place across disciplines and should focus on more holistic learning as opposed to the learning of isolated facts.
2. Increase opportunities for students to read informational texts throughout all levels of schooling. Students are very interested in such books but need more experience with reading and meaning construction in these different text structures.
3. Provide students with the experiences that will help them become strategic readers by scaffolding instruction and gradually releasing them to be responsible for their own reading. Model strategies using informational texts.
4. Keep students actively learning by helping them focus on what to do before, during, and after reading. Help them learn to monitor their reading, build connections with old knowledge, and use writing to improve their construction of meaning.

The more language-minority readers know about the content of the material, the better they comprehend the material (Scarcella, 1990); and teachers become as informed as possible about their students' cultures and historical backgrounds, incorporating the students' cultures whenever possible. As Scarcella said, texts are often difficult for language-minority students because these texts are "based on unfamiliar, culturally-determined assumptions" (p. 85). And the cultural assumptions are not those of the second-language learners! Authorities recommend the use of bilingual dictionaries for second-language learners as well as appropriate, native-language content texts that will allow these students to gain mastery of concepts while becoming familiar with the new language.

In attempting to account for the factors that "result in successful or effective education at levels beyond elementary school," Garcia (1992) suggested a number of instructional strategies that have been demonstrated as effective in promoting the linguistic minority students' literacy, mathematics, and English-language development in school. These approaches are listed in Table 7.1.

TABLE 7.1
Instructional strategies

Strategies	Examples
Thematic, integrated curriculum, and content-integrated instruction.	Weather conditions or geographic features of the students' native land and their new home in the U.S. mainland.
Small-group activities incorporating heterogeneous language grouping and peer tutoring; learning proceeds from concrete to symbolic.	Students of varying levels of language and proficiency work together in small language communication that focus around groups to enhance the area of study.
Interactive journals, silent reading followed by small-group discussion and interactive literature study, and mathematics logs.	Students record observations of a process, directions for doing a task, emotions or feelings related to personal events, or customs from their native countries.
Cooperative learning strategies that emphasize participation by students in processing curriculum materials.	Students work together cooperatively; use think-aloud or other processing and metacognitive strategies to solve problems.

Note: From Garcia (1992, pp. 132–133)

USING TECHNOLOGY IN THE CONTENT AREAS

Many educational publishers of commercial materials have come to realize the value of technology in the delivery of instruction to the students in schools today and into the approaching millennium (Van Dusen & Worthen, 1995). The term *technology* has changed in meaning over the past few years; previously it indicated the use of computerized programs, consisting primarily of software packages that offered content materials presented in colorful graphic displays. But it has now moved into the realm of interactive presentations and refers to distance learning (telecommunications) as well. The newer technologies provide students with the opportunity to pace their learning, similar to the programmed learning packages of the late 1960s and 1970s. Students respond to prompts or questions and receive feedback in terms of correctness and quality of their answers. Interactive programs allow students to give immediate answers, receive comments and explanations, and change or modify their responses if necessary.

The teacher's role changes in this scenario to one of facilitator and manager of the instructional programs. Students may work individually and independently or cooperate in small groups to problem solve, brainstorm, and complete activities. The teacher physically moves from group to group, checking with students, helping them to clarify their thinking, offering advice, and, in general, supporting their search for information. In addition, for limited-English-proficient students, the teacher may offer help in such areas as vocabulary, translations, and appropriate cultural and/or experiential references. Students become responsible for their own learning and manage the information that they receive. They share with their peers in a nonthreatening environment that allows them to take risks and figure out the "correct" responses from a number of possible options; or, they may obtain information about topics they knew nothing about previously or about which they may have had erroneous or incomplete knowledge. They are then able to put their ideas into a coherent format for themselves, their classmates, and their teachers.

Technology and the manner in which it delivers information to students is "fun"—to use a favorite word among today's youth. Programs are usually colorful and enhanced with graphics and sound effects. They allow students to proceed at a comfortable, noncompetitive pace. This is important to many Hispanic youngsters who learn best in an atmosphere reflecting their orientation to cooperation and group effort, which will not be characterized by a teacher as "cheating" when students are comparing answers or working together to solve a problem. The implications of technology in the classroom for teachers is that they themselves must become consumers of this technology. Just as they would with a text or other printed instructional package, teachers must become proficient with and comfortable using computerized instructional programs. These programs must be considered integral parts of the lesson and viewed as another mechanism for helping students to obtain information necessary to the development of skills and concepts; they are not to be viewed as "frills" or "add-ons" to the regular instruction that is too often built around dry, uninteresting textbook presentations. All content-area teachers must cease being "computerphobes." Just as mathematics and science teachers would never think of presenting certain lessons without manipulatives or laboratory equipment, or art teachers without crayons, paints, and brushes, so must they, and their colleagues in language arts, social studies, and other content areas become accustomed to using computer technology and all that it can offer to them and to their students in 21st-century schools. Technology is, after all, another tool to help teachers in their quest to assist their students in the areas of skills learning, concept development, and the ability to use higher order thinking skills.

Among the new technologies available to schools today are computer-based integrated learning systems (ILS) that include courseware and management software and run on networked hardware. They cover one or more curriculum areas across grade ranges, and usually include a management program that tracks and reports student progress. These programs center on basic instruction in mathematics and language arts, but many are now expanding to include computer skills, science, writing, social studies, foreign language, and even entire English as a second language (ESL) programs. Many of these ILS have moved beyond drill and practice and have required students to engage in problem solving and deep reflection about content. These technologies are increasingly popular for use with bilingual students who can continue using their native language, while being mainstreamed at a level they can handle.

There are many computer software packages available to teachers today. They are presented in Table 7.2.

Reading educators advise content-area teachers to help students sort, organize, and evaluate the enormous amounts of information that will greatly change teaching and learning in their classrooms. Teachers need to be prepared to continuously innovate, using such technology as integrated information programs, simulation programs, optical programs, and telecommunication programs.

Table 7.2
Computer software for content instruction.

Integrated Programs	Simulation Programs	Optical Programs	Telecommunications
AppleWorks	Revolution 76	Grolier Encyclopedia	Channel One
First Choice	Where in the World is Carmen Sandiego?	News Bank	National Geographic Kids' Network
The Children's Writing and Publishing Center	Oregon Trail	Reader's Guide to Periodical Literature	
Magic Slate II	The Golden Spike	The Time Machine	
The U.S. Constitution Then and Now	Time Navigator		
	The Ripple That Changed American History		

SAMPLE MATHEMATICS READING ACTIVITIES

Word problems and computations may present challenges to bilingual students in content-area classrooms. There are a number of differences between the reading processes used in mathematics texts and those found in texts in other areas. Mathematics concepts and skills are always presented in either oral or written language. In many instances, the textbook drives instruction in the mathematics class. Students' abilities to learn mathematics, then, greatly depend on their reading ability. Extensive research has documented the role that reading ability has on learning mathematics (Brasselton & Decker, 1994; Cox & Poe, 1991; Culyer, 1988; Henney, 1970; Kessler, Quinn, & Hayes, 1986; Muth, 1988, 1993). Thorndike (1912) asserted that "our measurement of ability in arithmetic actually is a measurement of two different things: sheer mathematical insight and knowledge, on the one hand; and acquaintance with language, on the other" (pp. 292–293). Teachers are often heard to say that their students would do better on standardized mathematics tests if they could just read them. Textbooks and worksheets, which depend on the written word, are a fundamental part of the resources used in math classes. It is essential, therefore, that students be taught how to "read" mathematics problems. The student's ability to read a basal reader or trade book does not guarantee that the student will be able to read a mathematics textbook. Reading instruction, necessarily, should be an essential component of mathematics classes. If students are to succeed in mathematics, their math teachers ought to understand the influence that reading has on their students' mathematical performance. In a similar vein, reading teachers should not limit their instruction to basal readers or literature books; they must also train students to read content-area textbooks to complement the efforts of their subject matter colleagues.

Mathematical writing is significantly different from the writing found in other, nonmathematical texts. Kane (1967) asserted that there is a substantial difference between mathematical English and ordinary English that requires different types of skills in order for the student to achieve comprehension. This "mathematical" English is a combination of ordinary English and a formal symbol system. Mathematics may be one of the most difficult content areas to read (Aiken, 1972; Culyer, 1988; Muth & Glynn, 1985). According to Culyer (1988), reading a math textbook is harder because it contains more concepts per word, per sentence, and per paragraph than any other content-area textbook. Mathematics texts contain features such as graphs, charts, symbols, and formulas. In addition, mathematics textbooks require a higher reading level than normally associated with the student's present grade. According to Cantieni and Tremblay (1979), the language skills needed to read math texts are 2 years ahead of the official grade placement system. Thus, a third-grade child would need a fifth-grade reading ability in order to successfully comprehend the math textbook. The following is a passage from a third-grade math textbook (McMillan/McGraw-Hill, 1991).

La Sra. Palanqueta decidió hornear pan. Su receta requiere 2 tazas y 1/4 de harina, 1 taza a 1/3 de pasa, 1/2 libra de avena, 2 cucharadas de canela y 1/2 cucharadita de sal. Pero la Sra. Palanqueta sólo tenía la sal y la canela, asi que fue a la casa de la Sra. Pancracia.

La Sra. Pancracia le dijo: "Lo siento, pero yo sólo tengo 2 tazas y 2/3 de pasas y 2 tazas a 2/8 de harina." La Sra. Palanqueta fue entonces a casa del Sr. Briollo. "No sé si puedo ayudarla," dijo el Sr. Briollo. "Yo sólo tengo 1 taza a 3/9 de pasas a 7/8 de libra de avena."

Finalmente, la Sra. Palanqueta fue a la casa de la Sra. Rosquita . . . "¡Qué lastima!" dijo la Sra. Rosquita. "Si hubieras venido ayer te hubiera podido ayudar, querida. Yo horneé mi pan y ahora sólo tengo 2 tazas y 2/3 de harina y 2/3 de harina y 2/4 de libra de avena."

¡Pobre Sra. Palanqueta! ¿La puedes tú a yudar? Explica su solución. (Macmillan/McGraw-Hill, 1991, p. 317A)

Note that this math passage is difficult to read. Mathematics writing (expository) requires a more careful and slower reading than other prose (narrative) because of the technical words and symbols and the heavy load of concepts that it presents. Mathematics writing is compact and content is limited to essential ideas (Henney, 1971). Reading verbal problems requires more intense concentration than that needed for reading narrative materials because of the mixture of symbols, graphs, charts, processing signs, and vocabulary used in a mathematics context. The vocabulary used in math textbooks may also be a source of difficulty to the reader. Understanding vocabulary is crucial to reading and solving mathematics problems. Usually, almost every word, number, and symbol carries a crucial meaning. Look at the following third-grade problem comprising only one sentence and one question:

Un terreno cuadrado mide 50 pies de lado. ¿Cual es el perimetro del terreno? (Macmillan/McGraw Hill, 1991, p. 376)

If students are not able to recognize and comprehend the word *perimetro,* they will not be able to solve the problem. Mathematics texts use vocabulary that in many instances coincides with the vocabulary of everyday Spanish. Words such as *producto, diferencia, cubo, volumen, factor, tabla, union, rayo, radio, cuarto,* and *primo* are some examples of words used both in everyday Spanish and mathematical Spanish. In mathematical Spanish, *producto* refers to the answer in multiplication, whereas in everyday Spanish, it refers to something produced by physical labor or intellectual effort. This example of content-specific use of this word is identical in English. What the teacher of mathematics, as well as the reading teacher, must do is teach special multiple-meaning words in different contexts. The same problem occurs with *cuarto.* In mathematical Spanish, *cuarto* refers to a customary unit of volume or a quarter of an hour on the clock, but for many Spanish-speaking students it also refers to a bedroom.

The complexity of understanding these kinds of words is compounded for the Hispanic child because some are used throughout the math textbook with both their everyday Spanish meaning and their mathematical Spanish meaning. For example, in the series *Matemáticas en Acción* (Macmillan/McGraw Hill, 1991) the term *diferencia* is used to refer to the answer in subtraction in the following situation: *¿Cual es la diferencia entre 9 y 3?* The same word, *diferencia,* is used in the same textbook on a different page with its everyday Spanish meaning. The following question appears on page 30: *¿Cuál es la diferencia entre estas dos figuras* [ ] ( )? In the previous question, the student may reply that one has four corners and the other does not. In the first question, if a student associates the word *diferencia* with its everyday Spanish meaning, then the student might respond that the nine is bigger than the three and be surprised to learn that the correct answer is six.

These examples show the importance of teachers (of both reading and mathematics!) alerting their students to the different meanings that these words have. It cannot be assumed that if students recognize a word while doing their math homework, that they are using its mathematical meaning. In fact, it may well be that they are using its nonmathematical, everyday Spanish meaning. Teachers can give students practice in identifying words that have multiple meanings. One appropriate activity would be to give students pairs of sentences that illustrate both the mathematical and nonmathematical meanings. The following are some examples:

La música está muy alta. ¿Podrías bajar el _____ del radio?

¿Cuál es el _____ de este vaso de agua?

Necesitarás un _____ de leche para hacer el bizcocho.

El _____ donde yo duermo es muy pequeño.

Students will also encounter words that have meaning only in mathematical Spanish, such as *paralelogramo* and *hipotenusa*. These words are usually of key significance to the understanding of those problems that contain them. Students' lack of understanding of these terms will undoubtedly affect their mathematical performance. In addition to lessons and activities that highlight how everyday and mathematical words are used, teachers should also pay special attention to words like *parallelogram* that have purely mathematical meaning. Teachers can also encourage their students to use glossaries.

As the Spanish language has dispersed through different countries, differences in vocabulary have arisen from country to country. In Spanish language classrooms in the United States, where one may find within any given class students from El Salvador, Puerto Rico, Peru, Mexico, and the Dominican Republic, for example, differences in vocabulary undoubtedly further confound students' understanding of mathematics passages. The following words, demonstrating the lexical variety of Spanish across Latin America, were taken from a third-grade math textbook: *fracciones, quebrados; entero, unidad, todo; tiras, bandas, cintas; bocadillos, entremeses, bocas, canapes, bocaditos, emparedados, picadera; popotes, sorbetos, pajillos, pajitas, canitas, calimetes.*

Teachers must provide students with alternative regional synonyms for these types of words in order to reach students from all Spanish-speaking countries. Several math textbooks provide this type of information in their teachers' guides.

Another complexity particular to mathematics writing is its lack of the usual context clues found in other types of writing, thus making it more difficult for those students who need them. Earp (1971) found that the context found in mathematics textbooks is not as rich as those found in other texts. Because these words are not part of the students' everyday language, teachers must make sure their students recognize and understand these words. They can do so by an explicit language approach to teaching these mathematical words. MacMillan's series *Matemáticas en Acción* has a section entitled "Language and Mathematics," which provides an integration of vocabulary skills important for communicating mathematically. The sample in Fig. 7.3 from the third-grade textbook shows how teachers can teach mathematics vocabulary (p. 374):

Completa las oraciones. Usa las palabras al final del ejercicio.

1. El ancho de una puerta es aproximadamente un _____.
2. A 3 3/4 se le llama un número _____.
3. La longitud del contorno de una figura es su _____.
4. El _____ es el número de unidades cuadradas que cubren la superficie de un objeto.

VOCABULARIO

perímetro	mixto	área
yarda	pie	entero

Fig. 7.2. Lenguaje y matemáticas. From *Mathematics in Action*, 3E (p. 374) by Macmillian/ McGraw-Hill. Copyright © 1991 by the McGraw-Hill Companies. Reprinted with permission.

Teachers assess the difficulty of the vocabulary used in math textbooks by checking whether words used appear to be familiar to their students, identifying those words that have multiple meanings, and considering whether sufficient context clues are provided for ambiguous words or if they appear in isolation. Unlike ordinary books, math textbooks not only provide the reader with information, but in many cases require the reader to do something. Take a look at this section from *Matemáticas en Acción* (p. 97):

Es difícil medir la longitud exacta de una curva. Pero puedes estimar la longitud usando una regla. Sigue estos pasos para estimar la longitud de una curva.

Paso 1 Marca varios puntos en la curva.

Paso 2 Une los puntos en la curva.

Paso 3 Mide los segmentos al centímetro más próximo.

Paso 4 Halla la suma de esos largos.

In order for students to understand that each content area requires a different kind of reading, Henney (1971) suggested that teachers devote at least one lesson to analyzing a page from each type of textbook used by students. Such lessons would incorporate discussion of the different ways each of these pages could be read. The major goal of mathematics instruction, as indicated by the National Council of Teachers of Mathematics (NCTM; 1989), is to develop in students the ability to solve problems.

Because problems are presented to students mostly in written language, it is crucial that students be taught the skills needed for reading mathematics materials. Teachers must realize that in addition to mathematics skills, students must also possess the reading skills necessary to cope with mathematics textbooks. Teacher-training programs and schools of education should place a heavy emphasis on the integration of reading and mathematics in their methods and curriculum courses. Mathematics teachers must become familiar with basic reading processes. Reading teachers must also be trained in the teaching of basic mathematics skills and vocabulary in order to incorporate mathematics content into their reading instruction.

CONCLUSION

The roles and responsibilities of educators of bilingual students are clear: They must prepare these students to be successful in their classrooms in the schools of the United States. To do so, teachers must understand and appreciate the cultural and linguistic backgrounds of these students. And they must have a thorough knowledge of the skills required of their students to master the content that they need in order to have mastery of concepts presented in their classrooms. The responsibility of teachers of bilingual students is to respond appropriately to their language needs; to build experiences that will enable them to understand concepts that are perhaps already familiar to their English-language-speaking classmates; and to be sensitive to the instructional materials and approaches that they employ, making certain that they pay attention at all times to the goal of helping their bilingual students attain mastery.

FOLLOW-UP ACTIVITIES

1. Select a mathematics or social studies topic, and for that topic:
   a. Prepare an instructional activity appropriate to the cultural and experiential backgrounds of the students you are teaching.
   b. Select two concepts of that lesson that will be stressed and identify the vocabulary and reading demands that each requires for the students to understand the concepts.
2. Identify and discuss two problems that might occur when trying to teach content and concepts to bilingual students using the materials and approaches with which you are familiar. For each problem, recommend a strategy or instructional material that will help to ensure students' success in the classroom.

3. Review the teacher's guide or manual that accompanies a reading series or content-area text. Check the skills presented and developed in the scope and sequence. What attention is paid in the content-area texts to the development of vocabulary in context; interpreting charts, graphs, symbols, and pictures; suggestions for relating new concepts to the students' cultural backgrounds and experiences?

4. Identify two software programs that are particularly useful for teaching content skills and concepts to bilingual students. Describe their strengths and discuss the reading skills emphasis that they have as well as how these skills are presented.

REFERENCES

Aiken, L. R. (1972). Language factors in learning mathematics. *Review of Educational Research, 42*(3), 359–381.

Braselton, S., & Decker, B. C. (1994). Using graphic organizers to improve the reading of mathematics. *The Reading Teacher, 48*(3), 276–281.

Cantieni, G., & Tremblay, R. (1979). The use of concrete mathematical situations in learning a second language: A dual learning concept. In H. T. Trueba & C. Barnett-Mizahi (Eds.), *Bilingual education and the professional* (pp. 246–255). Rowley, MA: Newbury House.

Cooper, J. D. (1993). *Literacy: Helping children construct meaning* (2nd ed.). Boston: Houghton Mifflin.

Cornell, C. (1995). Reducing failure of LEP students in the mainstream classroom, and why it is important. *Journal of Educational Issues of Language Minority Students, 15,* 123–146.

Cox, J. M., & Poe, V. L. (1991). The math–reading connection: A graded word list to estimate mathematics ability. *Reading Improvement, 28*(2), 108–112.

Culyer, R. C. (1988). Reading and mathematics go hand in hand. *Reading Improvement, 25*(3), 189–195.

Davison, D. M., & Pierce, D. L. (1992). The influences of writing activities on the mathematics learning of Native American students. *Journal of Educational Issues of Language Minority Students, 10,* 147–157.

Earp, N. W. (1971). Problems of reading in mathematics. *School Science and Maths.*

Garcia, E. E. (1992). Analysis of literacy enhancement for middle school Hispanic students through curriculum integration. *Journal of Educational Issues of Language Minority Students, 10,* 131–145.

Gonzalez, L. A. (1992). Tapping their language—A bridge to success. *Journal of Educational Issues of Language Minority Students, 10,* 27-39.

Henney, M. (1970). *Improving mathematics verbal problem-solving ability through reading instruction.* Paper presented at the Conference of the International Reading Association. (ERIC Document Reproduction Service No. ED 044 243), Anaheim, CA.

Kane, R. B. (1967). The readability of mathematical English. *Journal of Research in Science Teaching, 5,* 296–298.

Kessler, C., Quinn, M. E., & Hayes, C. W. (October, 1986). *Processing mathematics in a second language: Problems for LEP children.* Paper presented at the Delaware Symposium VII on Language Studies. (ERIC Document Reproduction Service No. ED 268 821)

MacMillan/McGraw-Hill. (1991). *Matemáticas en acción, edicion de tercer grado.* New York: MacMillan/McGraw-Hill.

Mather, J. R. C., & Chiodo, J. J. (1994). A mathematical problem: How do we teach mathematics to LEP elementary students? *Journal of Educational Issues of Language Minority Students, 13,* 1–12.

Muth, D. K. (1988). Comprehension monitoring: A reading-mathematics connection. *Reading Research and Instruction, 27*(3), 60–66.

Muth, D. K. (1993). Reading in mathematics: Middle school mathematics teachers' beliefs and practices. *Reading Research and Instruction, 32*(2), 76–83.

Muth, D. K., & Glynn, S. M. (1985). Integrating reading and computational skills: The key to solving arithmetic word problems. *Journal of Instructional Psychology, 12*(1), 34–37.

National Council of Teachers of Mathematics. (1989). *Curriculum and evaluation standards for school mathematics.* Reston, VA: National Council of Teachers of Mathematics.

Roe, B. D., Stoodt, B. D., & Burns, P. C. (1991). *Secondary school reading instruction: The content areas.* Boston: Houghton Mifflin.

Scarcella, R. (1990). *Teaching language minority students in the multicultural classroom.* Englewood Cliffs, NJ: Prentice-Hall.

Smith, C. B., & Elliott, P. G. (1979). *Reading activities for middle and secondary schools: A handbook for teachers.* New York: Holt, Rinehart & Winston.

Thelen, J. (1976). *Improving reading in science.* Newark, DE: International Reading Association.

Thorndike, E. L. (1912). The measurement of educational products. *School Review, 20,* 289–299.

Van Dusen, L. M., & Worthen, B. R. (1995). Can integrated instructional technology transform the classroom? *Educational Leadership, 53*(2), 28–33.

8

Teaching Reading to Bilingual Students With Disabilities

Frances Segan
Board of Education of the City of New York

Este capítulo pone énfasis en identificar quiénes son los estudiantes bilingües con necesidades especiales y qué estrategias y adaptaciones instruccionales usar para ayudar a los estudiantes en el proceso de desarrollar las destrezas de lenguaje, especialmente la lectura y la escritura. También se presentan sugerencias para integrar la literatura española en las áreas de contenido.

OBJECTIVES

After completing this chapter, the reader will:

1. Discuss varied literacy needs of bilingual students at-risk and those with disabilities.
2. Compare the use of literature-based, content-rich learning and reading experiences with those of remedial reading programs that focus on isolated skills as to their impact on success with bilingual students with disabilities.
3. Explain why home–school–community linkages are integral to the success of bilingual students at-risk or with disabilities.
4. Cite specific examples of Latino literature and how they can be utilized and adapted to meet diverse needs of bilingual students with disabilities.

5. List and describe varied whole-language and literacy approaches, including multiple intelligences theories as applied to bilingual students with disabilities.

GUIDE QUESTIONS

1. What are today's goals in teaching reading to bilingual students with disabilities?
2. How do bilingual instructional approaches for students with special needs compare today with previous approaches that focused on disabilities?
3. What are some recommended bilingual literature-based strategies to teach reading in Spanish to students at-risk or with disabilities?
4. Identify specific reading approaches and adaptations to help bilingual students with disabilities to succeed in content-area-based reading experiences.
5. What bilingual reading strategies may be useful for students with mild disabilities, emotional problems, or more severe impairments such as deafness?
6. How can the multiple intelligences theories be applied successfully with bilingual students with disabilities?
7. Describe the richness of diversity of Latino literature and explain how it can be used to meet the needs of immigrant students with disabilities.

INTRODUCTION

Today educators in the United States are faced with the challenge of helping each student develop strong literacy skills. However, bilingual educators face an even greater challenge because bilingual students who are developing literacy in two languages come to school with a variety of life experiences, levels of education, and specific individual needs as well as diverse disabilities. It is important to identify some of the bilingual students with whom teachers work and who may need bilingual prevention programs to avoid referral and inappropriate placement in special education programs. These students may have been born in the United States or may be recent immigrants. Bilingual special education students are bilingual students who have received a bilingual multidisciplinary assessment and who have been identified as in need of bilingual special education services. Special education disabilities may range from learning disabilities to emotional problems or more severe disabilities such as blindness, deafness, or autism (Carrasquillo & Baecher, 1990).

Often bilingual students with low literacy skills are termed at-risk and, if appropriate bilingual services are not provided, many are incorrectly referred to special education. Older immigrant students with low literacy skills become discouraged when they do not receive bilingual prevention/intervention programs, thus resulting in lack of academic success and increased numbers of dropouts. Some examples of bilingual students at-risk or with disabilities may include:

1. Bilingual students, born in the United States, but who have traveled back to their families' native countries and who have had interrupted educational experiences. These students may not have disabilities initially, but may develop emotional problems and difficulties with adjustment to school.
2. Bilingual students, born in the United States, who have gone through a bilingual program, but who exhibit learning disabilities or other disabilities and are bilingually assessed as in need of bilingual special education services.
3. Bilingual immigrant students, who have little or no formal educational experiences in their native country due to poverty, war, or rural location that prevented them from attending school. They may have also suffered physical or emotional damage in their native countries. Educational deficits may develop into learning deficits without bilingual prevention services in general education.
4. Bilingual immigrant students who have low literacy skills in their native language and who are also evaluated as having a disability and being in need of bilingual special education services.

MEETING THE LITERACY NEEDS OF BILINGUAL STUDENTS WITH DISABILITIES

School systems across the country are focusing on bilingual students with special needs in terms of their strengths rather than their disabilities. A major goal is to encourage participation of bilingual special education students in the least restrictive environment. Mainstreaming and integrated experiences in bilingual and monolingual settings can take place with the use of a variety of curricular and instructional adaptations and techniques. For example, bilingual students with disabilities can learn through activities that are multisensory as well as multicultural. Many literature books now also come with audiotapes, posters, and hands-on, follow-up activities. Bilingual students who are at-risk and bilingual special education students close to decertification can receive bilingual consultant teacher services. Other bilingual students with disabilities attend the bilingual resource room. Some will be in self-contained bilingual special education classes, but can be mainstreamed students for a content-area subject, as per their Individualized Education Program (IEP).

Crawford (1994) explained that when bilingual students exhibit difficulties, some are placed in remedial reading programs that use incomplete text and focus on isolated skills instead of reading instruction through culturally rich literature. Through curriculum alignment with bilingual/general education programs, bilingual students with disabilities need to be exposed to the same literature, books, and learning experiences as general education students to succeed and to be able to move to less restrictive instructional settings. Schifini (1995) looked at many immigrant students who have difficulty with reading in content-area subjects, starting from the upper elementary grades and continuing into intermediate and high school. He cited several causes: Some students lack linguistic skills to understand abstract content area material. Others do not have strong independent reading skills and find thick text and few graphic illustrations difficult to comprehend. Still other students in Latin America, for example, speak native American languages rather than Spanish as their native language.

Thus, these students need to strengthen literacy skills in their native language and also develop strong reading skills in Spanish and English when they come to the United States. In addition, lack of access to good health programs may result in bilingual students with vision and hearing problems that also impede progress in language development and literacy. Some may have attention deficits or need assistance in learning how to organize reading materials. Maldonado (1994) reviewed several issues related to specific learning disabilities in language and reading evidenced by bilingual students with learning disabilities and/or mental retardation. One problem was cited across the United States: Although students are entitled to receive bilingual services, due in part to teacher shortages, many receive instruction only in English. As a result of a lack of bilingual instruction, students with disabilities experience the following problems: language delay in both the native and second languages, delay in the development of bilingual reading and literacy skills, learning problems in the content areas due to lack of bilingual instruction and transfer from native language to English, behavior problems related to lack of success in general or special education in English-only settings, increased numbers of drop-out students, and problems in cultural identity and positive self-esteem.

With proper bilingual special education programs such students would be able to receive support from the use of bilingual, culturally relevant materials that would allow for increased academic success in both Spanish and English, using appropriate ESL methodologies. The students would also be able to match their own experiences to culturally relevant material and would interact with a bilingual teacher who could assist them in their native language and in English.

The importance of increasing culturally rich discussions on literature and reading experiences is highlighted by the ecobehavioral assessments utilized by Arreaga-Mayer, Carta, and Tapia (1994) to evaluate the quality of instruction for exceptional culturally and linguistically diverse students. The study analyzed student behaviors in 4 schools, in 26 classrooms, and across 213 days. Students did not use language or talk 92% of the time. Students used Spanish only 1% of the time and English 8% of the time. Only 5% of students' time was spent on "Academic Talk." Students read aloud in special education resource room on an average of 19%. Small group instruction facilitated silent reading 14% and writing 18% of the time. This research, among others, shows that exceptional culturally and linguistically diverse students had little time to interact and discuss stories with each other. Greater student participation utilizing all four languages skills will lead to more meaningful, contextually embedded language and literacy experiences in the students' native language.

Home–School–Community Support Systems

Several researchers address the importance of the home, school, and community support to bilingual students with disabilities. Chadwich and Scagliotti (1990) analyzed the relationships between family and school that impact on bilingual students' learning difficulties. How the students are perceived by their parents, other members of their families, and their teachers affects their own self-esteem and success. This study found that when the key focus is on the difficulties the students exhibit, rather than on activities leading to successful and enjoyable reading experiences, students are not encouraged to excel. De Leon, Ortiz, Sena, and Medina (1996) documented that Hispanic parents with preschool children with developmental disabilities believed that they could be most supportive by reading Spanish literature to their children at home. Parents in the study supported using both Spanish and English as well as their culture as important components of school instruction that could be supported through reading experiences in the home. Families who speak only Spanish or who are bilingual, but stronger in Spanish, believe that they can at least read and discuss picture storybooks with their children. Parents who are literate in Spanish and who are learning English can develop prereading and initial literacy skills in the children's native language.

Chang, Fung, and Shimizu (1996) also documented the importance of home–school–community collaboration in comparing literacy research with Chinese-American, LEP learning disabled students in Northern California and Chinese LEP students at-risk in New York City. Families that used libraries and afterschool community centers as resources to help students were better able to support literacy development for their children. The researchers noted that "literacy support across multiple sites is critical for those LEP children who are at-risk of school failure, identified as learning disabled, living in poverty and/or in non-mainstreamed working environments where English is not the dominant language" (p. 13).

The research points to the need for the school to work with parents as to how they can develop literacy skills in the native language at home. Linkages and programs need to be established to help families develop literacy skills together through libraries and the arts, at museums, zoos, and botanical gardens, and at cultural community centers and organizations.

RECOMMENDED STRATEGIES LEADING TO QUALITY BILINGUAL READING EXPERIENCES FOR BILINGUAL STUDENTS WITH LOW LITERACY SKILLS OR WITH DISABILITIES

There are a many creative approaches to presenting enjoyable literature-based, literacy experiences. The materials should be of high interest, but at an appropriate reading level for the students' functioning levels. García and Malkin (1993) provided several suggestions for literacy development by bilingual general and special education teachers: use of holistic approaches, integrated language experiences that are interdisciplinary, thematic literature units, and use of the language experience approach and writing journals.

Gersten (1996, p. 21) provided additional strategies to strengthen literacy skills for language minority students in both their first and second languages:

1. Use "evocative words as an explicit focus of lessons." Teachers who made the linkages between human experiences and feelings to literary

discussions were most successful. Students could also write about their own personal experiences related to stories and vocabulary from original literature.

2. "Use explicit strategies to help students become better readers." One bilingual teacher requested her students to give data or specific examples from the story to support predictions or interpretations.

3. "Teach children how to transfer into English what they know in their native language." Students with low literacy skills need to learn steps to use knowledge they know in their first language to apply to topics in English.

4. "Encourage students to speak and write about their lives." Such activities help students to share experiences with both the teacher and colleagues as well as to validate the students' own life experiences.

In noting key changes in society's view of literacy, which has become more "socially situated" and includes more than "one type of literacy," Rueda, Ruiz, and Figueroa (1995) highlighted several important features of useful instructional practices used by bilingual special education teachers:

- "They build strong connections to background knowledge.
- They build on existing competence or funds of knowledge.
- They provide activities that are perceived as meaningful and authentic by the students.
- They require active rather than passive participation, especially in joint productive activity.
- They value and incorporate the language of the students in high-level academic activity.
- They permit 'nonstandard' interactional patterns where appropriate to support learning." (p. 14)

Therefore, successful bilingual special education teachers would encourage students to apply their experiences in the native country and the United States to a story, such as *El Regalo Mágico* (Mohr, 1995), which tells about a Dominican boy, Jaime Ramos, who is forced to move to the United States with his family and finds himself lonely and without friends. His great uncle Ernesto sends him with a shell from Montaña Verde so he will be able to remember his friends and family there. *El Regalo Mágico* provides teachers with opportunities to develop students' advanced literacy skills as shown in the following examples:

1. Compare and contrast

Students' experiences when coming from native countries.	Jamie Ramos' experiences in *El Regalo Mágico*.

2. Cause and effect

Jamie listens to the shell.	He "sees" his hometown and friends.

3. High-level academic activity

An example of a high-level academic activity would be to ask the students to explain how the "magic occurs" when Jaime listens to the shell. Why does it sometimes not happen?

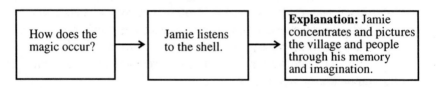

4. Participatory Activity

A participatory activity would be to give bilingual students with short attention spans or emotional problems a shell to hold up to their ears. They could concentrate and describe or write about people and things they remember from their native towns.

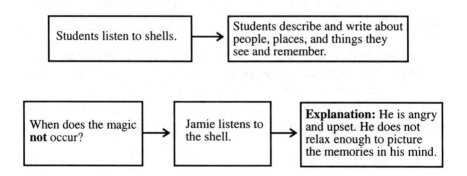

Respect for students' regional dialects and vocabulary in expressing ideas is important to building their self-esteem and sense of freedom to participate. Dominican students may use different vocabulary words than Colombian students. Students with language delays may use key words or two-word sentences to express ideas about the story or their own experiences.

Activities may include literature-based readings, the importance of which is strongly advocated by several researchers (Crawford, 1994; Freeman, Goodman, & Serra, 1995; Schifini, 1994). Freeman et al. (1995) described classroom scenes where bilingual resource room students enjoy the actual literary pieces in their native language and in English. By letting students have choices, they are able to explore author's intent; share different interpretations of the same story, poem, or play; and relate their own experiences and interests to literature selected. Students can plan with the teacher to answer specific questions and to write their own reactions to and reviews of the literature read. Students are also encouraged to create their own stories and to develop them into books to share with others. For example, students could either select *El Regalo Mágico* (Mohr, 1995) or *Vejigante/Masquerader* (Delacre, 1993). Those who read *El Regalo Mágico* could create individual booklets in the shape of a shell with their own book reviews and reactions. Other students who choose the bilingual book, *Vejigante,* can follow directions to create their own masks, and role play and form a parade, singing vejigantes' chants or estribillos. Such participatory activities increase interest and provide a variety of activities for bilingual students with disabilities.

Content-area Instruction

In reviewing educators' instructional approaches to content-area instruction, Schifini (1995) cited three important components.

1. All students should have meaningful activities that provide contextualized instruction rather than remedial instruction, which is passive and often focuses on memorization rather than on active learning experiences.

   Example: The bilingual teacher initiates song and dance "Arroz con leche."

2. When the students' knowledge and previous experiences are valued, it helps to connect the student with the topic of new material. Linkages

between the students' present life experiences and those of the future help to develop a strong self-image.

Example: *Arroz con leche: Popular songs and plays from Latin America* compiled by Delacre (1989): Teach students to read and follow a recipe for rice pudding or to describe changes that occur to the ingredients during cooking.

3. Authentic assessment allows students to show academic progress through a variety of activities, not just paper-and-pencil tests. The use of thematic portfolios is just one authentic assessment approach that enables students to demonstrate knowledge in several ways.

Example: Students could make their own arroz con leche to demonstrate mastery of reading a recipe. They could demonstrate a dance as a group after learning the song and movements. Some students might like to write about how their family makes arroz con leche for a holiday, and so on.

Crawford (1994) listed a variety of strategies to help bilingual students develop comprehension through literature and content-area subjects. Crawford suggested that the teacher read a story aloud to students. Students can then retell the story as a group process. The text can be used for a shared reading experience.

Example: A teacher could use one story from the *La Canción del Coquí y otros Cuentos de Puerto Rico* (1995) written by Nicholasa Mohr and beautifully illustrated by her collaborator Antonio Martorell.

The class and teacher can focus on survival reading through daily living items such as use of bottles, cans, calendars, signs on buses, billboards, and so forth.

Example: A bilingual teacher might take a walk through the neighborhood and have students copy billboard signs or take photos of signs on buses in Spanish.

The use of "scaffolding" types of support strategies help students become familiar with specialized vocabulary in science, music, social studies, and mathematics.

Example: Use *"En el Bosque Seco de Guánica" as described later in this chapter.*

Use of graphic charts, discussions, and sketches assist in comprehension of text. And directed reading questions help students analyze literature for interpretations or style.

Gersten and Woodward (1994) noted that special educators working with bilingual students need to move away from early training in task analysis to whole-language and natural-language approaches in the first and second languages. Working toward mainstreaming and decertification of students with mild disabilities requires bilingual and monolingual English special educators to align their curriculum materials and learning experiences to prepare bilingual special education students to succeed in general education settings. Segan (1990) also highlighted the need to move from task analysis and discrete skills through the use of experiential, interdisciplinary themes such as visiting a botanical garden to locate plants from students' native countries. After the trip, students can utilize map skills, identify climate conditions to grow plants, and read and create stories about plants or trees such as the flamboyan tree. Cloud (1993) also advocated for instructional changes in teaching culturally and linguistically diverse students. She recommended an integrated approach to intervention programs by not only considering the student's disability, but also the student's language and culture to organize effective teaching and learning environments. Teachers can focus on the student's potential and provide linguistically and culturally relevant, prereferred intervention services before students are inappropriately referred or placed in special education settings.

WHAT ARE SOME SPECIAL PROGRAMS THAT HAVE BEEN USED WITH BILINGUAL SPECIAL EDUCATION STUDENTS WITH MORE SEVERE DISABILITIES?

Bilingual students with more severe disabilities, such as deafness, actually develop literacy in several languages: Spanish sign language, American sign language (ASL), as well as reading and writing in English as a Second Language. Andrews, Winograd, and Deville (1995) described how using sign language summaries as well as other prereading activities (i.e., field trips and movies) can be helpful to introduce literature. A teacher can present the ASL summary technique as follows:

1. Teacher signs a summary of a culturally rich fable.

Example: "La guinea: El ave polizonte" by Nicholasa Mohr and

Antonio Matorell. It is a story about a guinea hen who was brought aboard a slave boat from Africa to Puerto Rico. She was pursued by everyone. She escaped and hid in the fireman's truck in the Parque de Bombas. She finally finds a home with Don Elías, el mascarero. He brings her a mate. The guinea hen inspires Don Elías to create the most famous and beautiful masks in all of Puerto Rico.

2. Students read the fable independently. The teacher can provide sign equivalents for key words or phrases.
3. Students individually retell the story through sign language all that they remember.
4. Students use ASL to discuss the moral of the story by explaining interpretations and inferences as the story applies to the individual student.
5. The teacher and student "discuss" the student's retelling and moral-lesson response.
6. The teacher fills in remainder and conceptual gaps. The teacher can highlight sequence or details about the characters. (pp. 31–32)

Note that bilingual teachers may use Spanish sign language if their students are more comfortable. Then, American sign language would be introduced later.

Additional adaptations include mime, role playing, and drawing pictures to help the students express their comprehension of the story in different ways. Clark and St. John (1995) described a program in South Monterey County, California, to present bilingual literature units to Spanish-speaking students from pre-K–13 with moderate to severe disabilities: Each staff member contributed a Spanish story. The literature units were read and reread across a 1-month period. Art, music, puzzles, and other manipulatives were utilized. Language and story grammar charts were used. Bulletin boards were also created by the students to display stories. Students were encouraged to retell the story in sequence. Key "descriptor words" were identified and students kept short journals using pictures and key words or descriptions.

> **Example:** Again using "La guinea: el ave polizonte" and the beautiful drawings, severely disabled students could create murals, arrange sequence cards, and match key pictures and words, for example, *la guinea, el coche de bomberos, el mascarero, un batey.*

ADDITIONAL EXAMPLES TO TEACH LITERACY SKILLS
THROUGH LITERATURE AND THE CONTENT AREAS

The following four figures present examples illustrating the use of literature in the different context areas.

Poem:
Canción de todos los Niños del Mundo (Ada, 1993, pp. 16–17)

Diferencias	Aquí	Allá
	Noche	Mañana
	Verano	Invierno-abrigos
	Un idioma	Otro idioma
Similaridades	Las similaridades incluyen como todos se ríen, aprenden y sueñan.	
Conclusión	"¡Somos hermanos!"	
Pregunta	¿Por qué concluye el poeta que "somos hermanos?"	
Actividades para estudiantes	• Dibujos en un mural para mostrar diferencias de vida en varias partes del mundo.	
	• Mapas del mundo para mostrar distancia y las diferentes estaciones en los hemisferios.	

Fig. 8.1. Charting differences and similarities.

"La guinea: El Ave Polizonte" (Mohr & Martorell, 1995)

a. ¿De dónde venía la guinea? (Africa)
b. ¿Quiénes trajeron la guinea? (los esclavos)
c. ¿Dónde está la ciudad de Ponce? (Puerto Rico)
d. ¿Cuál fue la reacción de la gente al ver la guinea? (Querían atacarla)
e. Dónde se escondió? (el coche de los bomberos)
f. ¿Quién era Don Elías? (el mascarero)
g. ¿Cuál fue el resultado de la inspiración de la guinea? (La creación de máscaras muy hermosas)
h. ¿Qué suerte le llevó? (Fama y fortuna)

Fig. 8.2. Guided questions and sequence chains.

"En el Bosque Seco de Guánica" (Torres, 1997, pp. 93–104)
Tema—"La contaminación del agua"
Tópicos—Variedad de plantas, animales y aves

1. **Linguistic**—Escriban un cuento o poema acerca de Don Carey "En el bosque seco de Guánica."
2. **Logical-mathematical**—Cuenten el número de animales que se mencionan en el cuento.
3. **Spatial**—Hagan dibujos del bosque seco de Guánica: Antes y después de la contaminación del agua.
4. **Bodily-kinesthetic**—Imiten los movimentos de los animales en el Bosque.
5. **Musical**—Piensen en sonidos de los animales en el Bosque Seco. Hagan imitaciones de las aves y las tortugas marinas.
6. **Interpersonal**—Compartan ideas sobre cómo miembros de su clase pudieran limpiar un río o una playa o parque cerca de su escuela o casa.
7. **Intrapersonal**—Haga una lista de 5 o 10 cosas que Ud. y su familia pueden hacer en su vida diaria para limpiar el agua.

Fig. 8.3. Utilizar ejemplos de las siete inteligencias múltiples.

- Taping a recording of a summary of the story in Spanish (linguistic)
- Taking a trip to a riverbank, beach or forest (bodily-kinesthetic)
- Create relief maps or diagrams of the Bosque Seco (Spatial)
- Writing journals about trip to beach or forest (intrapersonal)

Fig. 8.4. Adaptations that could be used with the story "El Bosque Seco de Guánica."

The Multiple Intelligencies theory can be successful with bilingual special education students because it can be used to interest them through a variety of learning experiences that are multisensory and active. Using several modes simultaneously helps students to recognize, interpret, and remember details from the story by using visual, auditory, kinesthetic, and tactile learning modes. "En el Bosque Seco de Guánica" presents the opportunity to create many interdisciplinary subthemes through the study of science (pollution), mathematics (age of trees or numbers of animals and plants), and social studies (location of Guánica on Puerto Rican map). Because "En el Bosque Seco de Guánica" is a long story, the bilingual special education teacher would present segments and activities across a period of time. Vocabulary and details would be selected, limited, and highlighted through charting each day.

CONCLUSION

Goals 2000 emphasizes that all students will develop strong literacy skills. Bilingual students with disabilities must be part of this national initiative, whether they begin in the U.S. educational system or enter at an older age. Today's multicultural society needs everyone to be literate and to contribute their individual expertise, becoming stronger as disabilities are bypassed to focus on the many talents of all bilingual students. Teaching reading and literacy skills to bilingual students with disabilities requires well-prepared bilingual special education teachers who can provide these students with the same literature-rich experiences that general education students receive. Activities must be based on students' experiences and interests as instruction interfaces with required curricula and instructional goals. Using literature created or compiled by Latino writers helps to provide value and support for Spanish-speaking bilingual students with disabilities. By developing the same skills as their bilingual and monolingual general education peers receive, the students are prepared to succeed as they move into less restrictive environments, integrated classroom settings, or as they become decertified and return to the general education setting. Flexibility must be given to such students to demonstrate learned skills in a variety of ways.

FOLLOW-UP ACTIVITIES

1a. Based on research and ideas presented in this chapter, discuss how bilingual students with disabilities can participate in literature-based literacy experiences that develop success and greater self-pride.
  b. What are some activities you could implement with other staff members in your school to encourage mainstreaming between bilingual general and bilingual special education classes?
2. Design a lesson using Latino literature that both a bilingual general education and bilingual special education teacher would use. Emphasize the instructional adaptations and techniques you would use to present the lesson to bilingual learning disabled or bilingual emotionally disturbed students.

3. List at least five specific resources such as libraries, museums, botanical gardens, zoos, and cultural community centers in your area that you, as a teacher, might use to support bilingual students with special needs and their families: for example, libraries that offer bilingual families and children access to literacy programs through storytelling or computers.

4. Read Armstrong's (1994) work on Multiple Intelligences. Using a selection from Latino literature or poetry, make a chart to demonstrate how you would develop all of the Multiple Intelligences with a specific group of bilingual students with disabilities. Identify which tasks you believe would be easy or more difficult for your students based on individual strengths as well as weaknesses. Present an adaptation to assist each bilingual student to succeed.

Latino Literature

Multiple Intelligence	Activity	Adaptations or Diverse Instructional Strategies
Linguistic		
Logical Mathematics		
Spatial		
Bodily Kinesthetic		
Musical		
Interpersonal		
Intrapersonal		

5. Using a bilingual content-area text, big book, or student-created materials, describe how you would develop literacy skills through a specific content-area topic for bilingual students with special needs.

6. Using a thematic, interdisciplinary approach, create a portfolio project that could be used with bilingual special education students. Explain how some choices would enable students to develop language experiences with peers and parents, as well as develop reflective intrapersonal skills.

REFERENCES

Andrews, J. F., Winograd, P., & DeVille, G. (1995). Using sign language summaries during prereading lessons. *TEACHING Exceptional Children, 28*(3), 30–35.

Armstrong, T. (1994). *Multiple intelligences in the classroom.* Alexandra, VA: Association for Supervision and Curriculum Development.

Arreaga-Mayer, C., Carta, J., & Tapia, Y. (1994) Ecobehavioral assessment: A new methodology for evaluating instruction for exceptional culturally and linguistically diverse students. In M. S. García

(Ed.), *Addressing cultural and linguistic diversity in special education: Issues and trends* (pp. 10–29). Reston, VA: Council for Exceptional Children.

Carrasquillo, A., & Baecher, R. E. (Eds.). (1990). *Teaching the bilingual special education student.* Norwood, NJ: Ablex.

Chadwich, M., & Scagliotti, J. (1990). Aproximación del enfoque sistémico a los trastornos de aprendizaje. *Lectura y vida, 11*(1), 17–25.

Chang, J., Fung, G., & Shimizu, W. (1996). Literacy support across multiple sites: Experiences of Chinese-American LEP children in inner cities. *NABE News, 19*(7), 11–13.

Clark, C., & St. John, K. (1995). Using bilingual literature with students who have severe disabilities. In B. A. Ford (Ed.), *Multiple voices for ethnically diverse exceptional learners* (pp. 47–49). Reston, VA: Council for Exceptional Children, Division of Culturally and Linguistically Diverse Exceptional Learners.

Cloud, N. (1993). Language, culture, and disability: Implications for instruction and teacher preparation. *Teacher Education and Special Education, 16*(1), 60–72.

Crawford, A. N. (1994). Estrategias para promover la comprensión lectora de estudiantes de alto riesgo. *Lectura y vida: Revista Latinoamericana de Lectura, 15*(1), 21–27.

De Leon, J., Ortiz, R., Sena, G., & Medina, C. (1996). Hispanic parent involvement in the education of their preschool child with developmental disabilities. *Journal of Educational Issues of Language Minority Students, 16,* 33–48.

Freeman, Y. S., Goodman, Y. M., & Serra, M. B. (1995). Revalorización del estudiante bilingüe mediante un programa de lectura basado en literatura auténtica. *Lectura y vida: Revista Latinoamericana de Lectura, 16*(1), 13–24.

García, S. B., & Malkin, D. A. (1993). Toward defining programs and services for culturally and linguistically diverse learners in special education. *TEACHING Exceptional Children, 26*(1), 52–58.

Gersten, R. (1996) The double demands of teaching English language learners. *Educational Leadership, 53*(5), 18–22.

Gersten, R., & Woodward, J. (1994). The language-minority student and special education: Issues, trends, and paradoxes. *Exceptional Children, 60*(4), 310–322.

Maldonado, J. A. (1994). Bilingual special education: specific learning disabilities in language and reading. *Journal of Educational Issues of Language Minority Students, 14,* 127–147.

Mohr, N. (1995). *El regalo mágico.* New York: Scholastic.

Rueda, R., Ruiz, N. T., & Figueroa, R. A. (1995) Issues in the implementation of innovative instructional strategies. In B. A. Ford (Ed.), *Multiple voices for ethnically diverse exceptional learners* (pp. 12–22). Reston, VA: Council for Exceptional Children, Division of Culturally and Linguistically Diverse Exceptional Learners.

Schifini, A. (1994). Language, literacy and content instruction: Strategies for teachers. In K. Spangenberg-Urbschat & R. Pritchard (Eds.), *Kids come in all languages: Reading instruction for ESL Students* (pp. 158–179). Newark, DE: International Reading Association:

Schifini, A. (1995). El contenido y los alumnos de alto riesgo: Estrategias prácticas para maestros. *Lectura y vida: Revista Latinoamericana de Lectura, 16*(2), 25–31.

Segan, F. (1990). Developing literacy skills in two languages. In A. L. Carasquillo & R. E. Baecher (Eds.), *Teaching the bilingual special education student* (pp. 132–147). Norwood, NJ: Ablex.

INSTRUCTIONAL RESOURCES

Ada, A. F. (1993). Canción de todos los niños del mundo. In A. Flor Ada & F. I. Campoy (Eds.), *Nuevo día* (pp. 16–17). Orlando, FL: Harcourt Brace.

Delacre, L. (1993). *Vejigante.* New York: Scholastic.

Delacre, L. (1989). *Arroz con leche: Popular songs and rhymes from Latin America.* New York: Scholastic.

Mohr, N. (1995). *El regalo mágico.* New York: Scholastic.

Mohr, N., & Martorell, A. (1995). La guinea: El ave polizonte. In *La canción del coquí y otros cuentos de Puerto Rico.* New York: Viking.

Torres, A. L. (1997). En el Bosque Seco de Guánica. In *Selecciones literarias* (pp. 99–103). Englewood Cliffs, NJ: Prentice-Hall.

9

Recursos a Utilizar en la Enseñanza de la Lectura en Español

Grisel López-Díaz
Jersey City Public Schools

The task of developing literacy skills can be a very challenging and exciting one, especially if teachers become fully aware of the numerous resources available to them. Children need to be exposed to and interact with a variety of genre, text types, and purposes in the process of reading and writing. This goal of teaching students to obtain meaning from the printed text cannot be accomplished with a basal reader or a reading text alone, but rather with every means of communication available that will require them to interact with different audiences for a variety of reasons. This chapter discusses the resources available (ranging from the classroom library to the computer) for the teaching of reading in Spanish. The use of all these resources creates a classroom atmosphere that celebrates literacy and encourages the emergence of a community of readers.

OBJETIVOS

Al finalizar el estudio de este capítulo, el lector podrá:

1. Describir lo que es la literatura "auténtica."
2. Explicar los diferentes tipos o clases de textos literarios que existen.
3. Describir cómo el maestro puede modelar el proceso de la lectura para el estudiante.
4. Identificar y explicar diferentes recursos audiovisuales que se pueden emplear en la enseñanza de la lectura.

163

5. Explicar la función de la tecnología en la enseñanza de la lectura y la escritura.
6. Introducir aspectos multiculturales en la enseñanza de la lectura.
7. Enumerar los pasos a seguir para crear una comunidad de lectores.
8. Buscar maneras de pedir ayuda a los padres y miembros de la comunidad con el fin de crear una comunidad literaria en la escuela y en el vecindario.

PREGUNTAS GUÍAS

1. ¿Cuál es la mejor filosofía sobre el uso de la lengua nativa al enseñar la lectura al estudiante bilingüe?
2. ¿Por qué es importante utilizar diferentes tipos de literatura en la enseñanza de la lectura?
3. ¿Qué beneficios académicos tiene el utilizar recursos audio visuales en la enseñanza de la lectura?
4. ¿Qué estrategias metodológicas se recomiendan para incluir la cultura de los estudiantes en el currículo y crear un ambiente multicultural en la enseñanza de la lectura?
5. ¿Cómo puede modelar el maestro los hábitos de un "buen lector?"
6. ¿Cómo crear una comunidad de lectores?
7. ¿Cómo involucrar a padres y miembros de la comunidad en el proceso del aprendizaje de la lectura?

INTRODUCCIÓN

La enseñanza de la lectura en español no puede resultar efectiva si no existe una filosofía previa que ponga énfasis en la importancia de la enseñanza de la lectura en la lengua nativa, en las contribuciones literarias que ha hecho la literatura de España y América Latina a la literatura mundial y al aspecto cultural de la literatura. Al enseñarle a leer al estudiante en español se le abren las puertas a una gran herencia literaria que los ayudará a comprender mejor su pasado. Carrasquillo y Segan (1984) afirman que es la lengua materna, o sea la lengua que se habla en el hogar, la que en realidad lleva a cabo la gran tarea de ofrecerle seguridad y confianza a ese niño. Si el propósito del sistema educativo y del maestro es el de mantener y desarrollar la lengua nativa del estudiante, entonces se le debe dar un lugar prominente al uso del idioma en la instrucción y en el uso de los materiales educacionales y de recursos que se emplean en el salón de clases. Por suerte, hoy en día existe una gran variedad de libros de texto, series de lecturas, libros, y materiales audiovisuales en español. Un distrito escolar afirma su creencia en el bilingüismo al utilizar sus recursos económicos para adquirir materiales educacionales en español para las clases, las biblotecas escolares y centros para padres. También se han publicado recientemente literatura narrativa e informativa en ediciones bilingües que reafirman la importancia de la comunicación en dos idiomas dándole oportunidad al estudiante de leer en el idioma en el cual tiene más proficiencia o en el cual prefiere leer. Un ejemplo es la publicación bilingüe de B. McMillan (1994) en inglés–español titulada *Sense Suspense: A Guessing Game for the Five Senses*. El uso del español también le abre las puertas a los padres de los estudiantes a participar y contribuir al desarrollo literario de sus hijos. El maestro debe alentar contínuamente a los padres a que utilicen la lengua nativa en el hogar.

RECURSOS DISPONIBLES

Las siguientes recomendaciones tienen el propósito de ayudar al maestro a facilitar la enseñanza del idioma español y de la lectura y escritura en español.

El Uso de Literatura Auténtica

Hoy en día, el uso de literatura "auténtica" se recomienda al enseñar a los niños a leer. Esta literatura abarca un sin fin de géneros y de tópicos y le brinda al lector una variedad inmensa de estilos, vocabulario e ideas para estimular la imaginación. Los libros de texto de lectura, al contrario de la literatura auténtica, están limitados en vocabulario y a veces son escritos basados en tópicos relacionados a la gramática o a la fonética; dándoles un tono artificial. Sin embargo, la literatura auténtica le brinda al joven lector estilos literarios que pueden emular y recursos literarios con los cuales pueden experimentar. Entre los diferentes géneros se encuentran los siguientes:

- Cuentos clásicos
- Cuentos folklóricos
- Fábulas
- Novelas
- Poesías
- Ensayos
- Dramas

Entre los materiales de lectura existen los siguientes:

1. **Narrativos.** Entre estos textos encontramos cuentos, novelas, poesías, y dramas.

2. **Informativos.** En este género se encuentran la información contenida en libros de texto, periódicos y revistas.
3. **Persuasivos o argumentativos.** Ensayos y editoriales son ejemplos de este tipo de texto.
4. **Textos de la vida diaria o relacionados con el mundo del trabajo.** Ejemplos de este tipo de lectura son manuales, solicitudes, recetas e instrucciones, entre otros.

Es de suma importancia que el estudiante se familiarice con todos estos tipos de textos, ya que todos son necesarios para tener éxito en el mundo académico y en el mundo del trabajo. El maestro debe empezar a coleccionar todos estos tipos de textos en la clase y variar las actividades y los tipos de lectura para que el estudiante adquiera las estrategias para comprender estos diferentes tipos de lectura. Se recomienda que después de proveer ejemplos, el maestro le pregunte al estudiante durante la clase de lectura qué tipo de texto es, cuál es el propósito del autor y qué estrategia metacognitivas va a utilizar para entender el mensaje. Esto se puede hacer oralmente, en hojas impresas o en una cartulina permanente en la pared de la clase.

Al hablar de literatura se incluyen otras formas de tradiciones literarias orales, tales como adivinanzas, trabalenguas, jeringonzas, retahilas y coplas; todo ese material que conocemos como parte del folklore y que en todas sus variaciones ha ido pasando de una generación a otra.

1. **Cuentos.** El cuento se puede definir como la relación oral, o en forma escrita, de un suceso falso o de pura invención. Un cuento es la narración de hechos fantásticos reales con que se entretiene a los niños. Aún antes de que el niño aprenda a leer, y como paso previo al aprendizaje de la lectura, se recomienda el uso de narraciones de cuentos infantiles. Los cuentos, leídos o narrados por el maestro, estimulan la imaginación infantil a la vez que despiertan la curiosidad, desarrollan la atención, aumentan el vocabulario y desarrollan la memoria. Más tarde, cuando el niño ya aprende a leer, estará motivado y buscará libros de cuentos, leyendas y fábulas, o libros basados en hechos de la vida real de acuerdo con sus intereses. Existen distintas clases de cuentos, entre ellos:
   • Cuentos de **hadas,** como por ejemplo *La Cenicienta,* y *Blanca Nieves y los Siete Enanitos.*
   • Cuentos **humorísticos,** como los cuentos de *Juan Bobo.*

- Cuentos **realistas** o que presentan hechos de la vida cotidiana, como la colección de libros de Carolina: *Carolina Viaja por Europa; Carolina en la Nieve,* publicados por la Editorial Juventud.
- Cuentos de la **naturaleza,** como *El bosque,* de Alain Grée.
- Cuentos de nunca acabar, como el *Cuento de la Buena Pipa,* o el Cuento del Gallo Pelón, en que el adulto pregunta o dice algo y, según la respuesta que recibe del niño, va repitiendo una y otra vez lo mismo, hasta que el adulto o el niño se cansan de este juego interminable.
- Cuentos **acumulativos,** como *La casa de Antón* (The House that Jack Built), en que, en cada nuevo fragmento, aparece un elemento nuevo que se acumula a los anteriores que a su vez, se repiten.

2. **Leyendas.** La leyenda es una relación de sucesos que tienen más de tradicionales o maravillosos que de históricos o verdaderos. Las leyendas han pasado de una generación a otra y aunque tienen mucho de fantasía, generalmente se piensa que se basan en algo que existió o sucedió. Cayetano Coll y Toste escribió las *Leyendas Puertorriqueñas,* publicadas por primera vez en 1924–1925; se inspiró en las fuentes históricas y logró crear verdaderas estampas de carácter nacional.

3. **Fábulas.** La fábula es una composición literaria, muchas veces en forma de verso, en la cual, por medio de una ficción alegórica y de la representación de personas o de la personificación de objetos o de animales, se ofrece una enseñanza útil o moral, conocida como moraleja. Cuando se habla de fábulas, generalmente se piensa en las fábulas de Esopo, figura casi legendaria que se supone fue un esclavo que vivió en el siglo VI antes de Cristo. Sus famosas fábulas han sido traducidas a todos los idiomas. También son muy conocidas las del escritor francés del siglo diecisiete, Jean de La Fontaine. Las fábulas de Samaniego, así como las del Iriarte, ambos españoles, constituyen parte de nuestra herencia cultural y deben ser conocidas por nuestros niños. Ejemplos:

EL BURRO FLAUTISTA
(Sin reglas del arte, el que en algo acierta, acierta por casualidad).

Esta fabulilla,
salga bien o mal,
me ha ocurrido ahora

por casualidad.
Cerca de unos prados
que hay en mi lugar,
pasaba un borrico
por casualidad.
Una flauta en ellos
halló, que un zagal
se dejó olvidada
por casualidad.
Acercóse a olerla
el dicho animal,
y dio un resoplido
por casualidad.
En la flauta el aire
se hubo de colar,
y sonó la flauta
por casualidad.
¡Oh! —Dijo el borrico—:
¡Qué bien sé tocar!
¡Y dirán que es mala
la música asnal!
Sin reglas del arte,
borriquitos hay
que una vez aciertan
por casualidad.

4. **Refranes y Proverbios.** Los refranes y proverbios contienen grandes verdades en forma breve. El Diccionario de la Lengua Española publicada por la Real Academia Española, define al refrán como *"dicho agudo y sentencioso de uso común."* En todos los países de habla hispana se usan mucho los refranes, que encierran la sabiduría o característica del pueblo, y que se van acumulando a través de generaciones y que se utilizan con acierto e ingenio. Los refranes son tantos, que siempre hay uno dispuesto para cada ocasión. Ejemplos:
• A buen hambre, no hay pan duro.
• En boca cerrada no entran moscas.
• Al que a buen árbol se arrima, buena sombra le cobija.

- En casa del herrero, cuchillo de palo.
- No se le pueden pedir peras al olmo.
- No todo lo que brilla es oro.

5. **Adivinanzas.** Las adivinanzas o acertijos constituyen la delicia de grandes y chicos. A los niños les gusta acertar las adivinanzas, y con esto no sólo se enriquece su vocabulario, sino que el niño también razona y descubre el sentido oculto de frases y oraciones o según el caso, descubre el juego de palabras que la adivinanza encierra. Ejemplos:

Mi madre es tartamuda,
mi padre cantador,
tengo blanco mi vestido
y amarillo el corazón
—El huevo.

Oro parece,
Plata no es,
el que no lo adivine
bien tonto es.
—El plátano.

Para bailar me pongo la capa,
porque sin capa no puedo bailar.
Para bailar me quito la capa,
porque con capa no puedo bailar.
—El trompo.

En el aire yo me muevo,
en el agua vivo bien,
si yo pico en el anzuelo
voy a dar a la sartén.
—El pez.

Río y no corre,
piedra y no es dura.
—Río Piedras.

Es venta y no se vende,
es Ana y no es de gente.
—La ventana.

6. **Trabalenguas.** Como su nombre lo indica, los trabalenguas son difíciles de pronunciar pero ayudan a articular y pronunciar correctamente las palabras. Son divertidos y a través de ellos, en forma de juego, los niños mejoran la dicción. Pueden utilizarse también en la enseñanza de la lectura, al presentar alguna letra, sonidos o combinaciones silábicas. Ejemplos:

Paco Peco, chico rico,

insultaba como loco

a su tío Federico,

y éste dijo: Poco a poco,

Paco Peco, poco a poco,

poco pico.

El gallo Pinto no pinta,

el que pinta es el pintor,

que al gallo Pinto las pintas,

pinta por pinta pintó.

7. **Retahílas.** Rimas o serie de rimas que se suceden unas a otras en cierto orden. Al igual que los trabalenguas, ayudan a mejorar la pronunciación, aumentan el vocabulario, desarrollan la atención y motivan al niño a leer a la vez que lo entretienen. Ejemplos:

Tilingo, tilingo,

mañana es domingo,

se casa la gata

con Juan Pirindingo ...

Aserrín, aserrán,

los maderos de San Juan

piden pan,

no les dan,

piden queso,

les dan ...

Cuando los niños van a echar suertes para ver a quien le toca empezar alguna actividad, suelen decir:

Tin marín de dos pingüés,
cúcara, mácara, títere fue.
El inglés cogió la espada
y mató al cincuenta y tres.
¿Cuántas patas tiene el gato?
Una, dos, tres y cuatro,
y levanta la cortina
y verás quién fue.

O también pueden decir:

Pito, pito, colorito;
¿dónde vas tú tan bonito?
A la acera verdadera ...
¡Pin, pon, fuera!

Audiovisuales

Vivimos en una época en la cual los estudiantes han estado expuestos a la televisión, los videos y a los juegos electrónicos desde la infancia. La instrucción con la asistencia de computadoras va a ser lo normal y no la excepción en las escuelas del futuro. Los recursos audio visuales le brindan al maestro una forma de alcanzar los siguientes objetivos:

* Familiarizar al estudiante con el mundo de la tecnología.
* Presentar una lección.
* Activar los conocimientos previos del estudiante.
* Proveerle más información al estudiante sobre el tópico a estudiar.
* Repasar un tema.
* Permitirle al estudiante ver o escuchar algo que no entendió la primera vez que fue presentado.
* Presentar el tópico en un estilo que se acerque más al estilo de aprendizaje del estudiante, que puede ser auditivo o visual
* Darle la oportunidad al estudiante a que vea dos formas diferentes de presentar la misma historia o idea y de analizar las similitudes y los contrastes, como por ejemplo al leer una novela y después ver la película basada en ella y discutir los dos géneros.

Entre los recursos audiovisuales se encuentran:

* Los "cassettes" que contienen cuentos, novelas, dramas o poesías grabadas.
* Los videos de películas basados en novelas y dramas.

- Los videos de documentales que ayudan al estudiante a obtener una mejor base para prepararlo para lo que va a estudiar.
- Los "CD roms," muy efectivos para organizar información.
- Los programas de computadoras.

Es muy común que las compañías que publican libros en español tengan también materiales audiovisuales o materiales para usar en la computadora que sirven de suplemento a la serie o al libro de texto. La tecnología da acceso a más información de una forma rápida y eficiente. Es fácil individualizar la instrucción y ajustarla al estilo de aprendizaje del estudiante, a la rapidez con la cual aprende y a sus intereses. Desde el punto de vista práctico, se necesita mucho menos espacio para guardar recursos cuando se encuentran contenidos en un CD Rom o en un cassette. El CD Rom es una forma práctica de mantener portafolios de estudiantes.

Entre las desventajas de la tecnología se encuentra su aspecto impersonal. En el aprendizaje del idioma, el intercambio humano entre estudiantes y maestros y entre estudiantes y estudiantes es indispensable. El maestro tiene que controlar y facilitar este tipo de instrucción y utilizarlo para alcanzar las metas académicas deseadas. Muchas veces este aspecto personal y humano desaparece al hacer uso de la tecnología.

El Uso de Material de Referencia

Una parte importantísima de la lectura es la de tener las destrezas para buscar información que ayude al estudiante a extender y profundizar sus conocimientos. Entre los recursos de referencia encontramos los sigientes:

- **El Diccionario.** Se puede utilizar para buscar el significado de palabras, el origen de palabras, sinónimos, antónimos, silabicación o acentos. En una clase bilingüe es imprescindible tener diccionarios en español, en inglés y en inglés-español. Estas referencias proporcionan al estudiante una forma de desarrollar el vocabulario, entender mejor su idioma y compararlo a otros idiomas.
- **La Enciclopedia.** Se utiliza para escribir informes o monografías o para obtener más información sobre un tópico. Actualmente existen programas de enciclopedias en CD rom que se pueden utilizar en la computadora y no ocupan el espacio de una enciclopedia de muchos volúmenes.
- **El uso del "internet."** Este modo de comunicación electrónica le abre las puertas del futuro al estudiante. Al aprender a utilizarlo, el

estudiante prodrá obtener información sobre cualquien tópico en segundos y también podrá comunicarse por medio del correo electrónico en el mundo entero. También tendrá alcance a muchas fuentes de información, como bibliotecas, museos, negocios u otras escuelas en diferentes partes del mundo.

- **Otros materiales de referencia.** Estos incluyen los atlas, libros telefónicos y antologías.

Es muy importante tener en cuenta que para poder usar estos materiales de referencia, el estudiante necesita entender su uso, familiarizarse con su forma y contenido y tener muchas oportunidades para practicar su uso con la ayuda del maestro. Después de esta etapa de entrenamiento, el maestro puede pedir a los estudiantes que utilicen estos materiales en sus trabajos, proyectos y presentaciones.

El Periódico como Recurso

El periódico resulta un recurso variado, contemporáneo y económico para uso en una clase. El periódico le brinda al maestro que enseña desde el cuarto grado hasta el último año de escuela secundaria, una fuente de lectura variada que contiene tópicos de intereses tan diferentes que se pueden utilizar para motivar a todos los estudiantes. La mayoría de los principales periódicos de las ciudades grandes tienen un departamento dedicado a la educación y no solamente ofrecen un precio especial para las escuelas sino que también ofrecen talleres y valiosas guías para maestros. Por ejemplo, *El Daily News,* publicado en Nueva York, ha creado una guía llamada *Newsworthy* que sirve de importante recurso para el maestro. Desafortunadamente el periódico *El Daily News* ha suspendido temporalmente su edición en español. Periódicos publicados tales como *Noticias del Mundo* y *El Diario* publicados en Nueva York tienen secciones para usarse en las escuelas, especialmente en los programas bilingües.

No es necesario suscribirse al periódico diariamente. El periódico ofrece tantas secciones diferentes que un maestro puede utilizar el ejemplar de un día de la semana y concentrarse en diferentes secciones cada día. La figura 9.1 presenta un ejemplo de cómo usar el periódico durante toda una semana.

El periódico le ofrece a los estudiantes una variedad de textos, una fórmula a seguir para escribir textos informativos y persuasivos. El maestro puede utilizar los artículos y editoriales para llegar a alcanzar metas tales como:

Día	Actividad
Lunes	Las noticias del mundo. Diferentes grupos puden seguir una noticia diferente.
Martes	Diferentes grupos pueden reportar sobre diferentes eventos deportivos en una forma oral o escrita.
Mi!rcoles	Entretenimiento; incluyendo el teatro, el cine, la televisión y otras diversiones.
Jueves	Ciencias, enfocándose en tópicos relacionados con la salud y la medicina, la exploración del espacio y la tecnología.
Viernes	Editoriales y opiniones del lector.

Fig. 9.1. El Uso del Periódico.

- Proporcionarle al estudiante un suplemento al libro de texto que refleja mejor la actualidad.
- Individualizar la instrucción basada en las preferencias del estudiante, lo cual ayuda a motivar al estudiante al permitirle escoger un tópico de interés.
- Facilitar la expresión de opiniones sobre las noticias del día.
- Ofrecer un modelo al estudiante para escribir un periódico de la clase.
- Motivar al estudiante a continuar leyendo el periódico diariamente.

Las siguientes actividades se pueden llevar a cabo haciendo uso del periódico:

- Estudiar las carteleras y crear sus propias carteleras. Esto le ayuda al estudiante a comprender mejor el concepto de idea principal e ideas suplementarias.
- Entender cómo el periodista utiliza preguntas tales como *quién, qué, dónde, cuándo,* y *cómo,* en una forma concisa o estilo periodístico.
- Entender cómo expresar opiniones y cómo persuadir.
- Entender cómo se utilizan los anuncios para convencer al consumidor.
- Entender el humor y cómo se utiliza en las tirillas cómicas.
- Familiarizarse con las partes del periódico.
- Utilizar la tecnología para publicar un periódico de la clase.

Las Revistas

Una colección de revistas en la clase representa un gran recurso en la enseñanza de la lectura y la escritura. No solamente le brinda una gran variedad de tópicos al estudiante, sino que también se pueden utilizar de las siguientes formas:

- Le brindan una motivación al estudiante para escribir.
- Se pueden recortar y utilizar las ilustraciones para ilustrar los trabajos escritos de los estudiantes.
- Para suplementar la instrucción en otras asignaturas como ciencias y estudios sociales.
- Se pueden utilizar los anuncios para estudiar la propaganda comercial.
- Pueden servir de modelo para que los estudiantes creen sus propias revistas en grupo.

RECURSOS MULTICULTURALES

Los niños hispanoparlantes en las clases bilingües frecuentemente representan diferentes países y varios aspectos culturales. Aunque el español los une, existen muchas variedades dialécticas y socioculturales que pueden causar confusión en la clase. Es el deber de todo maestro el de escoger y brindar una variedad de literatura española y latinoamericana a nuestros estudiantes que refleje las diferentes culturas que están representadas en la clase. Existen varias bibliografías que contienen listas de libros recomendados por bibliotecarios y maestros para niños en escuelas elementales y secundarias. Estas listas se pueden utilizar para planificar las selecciones anuales basadas en temas o unidades que tratan de integrar varias disciplinas académicas alrededor de un tópico. En *Recommended Readings in Literature: Kindergarten through Grade Eight* (California Department of Education, 1990), por ejemplo, la extensa bibliografía está clasificada por grado, género literario y cultura. Dentro de cada categoría se encuentran dramas y libros escritos en otros idiomas.

Los regionalismos que existen en español pueden servir de base para el enriquecimiento del vocabulario. El maestro no debe asumir que los estudiantes conocen el significado de las palabras simplemente porque están escritas en español. Una forma efectiva para asesorar la comprensión y enriquecer el vocabulario es el de preguntar qué nombre se le da al mismo objeto en diferentes países. Por ejemplo:

globo	chiringa	cometa	papalote
guagua	autobús	camión	colectivo
maní	cacahuates		
frasco	pomo	botella	
guaraches	chancletas	sandalias	pantuflas
anillo	aro	sortija	
lentes	gafas	anteojos	espejuelos

Las selecciones literarias que escogemos para las clases deben reflejar las diferentes experiencias de individuos de distintas culturas y deben estimular a los estudiantes a que analicen los factores diferentes y en común que tienen estas experiencias. El genio creativo de poetas latinos como Sandra Cisneros y Gary Soto se refleja en el libro *Cool Salsa: Bilingual Poems on Growing Up Latino in the United States* (Carlson, 1994). Según Bishop (1987), el uso de la literatura multicultural puede ayudar a preparar a nuestros estudiantes a vivir en una sociedad multicultural al guiarlos a reconocer las emociones, aspiraciones y necesidades humanas que tenemos en común y ayudarlos a comprender y apreciar las diferencias culturales y lingüísticas que nos hacen únicos y que representan una contribución a la sociedad en la que vivimos. Sin embargo, durante el proceso de selección de libros para una clase, el maestro necesita leerlos y determinar si los personajes reflejan la cultura, la historia y el idioma de un grupo étnico particular de una forma objetiva y no estereotipicada.

EL MAESTRO COMO MODELO Y RECURSO HUMANO PARA EL ESTUDIANTE

El papel más importante para el maestro es el de modelar para sus estudiantes estrategias que los estudiantes puedan imitar. El maestro puede demostrar contínuamente en la clase los pasos a seguir durante el proceso de comprensión cuando se obtiene significado de la lectura. Entre estas actividades se encuentran las siguientes:

Los estudiantes tienen la oportunidad de observar al maestro leyendo con frecuencia.

El maestro modela las estrategias que usan los buenos lectores para descifrar y para comprender el significado del mensaje del autor o para entender el contenido de un texto.

Dos tipos de métodos para demostrar estos procesos mentales son descritos por Roehler y Duffy (1991); uno es el de "hablar en voz alta" y el otro es el de "pensar en voz alta." En el proceso de hablar en voz alta, el maestro guía al estudiante con una serie de preguntas o diálogos sobre el tópico de la lectura mientras este proceso está ocurriendo. Por ejemplo:

• ¿Cuál es el título de la historia?
• Basado en el título, ¿de qué creen que se trata la historia?
• ¿Qué nos dice la carátula del libro?

Este método también se puede demostrar utilizando transparencias con texto impreso o con texto e ilustraciones. Por ejemplo:

⇒ Busca la palabra "indicios" en el título.

⇒ Piensa en la palabra clave.

⇒ Estudia las ilustraciones en la carátula.

En el método de "pensar en voz alta," el maestro expresa oralmente el proceso mental que está llevando a cabo para poder obtener el significado de la lectura. Por ejemplo:

• Aquí dice que el personaje se puso la mano en la frente.
• Esto quizás quiere decir que está preocupado o sorprendido.
• Voy a buscar otros indicios que pueden confirmar esto.

La enseñanza más efectiva es la que le demuestra al estudiante contínuamente el proceso de aprendizaje para emular y adaptar a sus propias necesidades. El buen maestro modela estas estrategias contínuamente.

Como Crear una Comunidad de Lectores y Escritores

Para alentar al estudiante a leer, el maestro debe presentar la lectura como una aventura, una especie de alfombra mágica que los puede transportar a mundos desconocidos. Para alcanzar esta meta, es imprescindible tener una biblioteca en la clase que refleje los intereses de los estudiantes, varios niveles de lectura, y varios géneros. La biblioteca debe contener libros, periódicos, revistas y materiales creados por los estudiantes. Es muy importante que si los estudiantes son bilingües, la biblioteca contenga libros en ambos idiomas.

El centro dedicado a la lectura independiente debe ser atractivo y debe contener libros y materiales audiovisuales arreglados de una forma agradable y que se puedan localizar fácilmente. Este lugar o rincón especial debe ser cómodo; con pequeñas sillas, cojines o pedazos de alfombra para crear un ambiente relajado. Es recomendable que el maestro busque la cooperación de la bibliotecaria o bibliotecario de la escuela cuando esté planeando este centro de lectura. El centro de escritura puede ser muy sencillo y reducirse a un par de mesas con sillas, cajas que contengan lápices, plumas, creyones, gomas de borrar, tijeras y materiales para crear las carátulas de los libros. Sería ideal tener una computadora en este centro, ya que el uso de la tecnología ayuda mucho a simplificar el proceso de editar y le permite al estudiante ser más creativo. El centro de escritores debe tener espacio para guardar los trabajos en diferentes etapas de edición, ya sea en pequeños archivos de cartón, o libreros. También es importante crear espacio para celebrar la creación de los estudiantes, ya sea un tablero de corcho, una tendedera o un pedazo de pared para "publicar" estos trabajos. Para estimular al estudiante, el maestro debe presentar los libros nuevos de varias formas:

- hablando sobre el libro.
- leyendo partes del libro en voz alta.
- presentando el libro de una forma especial—ya sea un drama o un video.
- dejándolo en un lugar prominente en la clase.
- dándole la oportunidad a otros estudiantes para que le hablen a sus compañeros sobre el libro que han leído.

Es importante que ciertas actividades ocurran después de haber leído un libro. Entre estas actividades se recomiendan:

- Un reporte que se ponga en exhibición en la clase.
- Discusión oral sobre el libro.
- Discusión entre el grupo que leyó el mismo libro.
- Dramatización de ciertas partes del libro.
- Una crítica del libro en el periódico de la clase.

Si queremos crear una comunidad de lectores, hay que dedicarle tiempo a la lectura formal y recreativa. Las siguientes actividades pueden ser planificadas:

- El maestro le lee a los estudiantes.
- Los estudiantes leen con el maestro.
- Los estudiantes leen el mismo libro en grupos pequeños.
- Los estudiantes le leen a otros estudiantes.
- Los estudiantes leen en silencio en pequeños rincones o centros que han sido dedicados a la lectura.
- Los estudiantes visitan la biblioteca de la escuela semanalmente.

Cooper (1993) considera la creación de este ambiente literario como esencial en cada salón de clases cuya meta es la de crear buenos lectores.

Es una comunidad donde los maestros, estudiantes y padres aprenden juntos.

La Creación del Estudiante

Es de suma importancia celebrar la creacion de los estudiantes. Esta celebración puede tomar las siguientes formas: (a) libros y poesías escritos por los estudiantes, (b) dramas escritos o presentados por los estudiantes, (c) diarios, (d) periódicos, y (e) creaciones audiovisuales. No es suficiente asignar trabajos en los cuales se les pide a los estudiantes que escriban o creen un proyecto, esta asignación no adquiere importancia en la vida del estudiante hasta que lo siguiente ocurra: (a) el libro tiene forma de libro y forma parte de la biblioteca de la clase, (b) el tema escrito por los estudiantes es presentado en el salón de conferencias, (c) el periódico de la clase es distribuido en la escuela, y (d) otros estudiantes y adultos lo disfrutan y reaccionan a la creación.

PADRES COMO RECURSOS

Está comprobado que la participación de los padres en la educación de sus hijos es esencial para el éxito académico de los niños. Shanahan, Mulhern, & Rodriguez-Brown (1995) documentan en su artículo sobre el proyecto de lectura familiar FLAME que el brindar oportunidades de aprendizaje para niños y padres en el hogar ayuda a establecer conexiones sociales que ayudan en el desarrollo de la lectura. Al establecer este tipo de programa, abrimos las puertas de la escuela a los padres latinos que muchas veces se sienten aislados y enviamos el mensaje que su idioma nativo es valorizado en la escuela. Debemos hacerle entender a los padres que estos programas son un tipo de contrato entre ellos y la escuela.

Ya que la lectura tiene un gran contenido cultural, un proyecto de lectura entre escuela y hogar tiene que tomar en consideración los tópicos de interés, el idioma de los padres, su nivel de educación, y sus métodos de comunicación. Estos proyectos tendrán mucho más exito si las siguientes condiciones existen:

1. Ofrecer una explicación a los padres en una reunión escolar sobre el proyecto, incluyendo la importancia de la lectura en la casa.
2. Enviar materiales a la casa que estimulen la lectura en la casa; incluyendo libros, copias de cuentos, artículos de revistas y videos.

3. Dar sugerencias sobre el ambiente que se debe crear para estimular la discusión sobre la lectura.
4. Modelar para los padres en diferentes talleres varias actividiades relacionadas con la lectura y la escritura.
5. Explicar a los padres cómo utilizar la biblioteca pública.
6. Enviar a la casa comunicaciones frecuentes que pueden tomar las siguientes formas: (a) cartas; (b) contratos entre padres, estudiantes y maestros; cuestionarios sobre sus hijos; y (c) boletines familiares que describen los temas que se están estudiando y ofrecen sugerencias sobre tópicos para discutir en la casa.
7. Sugerir pequeñas excursiones con sus hijos por el vecindario con tópicos para discutir después de la excursión.

No debemos olvidar la importancia de invitar a los padres a la clase o a la escuela para participar en eventos relacionados con la lectura. Algunos ejemplos de ocasiones para invitar a los padres a participar en eventos escolares son:

• Servir como voluntarios para hacerle cuentos a la clase o para leer cuentos.
• Hablar sobre su país, historia u otros aspectos culturales.
• Invitar a los padres a observar clases de lectura en la escuela.
• Participar en clases o talleres que han sido escogidos previamente por los padres.
• Pedirles sugerencias o donaciones de libros infantiles para la biblioteca escolar.
• Compartir el progreso de sus hijos y compararlo con el progreso que han observado en la casa.
• Compartir los trabajos o los portafolios que contienen un ejemplo del trabajo del estudiante a través de cierto tiempo.

Existe una extensa bibliografía publicada por la Fundación Germán Sánchez Ruiperez (1993), que contiene títulos de libros en español para niños y jóvenes basados en temas relacionados con varios aspectos de la familia.

LA COMUNIDAD COMO RECURSO

A veces no reconocemos los valiosos recursos que representan los miembros de la comunidad en la educación de los niños. Encontramos que existen muchas empresas privadas cuyos empleados se ofrecen como voluntarios para ir cierto número de horas al mes a hablar con los estudiantes o servir de tutores. Muchos de estos individuos son expertos en su campo. También encontramos personas retiradas que se ofrecen como voluntarios en las escuelas para leer a los estudiantes y ofrecer instrucción individualizada para aquellos que la necesitan. Los beneficios para el maestro y los estudiantes son los siguientes:

1. Al abrir las puertas de la clase ofrecemos una oportunidad al público de observar todas las cosas positivas que están ocurriendo en la escuela.
2. Al tener expertos en varias áreas hablándoles a los estudiantes, enriquecemos sus experiencias.
3. Tener visitantes en la clase le ofrece una variedad a la rutina escolar.
4. Los voluntarios representan diferentes posiciones y ocupaciones que pueden servir para orientar a los estudiantes sobre las carreras que consideren para el futuro.
5. Los voluntarios pueden ofrecer cierta ayuda individual a algunos estudiantes que le resulta difícil ofrecer al maestro que tiene una clase muy grande.

La biblioteca pública debe considerarse también como uno de los recursos más importantes de la comunidad. El maestro debe considerar hacer arreglos al principio del año escolar para visitar la biblioteca pública más cercana, ya que de este modo los estudiantes recibirán instrucciones de la biliotecaria y se familiarizarán con el uso de la biblioteca.

EL AUTOR COMO MODELO

El autor, ya sea poeta, novelista o periodista, sirve de inspiración al estudiante. Al darle la oportunidad al estudiante de leer literatura escrita en español, en vez de traducida, le presentamos diferentes formas artísticas y creativas de utilizar la lengua nativa. Es importante presentarle el autor al estudiante como una persona auténtica antes de leer su obra. Esto se puede hacer de las siguientes maneras:

• Hablar sobre el autor.
• Leer una pequeña biografía del autor.
• Hablar sobre los problemas que tuvo que enfrentar el autor antes de ser reconocido.

• Discutir el estilo del autor.

Si es posible se recomienda leer varias obras del autor, ya sean cuentos, poesías y ensayos, para poder hacer generalizaciones sobre su estilo y discutir su desarrollo como autor. Los estudiantes deben sentirse que ellos también son autores desarrollando su propio estilo basados en sus experiencias, preferencias y raíces culturales.

CONCLUSIÓN

La enseñanza de la lectura en español requiere el desarrollo de una filosofía que incluya el uso de la lengua nativa y el empleo de materiales instruccionales que reflejen la literatura española e hispanoamericana. La variedad de materiales es esencial y debe incluir diferentes tipos de texto, tópicos y niveles. El maestro debe estar consciente de la importancia de la creación de una comunidad de lectores y debe planear cuidadosamente el ambiente del salón de clases para que refleje la riqueza de la literatura. Este ambiente estimulará al estudiante a leer y a escribir con libertad y lo motivará a ser más creativo. En este ambiente es muy importante utilizar una gran variedad de recursos para suplementar los libros de texto. La conexión entre los padres, la comunidad y el estudiante se debe fortalecer, estableciendo un diálogo continuo entre la escuela y el hogar que ponga énfasis en la importancia de la lectura en el hogar.

Quizás, la característica más importante para un maestro de lectura es la de demostrar un verdadero entusiasmo por la lectura. El acto de leer debe presentarse como un descubrimiento constante que lleva al estudiante a desarrollar ideas y conocimientos previos y a crear otros nuevos. Esto solamente ocurre en un ambiente que acepta variedades de opinión y crea oportunidades para discusión y experimentación. El maestro es el arquitecto principal en este proyecto.

EJERCICIOS DE APLICACIÓN

1. Escriba un ensayo describiendo su filosofía sobre la importancia de la lectura en español para compartirla con otros maestros y con los padres de los estudiantes.
2. Haga una lista de libros suplementarios para leer durante el año escolar basados en los temas de estudios sociales y ciencias.
3. Diseñe un centro de lectores y escritores para el salón de clases.

4. Planifique cinco actividades instruccionales relacionadas con el uso del periódico o revistas.

5. Desarrolle un plan de lectura o contrato entre la escuela, los estudiantes y los padres.

REFERENCIAS

Bishop, R. (1987). Extending multicultural understanding through children's books. In B. Cullinan (Ed.), *Children's literature in the reading program* (pp. 60–67). Newark, DE: International Reading Association.

California Department of Education. (1990). *Recommended readings in literature: Kindergarten through grade eight. Annotated edition and 1990 addendum.* Sacramento, CA: Author.

Carlson, L. M. (Ed.). (1994). *Cool salsa: Bilingual poems on growing up Latino in the United States.* New York: Holt, Rinehart & Winston.

Carrasquillo, A., & Segan, P. (Eds.). (1984). *The teaching of reading in Spanish to the bilingual student: La enseñanza de la lectura en español para el estudiante bilingüe.* Madrid, España: Ediciones Alcalá, S.A.

Cooper, J. D. (1993). *Literacy: Helping children construct meaning.* New York: Houghton Mifflin.

Fundación Germán Sánchez Ruiperez. (1993). *Historias familiares: Una selección para niños y jóvenes.* Salamanca, Spain: Author.

McMillan, B. (1994). *Sense Suspense: A guessing game for the five senses.* New York: Scholastic.

Roehler, L. R., & Duffy, G. G. (1991). Teacher's instructional actions. In R. Barr, M. L. Kamil, P. Mosenthal, & P. D. Pearson (Eds.), *Handbook of reading research* (Vol. 2, pp. 861–883). New York: Longman.

Shanahan, T., Mulhern, M., & Rodriguez-Brown, F. (1995). Project FLAME: Lessons from a family literacy program for linguistic minority families. *The Reading Teacher, 48*(7), 586–593.

LECTURAS RECOMENDADAS

Escobedo, T. H. (1983). *Early childhood bilingual education: A Hispanic perspective.* New York: Teachers College Press.

Crawford, A. N. (1992). Literature, integrated language arts, and the language minority child. In A. Carrasquillo & C. Hedley (Eds.). *Whole language and the bilingual learner* (pp. 61–75). Norwood, NJ: Ablex.

Cullinan, B. (1987). *Children's literature in the reading program.* Newark, DE: International Reading Association.

Cummins, J. (1979). Linguistic interdependence and the educational development of bilingual children. *Review of Educational Research, 49,* 222–251.

Dixon, C. N., & Nessel, D. (1983). *Language experience approach to reading and writing: LEA for ESL.* Hayward, CA: Alemany.

Edelsky, C. (1986). *Writing in a bilingual program: Había una vez.* Norwood, NJ: Ablex.

Ferreiro, E. (1991). La construcción de la escritura en el niño. *Lectura y Vida, 22*(3), 5–14.

Freeman, Y. S. (1988). Do Spanish methods and materials reflect current understanding of the reading process? *The Reading Teacher, 41,* 654–662.

Goodman, K. (1986). *What's whole in whole language?* Portsmouth, NH: Heinemann.

Hudelson, S. (1987). The role of native language literacy in the education of language minority children. *Language Arts, 64,* 827–841.

Pérez, B., & Torres-Guzmán, M. E. (1992). *Learning in two worlds: An integrated Spanish/English biliteracy approach.* New York: Longman.

Teberosky, A. (1990). El lenguaje escrito y la alfabetización. *Lectura y Vida, 21*(3), 5–15.

10

Spanish Reading Assessment

Philip Segan
Long Island University

El enfoque de este capítulo es la evaluación de las habilidades y las dificultades en la lectura del estudiante bilingüe. La información describe métodos e instrumentos recomendados que ayudan al desarrollo académico en la lectura. El capítulo describe las características de los exámenes estandarizados y provee recommendacciones generales para evaluar a los estudiantes bilingües.

OBJECTIVES

After completing this chapter, the reader will be able to:

1. Describe typical assessment procedures and discuss their appropriateness for use with bilingual students.
2. Identify problems associated with currently used, standardized tests, identifying alternative assessment instruments.
3. Determine the role of native and second-language proficiency of bilingual students.
4. Describe the characteristics of portfolio assessment as an alternative form of evaluation.

GUIDE QUESTIONS

1. What are some of the traditional uses to which assessment is put in the schools today?

2. Should there be differentiated assessment instruments and procedures for Hispanic bilingual students? If so, what kinds?
3. What are some of the possible problems that may be caused by using standardized, norm-referenced assessment instruments on a nonmainstream group of students?
4. What are some of the characteristics of second-language learners that must be taken into account when making assessment and placement decisions?
5. What are the characteristics of portfolios? How can they be used successfully with bilingual learners?
6. How can parents successfully be involved in the assessment process so that they can contribute to their children's success in school?

INTRODUCTION

What is assessment? How is it conducted? And for what purposes are the results of assessment used? Should all students be assessed using the same instruments? And are all instruments equally valid for identifying skills mastery? What about the assessment of non-English-speaking, second-language learners? These questions, and others like them, will be raised and answered in this chapter. The purpose is to review currently used assessment instruments and decide if—and how—they are appropriate for use with Hispanic, limited-English-proficient students.

Assessment results should be put to formative uses; that is, they should help to determine not only where students are on a developmental skills continuum, but also provide feedback about the success of instructional strategies and interventions. These indicators allow school administrators and teachers to make informed decisions about such items as placement of students in cooperative work groups, the instructional approaches and materials to be used, the need to reteach concepts, the pacing of instruction, and the general success of the units or lessons being taught or the activities being engaged in. Notice that this purpose moves some of the onus of responsibility from the students to the school. In other words, not every performance indicator that falls short of mastery should be laid at the feet of the students in the classroom. To be honest, educators must view results of assessments from a larger perspective than the students to include all of the pedagogical features that constitute their teaching repertoires and approaches.

Any discussion of assessment of student abilities in reading must be presented within the context of the purposes for which school personnel assess student progress; and the concept of assessment must itself be defined both in general terms and in relation to the population—bilingual students, mainly Hispanics—that it intends to measure. Eisner (1994) suggested that assessment, like educational evaluation, is not one but several things. It performs different functions and needs to be regarded in light of the educational functions it is intended to perform.

Assessment also needs to be viewed in the context of the purposes for which schools and school systems use the results of assessments to make decisions about placing students, the instructional program and materials used, as well as the promotion of students. The admitted goal of many of the educational endeavors is to produce students who are "independent thinkers and problem solvers." Proof of this goal is apparent in most of the vision or mission statements written by schools or districts and put forth to the larger community as the recognized, worthy purposes of the schools. Along with respect for cultural and linguistic diversity, independent thinking and the ability to solve problems rank high among the goals of all educators of the children in public and private schools at the end of the 20th century. Indeed, these statements echo many of the principles put forth at the national and many state levels in a variety of documents (e.g., *Goals 2000: Educate America Act* and *A New Compact for Learning*).

Far too often, however, there has been a differentiated set of expectations for special populations of students, especially those who are culturally and linguistically diverse (as well as those with "special needs"), in this case, non-English-speaking or limited-proficient-speakers of English. In many instances, assessment instruments and procedures are designed for use with a mainstream (Anglo-Western), dominant linguistic and cultural group in the schools and the general society (Hughes, 1989; McGintie, 1993; Oller, 1992; Perrone, 1991; Winograd, Paris, & Bridge, 1991). The results of these assessments, when applied to student populations different from those with whom they were originally intended to be used, can be devastating to these students in terms of the perceptions of their abilities, the educational decisions made about them, and their own self-esteem. The varieties of cultures, languages, and values represented by diverse students require that special considerations be taken into account both in developing and implementing assessments as well as in their interpretations and implications for placement of and instructional practices and materials used for these students.

The purposes of assessment also must have a future orientation; that is, educators, students, and their parents must be able to predict the achievement potential of the children being educated in the schools today for success in the approaching millennium. There must be among these groups, as well as other concerned citizens, a sense of confidence in the abilities of the future workers and contributors to society who are graduating from public schools and entering vocational schools, universities, and the employment ranks. All constituents must feel secure that schools are turning out literate, productive members of society who will succeed in their professional endeavors and who will contribute to the overall well-being of the United States for themselves and for the generations that will follow them. In short, education must prepare students to succeed not only in the school environment, but in the larger world that they will confront daily after they have graduated from school. With the recognition that the Hispanic population is the fastest-growing minority group in the schools, as well as in the general U.S. population, there is a special need, and a responsibility, to adequately and appropriately assess students in terms of their educational achievement and problem-solving ability.

THE NEED TO PROPERLY ASSESS HISPANIC STUDENTS

The assessments that are used traditionally have viewed students and their achievement in relation to other members of similar groups. The assessments used for these purposes are usually called standardized, norm-referenced tests. That is, they are uniform in their presentation; administered to groups (to the extent possible) under identical, "ideal" conditions; and they measure all students against a yardstick that is a comparison of other students in the same grades throughout the targeted or similar testing area. So, for example, Hispanic students in New York City, along with white and African American students, will take the same reading test as, and their results will be compared with, those of analogous populations in Chicago, Detroit, and Los Angeles. There will be little, if any, consideration given to any issues other than the length of time the students have been in English-language school settings and the grade in which they are currently to determine if they should be tested and which level of the test should be administered to them. What purposes do these tests serve; and to what use should their results be put? Eisner (1994; Worthen, 1993), among others, looks at these tests in view of the nature of the group process inherent in schools today and the need to achieve success in an outside world of group tasks. These authorities agree in stating that assessment tasks need not be limited to solo performance, many of the most important tasks undertaken require group efforts, assessment has to provide a place for assessing growth on group tasks, and school programs need to be designed to provide students with opportunities to learn how to contribute to the realization of group goals (pp. 205–206).

The purposes of group-administered tests may appear to be valid from this perspective; but there are inherent problems in the instruments used in terms of content, language, cultural expectations/understandings, and the biases of those who would interpret the results and make judgments about the students based on their performance on these tests. In discussing the language issue in standardized testing, Eisner agreed with Conroy (1992) when he stated that, having established that much of what is assessed in standardized testing is based on a student's knowledge of standard American English, students are linguistically at a disadvantage and would score lower as a group than mainstream, standard-English-proficient students.

What often needs to be considered and assessed first for second-language learners of English is their level of native proficiency in speaking and reading. The extent of their native literacy may be a crucial factor in the degree to which they are able to transfer already attained skills in Spanish reading to English, or their ability to learn to read in the new language at the same time that they are developing concepts and vocabulary in English. DeLain (1995), herself a member of a minority group, addressed the issue of differentiated assessment for different groups of students. She felt that there needs to be "equity" in all endeavors to assess students' achievement and/or intelligence. DeLain believed public school staffs have a special responsibility for educating and assessing students in their schools:

> Expectations for success should not vary dependent upon race, gender, ethnicity, where you live, how many parents you have, or whether your mom went to college. We teach the mix of students who walk through the door—black, white, yellow, tall, short, rich or poor. Our responsibility does not change. The paths we take to actualizing and evaluating success for our students may vary, but the bottom line stays the same. All children need to be given the tools they need to 'be all that they can be.' However, for years, the definition of what children are and what they can be has been influenced by the results of assessments. (p. 440)

Quintana (1996) listed the purposes of evaluation, of which assessment is a part, as:

- Provee los medios para clarificar lo que estamos enseñando.
- Nos ayuda a refinar nuestras expectativas sobre el nivel y la calidad del trabajo de los estudiantes.
- Provee un instrumento para involucrar activamente el alumno en su proceso de aprendizaje.

- Nos exige adaptar la intervención pedagógica a las necesidades de aprendizaje del estudiante.
- Nos provee información sobre cómo están funcionando nuestras estrategias de enseñanza con cada alumno.
- Promueve la colaboración de otros miembros de la comunidad educativa. (p. 40)

In summary, once school staff members have determined the purposes of and uses for the evaluations that can be made based on student assessments, they have a responsibility to be sure that the assessment instruments selected have been designed appropriately for a non-English-speaking population. These instruments need to be linguistically and culturally relevant and correct if they are to yield usable results.

Characteristics of Assessments and Students

If there is agreement that there is a need to revisit the issue of assessing the abilities, strengths, and weaknesses of second-language learners, then instructors must at once look at both the characteristics of the assessment tools as well as the characteristics of the learners for whom they are to be used. The instruments themselves as well as the populations for whom they are used differ greatly in terms of linguistic complexity, vocabulary skills, and conceptual and experiential knowledge bases.

Leung (1994, p. 96) pointed to "psychocultural incompatibility" in discussing "differential student achievement patterns" of culturally diverse students. He described the historical tendencies to view psychological differences as indicators of the abilities or lack of abilities of these students. He also discussed the controversial history of developing assessments according to the perspectives held by persons of one cultural group about another:

> Its controversy is primarily due to an historically presumed truth that Anglo cultures represent the norm to which others should be compared. This assumption led to the tools of psychological studies (e.g., development of tasks, instruments of measurement, etc.) being based solely on the Anglo-western society. When non-Anglo, nonwestern people did not perform at the same level, many psychologists made leaps to conclude cultural or ethnic inferiority of non-Anglo individuals. (p. 97)

It is in these perceptions of "inferiority," rather than in differences, that the unfortunate, negatively self-fulfilling prophecies about minority and linguistically and culturally diverse students seem to find their bases. The expectations about how these students will perform—or fail to perform—on currently administered tests lead to decisions about such things as whether to include them in the testing program (for fear that their poor scores will lower the overall achievement levels, and the resulting rankings of the schools). If they are included, there is the question as to whether to test them "on level" or to use the excuse that they are achieving at a lower level than their age-mates, hence making an erroneous case for testing them on a lower level of the test to be administered. Also what are the implications if their scores should somehow be higher than expected—an anomaly for sure? Did they somehow take the test under less than "honest" conditions (DeLain, 1995; Valdez-Pierce & O'Malley, 1992)? Did the teacher, perhaps, "teach to the test" (a practice that has become all too real as students', teachers', and schools' worth are measured in terms of the scores achieved on these tests)?

And, what placement and instructional decisions can or should be made on the basis of these one-time scores achieved under "optimal" conditions, with students putting forth tremendous effort in a short period of time? If their scores are low, do teachers and administrators judge these students to be generally low performers? Are they candidates for special education programs? Obviously, they are considered to be at-risk of something. If their scores are high, should the assumption be made that they can perform consistently at such a high level of achievement? And, should their instruction and the instructional materials used be at correspondingly high levels? One should hope not. These test scores are merely one indicator of student potential. As discussed earlier, they are not always accurate indicators of the potential of these students.

The situation, however, is not a hopeless one; and it is certainly possible to appropriately assess culturally and linguistically different students in the schools. A partial solution to the assessment issue lies in the use of "portfolios," part of the movement that has come to be known as "authentic," or "alternative," assessment. What are portfolios? What goes into them? Why, and in what ways, are they "authentic"? How do they differ from other, previously and currently used assessments? What are the purposes of these assessments? And, to what uses will the results of these assessments be put? These questions are answered in the next section.

NEW ASSESSMENT STRATEGIES

The author of this chapter recommends that because of all the flaws in standardized assessment instruments in assessing bilingual students' learning strengths and weaknesses that this assessment be considered as only one of a number of evaluation devices. Natural (authentic) assessments should also be included in trying to get a picture of the bilingual students' abilities. A defining characteristic of authentic assessment is that it is performance based, that is, it measures objectively those skills and knowledge that students have based on what they have experienced or learned in a school setting or another learning environment, such as a trip in the community, a visit from a performing group or a guest speaker, or interacting with some artifacts or other realia inside or outside of the classroom. Paris et al. (1992) provided the following partial definition:

> Assessments grounded in performance may provide dynamic descriptions of students' rates of learning and degrees of change.... Performance-based assessments [should] be judged by expanded notions of validity that include concepts such as the consequences of assessment, the fairness of tasks and scoring, the generalizability of results, and the quality and complexity of the content of the assessments. (p. 9)

Valdez-Pierce and O'Malley (1992) distinguished among *alternative* assessment, *performance* assessment, and *portfolio* assessment. Figure 10.1 provides a descriptive summary.

Performance-based assessment involves actual demonstrations, which involve integration of several processes, skills, and concepts. Student achievement is assessed by evaluating some type of student product that is planned, constructed, or developed (DeLain, 1995). Bilingual students can benefit from this type of assessment. DeLain (1995, p. 441) suggested some important characteristics of performance-based assessment for minority students. Performance-based assessment can be aligned with instructional practice; provide students opportunities to express or represent their knowledge in different ways; provide better indicators of the depth of a student's knowledge; stretch students' minds by requiring them to construct, design, compose, model, or build their response rather than select it from an array of choices; be aligned with ongoing classroom instruction so that it ceases to become an end in and of itself; answer all questions about what a child knows and is able to do; and be a panacea to all the assessment and instructional ills of the current educational system.

DeLain recommended using a variety of alternative assessment approaches that include, among others, interest inventories, interview protocols, classroom observation checklists, and informal teacher judgments based on observations of the student in the classroom in both academic and social situations.

Alternative assessment

Any method of finding out what a student knows or can do that is intended to show growth and inform instruction; based on activities that represent actual progress toward instructional goals and reflect tasks typical of classrooms and real-life settings requires integration of language skills; and may include teacher observation, performance assessment, and student self-assessment.

Performance assessment

A type of alternative assessment; an exercise in which a student demonstrates specific skills and competencies in relation to a continuum of agreed-upon standards of proficiency or excellence; reflects student performance on instructional tasks; relies on professional rater judgment in its design and interpretation.

Portfolio assessment

The use of records of a student's work over time and in a variety of modes to show the depth, breadth, and development of the student's abilities; the purposeful and systematic collection of student work that reflects accomplishment relative to specific instructional goals or objectives; can be used as an approach for combining the information from both alternative and standardized assessments; has as key elements student reflection and self-monitoring.

FIG. 10.1. Authentic assessment models.

Paris and his colleagues (1992) looked at the purposes of authentic assessments and suggested how they can be used to make meaningful instructional decisions about students as well as how they can provide insight into students' developmental levels; they also suggested how such assessments may be useful to parents and administrators. They stated that richer diagnostic information about students' skills can be derived from alternative assessment development than from more traditional assessment instruments used because these authentic assessments are tied directly to and grow out of the curriculum objectives and instructional procedures and goals in the classroom. For example, if students are reading an English-language biography of Simon Bolivar, they will be tested on the content of the factual material presented in the text and on the vocabulary as ways to assess their understanding or comprehension. Further, the data yielded by such alternative assessments can provide parents with information on their children's progress in the bilingual program. For example, student folders of work prepared during the course of the semester can be available for parents to review at afterschool parent–teacher conferences or at other meetings with their child's teachers. In addition, the sequence of work presented can inform parents about the topics being covered in classes. Authentic assessment can be used by students engaged in monitoring and evaluating their own work, reflecting on their efforts and accomplishments, and developing learning strategies that will help them in future tasks. Here, the implication is that students will begin to take responsibility for evaluating their own progress toward mastery of skills; they will develop a sense of how to form valid judgments about their work, demonstrate the ability to edit and improve their output, and will learn to budget their time to allow completion of activities. Finally, results of such assessments can provide administrators with summative data that can serve as reliable quantitative indicators of accountability. Administrators need to be able to provide information to parents, school board members, and other interested constituents about students' progress and achievement, especially in reading. Furthermore, they need interim progress checks in order to adjust curricular objectives, teaching approaches, and strategies to help students increase their achievement levels during the course of the school year.

With the burgeoning involvement of parents in the educational decision-making process, especially on school-site committees and school-based councils, there is a need to provide them with sound information on which to base their decisions. They must be able to decide on the best instructional program and course offerings for all children, not only their own, in the school. One method of obtaining some information about the achievement levels of these students is to be knowledgeable about the assessments used to determine skills proficiency and levels of mastery. Besides playing a role as the "at-home partners" of the school and working on reading and math skills with their children to reinforce classroom learning, parents need to be actively involved in the assessment process. Fredericks and Rasinski (1990) pointed out that inviting parents to take an active role in assessing individual literacy growth is predicated on three interdependent principles: Involving parents in the assessment process must be an integral part of that program, parent assessment procedures must be conducted comprehensively, and parents' involvement in assessment should be approached systematically.

It is only when parents become part of the assessment decision-making process that they will be in a position to make other important decisions about curriculum designs, instructional practices, and materials to be used that will best meet the needs of their own children as well as those of all the students in the entire school population, not the least important of whom are the bilingual, culturally and linguistically diverse learners. Some suggestions for informing and involving parents are provided by Cornell (1995, p. 135):

> Promote positive communication with parents. Early on, send home samples of student's best work—with praise. (In each case, use a translator if necessary). Parents will come to view their child's school favorably as a place where the child can succeed and where his or her self-esteem is raised. And parents will feel that the school really cares about their children and about sharing information with them about their children's progress. A hoped-for outcome might be the eventual involvement of parents on school committees for planning curriculum, instruction, and assessment strategies to be used in the schools.

PORTFOLIOS: AN IMPORTANT COMPONENT OF THE AUTHENTIC ASSESSMENT PROCESS

The linguistic and cultural backgrounds of second-language learners are important factors in the totality of their schooling experiences. Especially relevant contexts include the ability of these students to learn to read as well as to be correctly assessed in terms of overall ability, intelligence, and reading skills attainment. There must be careful attention paid to the language facility of these students in the L2, in this case, English. Portfolios lend themselves well to this assessment. Recently, Moya and O'Malley (1994) described authentic language assessment activities. Figure 10.2 presents a summary of their model.

Moving from the larger school program of general instructional practices, it is appropriate to look specifically at the role of assessment in measuring reading, or the preferred term, literacy, skills development of students in classrooms. In studying the factors related to equity and assessment for "minority" students, DeLain (1995) presented the assessment practices that too often have characterized much of what school folks have done:

> Until recently, assessment has been based upon the validity of breaking reading processes into discrete pieces; the assumption has been that if you know the pieces, you know the whole. Therefore, assessment of the pieces was presumed to provide evaluative information on a student's achievement of the processes. In reading, this meant testing vocabulary knowledge using lists of words or testing comprehension using short, artificially created paragraphs. (p. 440)

1. Identify purpose and focus of portfolio
   • Establish a portfolio committee.
   • Focus the portfolio.

2. Plan portfolio contents
   • Select assessment procedures.
   • Specify portfolio contents.
   • Determine frequency of assessment.

3. Design portfolio analysis
   • Set standards and criteria.
   • Determine procedure to integrate information.
   • Schedule staff responsibilities for analysis.

4. Prepare for instruction
   • Plan instructional use.
   • Plan feedback to students and parents.

5. Plan verification of procedures
6. Establish a system to check reliability.
7. Establish a system to validate decisions.
8. Implement the model.

FIG. 10.2. Portfolio assessment model.

In summary, it is important that the assessment instruments that school personnel use for bilingual students in U.S. schools be not only linguistically and culturally appropriate for these students, but also that they provide realistic, usable results that can be understood by parents as well as school personnel. They must provide information that can help in the design and implementation of literacy programs that address the weaknesses of these students as well as allow teachers the opportunities to capitalize on the strengths of their students. And parents need to be able to participate in placement and instructional decisions for their children that are based on sound, valid assessment results.

ASSESSING READING SKILLS OF THE HISPANIC BILINGUAL STUDENT

In light of the information presented, keep in mind a few suggestions for assessing the reading skills of bilingual students in the classroom. Teachers must know, or be able to determine, the child's reading and communicative proficiency in the native language; understand the experiential background (and schooling) that the non-English-speaking student brings to the task; be familiar with linguistic and cultural similarities and differences between the child's culture and the new language and culture of the school; be aware of the child's preferred learning style (e.g., cooperative/group or individual oriented, competitive, etc.); and understand the role that the child's parents and other significant family members play in receptivity to learning to read and communicate in English.

CONCLUSION

Armed with the knowledge presented earlier, the teacher of Hispanic, bilingual learners should confidently be able to promote successful literacy skills in these students in the classroom. There must also be careful coordination between and among the professionals on the staff who provide such services to these students as ESL, enrichment, or tutorial and, if appropriate, special education instruction. As the new millennium approaches, teachers should do so strongly committed to the proposition that "All Children Can Learn" and that they have the knowledge, ability, and skills to make universal learning a reality for all the students. It is only if teachers are so committed that the students will be successful in the decades ahead; and they will ensure that they and their children live in a more truly bilingual, literate world than they are now experiencing.

FOLLOW-UP ACTIVITIES

1. Obtain the test administration manuals (instructions to the teacher) for a standardized test and a diagnostic test. As you review each manual, look for and list information about: skills tested (English/Spanish); how scores are presented and interpreted; suggestions given to the teacher for grouping, placement, individual or small-group follow up, and reporting results to parents and community; subject matter passages used in test for reading selections; and grade/age levels tested (and provisions, if any, for out-of-level testing).

2. For two grade and content areas (reading, social studies, science, etc.) of your choice—one in English, one in Spanish—secure a scope and sequence or curriculum guide. Pick out a unit or topic of study and the learning objectives for the students. Design three criterion-referenced questions for two of the objectives.
3. Prepare the format for a suggested portfolio for bilingual students that you might teach. Discuss the kinds of documents that you would ask students to include, how often they would place materials into their portfolios, how they and you would evaluate the progress indicated, and how the items would be interpreted for parents reviewing the portfolios.
4. Describe the characteristics that should be identified in attempts to assess successfully the abilities of bilingual students in both native- and second-language proficiency. How are these factors important in decisions about class/grade placement, attainment of skills and concepts in L2, and reporting of progress?

REFERENCES

Conroy, A. A. (1992, Winter). The testing of minority language students. *Journal of Educational Issues of Language Minority Students, 11,* 175–186.

DeLain, M. T. (1995). Equity and performance-based assessment: An insider's view. *The Reading Teacher, 48*(5), 440–442.

Eisner, E. W. (1994). *The educational imagination: On the design and evaluation of school programs* (3rd ed.). New York: MacMillan.

Fredericks, A. D., & Rasinski, T. V. (1990). Involving parents in the assessment process. *The Reading Teacher, 44*(4), 346–349.

Leung, B. P. (1994). Culture as a contextual variable in the study of differential minority student achievement. *Journal of Educational Issues of Language Minority Students, 13,* 95–105.

MacGintie, W. H. (1993). Some limits of assessment. *Journal of Reading, 36*(7), 556–560.

Moya, S. S., & O'Malley, J. M. (1994). A portfolio assessment model for ESL. *Journal of Educational Issues of Language Minority Students, 13,* 13–36.

Paris, S. G., Calfee, R. C., Filby, N., Hiebert, E. H., Pearson, P. D., Valencia, S. W., & Wolf, K. P. (1992). A framework for authentic literacy assessment. *The Reading Teacher, 46*(2), 88–98.

Perrone, V. (Ed.). (1991). *Expanding student assessment.* Alexandria, VA: Association for Supervision and Curriculum Development.

Quintana, H. (1996). El portafolio como estrategia para la evaluación de la redaccion. *Lectura y Vida, 17*(1), 39–41.

Valdez-Pierce, L., & O'Malley, J. M. (1992). *Performance and portfolio assessment for language minority students. Performance Information Guide Series.* Silver Spring, MD: National Clearinghouse for Bilingual Education.

Winograd, P., Paris, S., & Bridge, C. (1991). Improving the assessment of literacy. *The Reading Teacher, 45*(2), 108–116.

Worthen, B. R. (1993). Critical issues that will determine the future of alternative assessment. *Phi Delta Kappan, 74*(6), 444–456.

Appendix I

Competencies for Teaching Reading and Language Arts in Spanish

The competent teacher of Spanish reading and language arts is able to:

1. Define the role of Spanish reading and language arts within bilingual–bicultural education.
   a. Describe varied patterns of organizing Spanish language arts within several educational programs such as bilingual education, foreign languages, and dual language programs.
   b. Summarize the history of Spanish reading and language arts in bilingual education.
   c. Write a rationale for the teaching of Spanish reading and language arts within bilingual education.

2. Demonstrate knowledge of and proficiency in the Spanish language in listening, speaking, reading, and writing.
   a. Pronounce Spanish words correctly.
   b. Speak and write grammatically correct Spanish.
   c. Identify and practice nonverbal aspects of the Spanish language.
   d. Identify and practice paralinguistic aspects of the Spanish language such as stress, intonation, and phrasing in a nativelike manner.
   e. Correctly use punctuation, form (style), vocabulary, and idiomatic expressions.
   f. Answer, correctly in oral and/or written form, comprehension questions related to Spanish reading selections.

3. Demonstrate familiarity with the linguistic and cultural systems of Spanish.
   a. Enumerate and discuss universal characteristics of language as they apply to Spanish.
   b. Identify and explain different factors affecting the status of the different Spanish language dialects.
   c. Identify and describe the possible effects of contact between the Spanish and English languages in terms of the following:
      • phonological interference
      • morphological interference
      • syntactic interference
      • code switching
   d. Design and implement activities that minimize linguistic interference.
   e. Differentiate among the various purposes and types of Spanish language used in appropriate social contexts.
   f. Describe how planning considerations affect bilingual education programs.
   g. Analyze differences in family structures and patterns of authority across cultures and within a culture.
   h. Accept the language diversity and variety of the student and the standard variety as valid systems of communication, each with its own legitimate function.

4. Make reference to current research in Spanish reading and language arts.
   a. Read and critique professional articles and books related to research in Spanish reading and language arts.
   b. Use research findings to improve reading and language arts instruction in Spanish

5. Demonstrate knowledge of, and skills in employing, assessment tools in Spanish reading and language arts.
   a. Identify and select tests and instruments appropriate for use with Hispanic bilingual populations.
   b. List and implement techniques of informal assessment.
   c. Adapt and employ appropriate assessment batteries for diagnosis and prescription.
   d. Interpret test scores correctly.

e. Use item analysis and profile sheets in interpretive testing data.
f. Create and utilize test questions that are criterion referenced in a valid and reliable form.
g. Identify, describe, and use a variety of assessment tools and procedures, including checklists, questionnaires, and interview forms appropriate for Hispanic students.
h. Prepare an informal reading test in Spanish.
i. Assess students' reading and language arts performance and progress effectively.

6. Identify the developmental stages of Spanish language acquisition.
    a. Identify and explain different theories of child development and native language acquisition.
    b. Identify and explain the major theories and studies related to the acquisition of two languages simultaneously (i.e., the linguistic development of the bilingual child).
    c. Apply Spanish language theories in the teaching/learning process.

7. Demonstrate knowledge of the student's cultural environment and the ability to reflect the cultural values of the Spanish learner.
    a. Develop and implement activities, materials, and other aspects of the instructional environment related to the culture and history of the group's ancestry, the contributions of the group to the history and culture of the Untied States, and the contemporary lifestyles of the group.
    b. Recognize and identify the effects of cultural and socioeconomic variables on the students' learning.

8. Demonstrate effective teaching strategies and techniques for instructing Spanish-speaking students.
    a. Identify, describe, and utilize Spanish reading strategies (e.g., *el método fonético, el método global*), as well as other synthetic and analytical reading methods.
    b. Use literary materials relevant to the Spanish culture and appropriate to the levels of proficiency of the Spanish students.
    c. Identify cognitive levels and implement reading instruction reflecting knowledge of these levels.

    d.   Describe, develop, and implement activities that take into consideration contrastive linguistic characteristics between Spanish and English.

    e.   Develop a comprehensive readiness program based on the needs of beginning readers in Spanish.

    f.   Develop reading and language arts programs of instruction that take into account the entry skill of the student in English and Spanish.

    g.   Utilize techniques that enhance student–student, student–teacher, and student–material interactions.

    h.   Employ techniques that develop self-motivation in students such as reinforcement procedures, verbal and nonverbal feedback, and positive interpersonal relations.

    i.   Formulate questions that will elicit various levels of thinking in students.

    j.   Describe the various types of questions students and teachers generate for comprehension purposes.

    k.   Implement activities that take into consideration oral language skills.

    l.   Utilize appropriate techniques to develop grammar skills.

    m.   Develop and implement activities to improve comprehension and critical reading skills of bilingual learners.

    n.   Write competencies and objectives for Spanish reading and language arts.

    o.   Define the terminology relevant to the area of Spanish reading and language arts such as *método global, apresto, destreza,* and *cartel de experiencias.*

9. Demonstrate knowledge of effective classroom management techniques.

    a.   Demonstrate skills in assessing the limitations and strengths of various instructional patterns and groupings.

    b.   Arrange the physical environment of the classroom and utilize available resources of the school to achieve optimal learning for each student.

    c.   Work effectively with and plan for professionals and other adults in the classroom.

    d.   Develop record-keeping systems to monitor reading and language arts progress of Spanish-speaking students.

10. Demonstrate skills in utilizing resources in and out of the school.

    a. Identify and use resources from Spanish reading and language arts materials that are appropriate to the bilingual/cross-cultural classroom.

    b. Review and select suitable commercially prepared materials for reading and language arts in Spanish.

    c. Select audiovisual materials to enrich instruction in reading and language arts.

11. Demonstrate skills in evaluation/assessment procedures.

    a. Assess strengths and weakness of students' academic development in Spanish reading and language arts.

    b. Identify and assess other factors related to success and failure of the reading process including intellectual, social, cultural and linguistic factors

12. Appreciate the artistic and aesthetic contributions of the Hispanic culture.

    a. Select appropriate library and enrichment books.

    b. Select biographical, autobiographical, historical, cultural, or other pertinent Spanish literature.

    c. Identify and integrate various forms of Hispanic literature into the reading and language arts programs to integrate all aspects of Hispanic music and dramatic arts within the Spanish language arts curricula.

Apéndice 2

Introducción

1. **Acento (stress)** - Intensidad de la voz para pronunciar ciertas sílabas en las palabras. Determinadas inflexiones de la voz, por las que se diferencian y distinguen las naciones, pueblos o provincias en su peculiar modo de hablar (i.e., acento catalán, alemán, ruso, hispano-americano).

2. **Actividades de Enriquecimiento (enrichment activities)** - Grupo de actividades encaminadas a refozar lo que se ha estudiado o leído.

3. **Adiestramiento para el Maestro (teacher training)** - Preparación para poder cumplir con los deberes de un trabajo, en este caso, el de la enseñanza.

4. **Agrupación (cluster)** - En fonética, un grupo de fonemas que no constituyen necesariamente una sílaba.

5. **Agrupación por Habilidad (ability grouping)** - Agrupación del estudiante de acuerdo a su nivel o capacidad intelectual.

6. **Alfabeto Inicial de la Enseñanza (initial teaching alphabet, ITA)** - Alfabeto usado en la instrucción primaria de lectura y escritura.

7. **Alófonos (allophones)** - Diversos variantes de los sonidos del lenguaje los cuales constituyen un fonema.

8. **Análisis estructural (structural analysis)** - Procedimiento mediante el cual se identifican unidades estructurales significativas del lenguaje (como la raíz y los morfemas).

9. **Apresto o Preparación para la Lectura (reading readiness)** - Es el período del trabajo escolar donde se desarrollan actitudes, hábitos y destrezas que son indispensables antes de comenzar a aprender a leer.

10. **Artes de Lenguaje (language arts)** - Comprende las formas del lenguaje relacionadas con la expresión oral y escrita.

11. **Biblioteca (library)** - Local donde se mantienen libros ordenados para el uso personal.

12. **Bosquejo (outline)** - Plan general sin detalles.

13. **Cacofonía (cacaphony)** - Disonancia que resulta de la repetición de los elementos acústicos de la palabra.

14. **Cadencia de la Voz (cadence)** - Modulación de la voz al hablar que produce el flujo del lenguaje, especialmente la subida y bajada de la voz al final de una oración.

15. **Caligrafía (penmanship)** - Arte de escribir con letra correctamente formada.

16. **Cartel de Experiencias de Lectura (reading experience chart)** - Desglose visual de las experiencias y habilidades de lectura del estudiante: hablar, leer, comprender y escribir el lenguaje.

17. **Cita (quotation)** - Referenia directa que hacemos de un trabajo.

18. **Clave (clue)** - Explicación de los signos convenidos para escribir en cifra, o de cualesquiera otros distintos signos de los conocidos o usuales.

19. **Claves de Configuración (configuration clues)** - Ayudan a reconocer palabras utilizando la forma de las letras y patrones de letras en una palabra.

20. **Claves de Contexto (context clues)** - El proceso de captar la significación de la oración o selección a través de la lectura rápida y global.

21. **Coeficiente Intelectual (intelligence quotient (IQ))** - Medida de la viveza de ingenio/habilidad que tiene en cuenta la marca de un examen de inteligencia y la edad del individuo.

22. **Coherencia (coherence)** - Conexión, relación o unión de unas cosas con otras.

23. **Combinación de dos o tres Consonantes (consonant blend)** - Unión de consonantes que al pronunciarse se producen solas o acompañadas de una vocal.

24. **Compilar (encode)** - Convertir un mensaje o cierta información en una forma de clave o cifra.

25. **Comprensión (comprehension)** - Facultad o capacidad para entender.

26. **Conjugación (conjugation)** - Serie ordenada de todas las voces de variada inflexión con que el verbo expresa sus diferentes modos, tiempos, números y personas.

27. **Consonat e (consonant)** - Letra que no puede pronunciarse sin el auxilio de alguna vocal.

28. **Contenido de la Lectura (content of reading)** - Información que se obtiene sobre un tema por medio de la lectura.

29. **Contexto (context)** - Hilo o contenido lógico de la narración o texto.

30. **Crucigrama (cross word puzzle)** - Cruzamiento o mezcla de palabras.

31. **Deductivo (deductive)** - Proceso de llegar a la comprensión general usando las partes o detalles.

32. **Destrezas para Descifrar (decoding skills)** - El proceso que ayuda al individuo a leer o pronunciar palabras nuevas utilizando los sonidos o la estructura de las palabras.

33. **Diagnóstico (assessment)** - Forma de medir las deficiencias y habilidades de un individuo en la lectura.

34. **Diagrama/Gráfica (graph)** - Dibujo o representación que sirve para resolver un problema, para mostrar la disposición interior de una cosa o las variaciones de un fenómeno.

35. **Diptongo (diphthong)** - Combinación de dos vocales, una débil y otra fuerte o dos débiles y que forman una sílaba.

36. **Discusión Improvisada (brainstorming)** - Ideas que se discuten en forma improvisada, sin seguir un orden o una agenda determinada.

37. **Distinción Auditiva (auditory discrimination)** - La habilidad de distinguir, separar y diferenciar una cosa de otra, en lo que se oye por las cualidades sensibles que le son inherentes.

38. **Dominio Afectivo (affective domain)** - La sensibilidad del individuo.

39. **Dominio Cognoscitivo (o cognitivo) (cognitive domain)** - Se aplica a lo que se es capaz de conocerse a través del proceso de la comprensión analítica.

40. **Educación Especial (special education)** - Programa de instrucción individualizada donde se atienden las necesidades de cada estudiante ya sean mentales, de aprendizaje o de comportamiento general.

41. **Ejercicios de Práctica (pattern drills)** - Trabajos que tienen por objetivo la adquisición de una destreza.

42. **El Enfoque Psicolingüístico (psycholinguistic approach)** - La enseñanza de la lectura teniendo en cuenta el acondicionamiento de los factores psicológicos del individuo.

43. **El Pensamiento Crítico (critical thinking)** - El proceso mental que utiliza el lector para criticar lo que ha leído con respecto a su exactitud y veracidad.

44. **Enfoque (approach)** - Estrategia sistemática o método que se sigue al presentar una lección.

45. **Enseñanza Individualizada (individualized instruction)** - Método de lectura que recalca que el individuo lea aquel contenido que le interesa y que lo lea al ritmo y nivel que su capacidad mental le permita.

46. **Epíteto (epithet)** - Adjetivo o participio que se coloca antes del substantivo para destacar una característica sobresaliente.

47. **Etapas del Desarrollo (developmental stages)** - El proceso, por secuencias, del desarrollo mental del individuo.

48. **Evaluación/Avaluación (evaluation/assessment)** - Proceso sistemático de recopilar información del estudiante con el propósito de organizarla y analizarla para mejorar el proceso de enseñanza-aprendizaje.

49. **Examen Anterior (pre-test)** - Examen que se administra a principios del curso para determinar las necesidades del estudiante.

50. **Examen de Aprovechamiento Académico (achievement test)** - Grupo de ejercicios que determinan hasta qué punto los conocimientos y destrezas que se han enseñado anteriormente han sido adquiridos por el estudiante.

51. **Examen de Referencia de Criterio (criterion-referenced test)** - Examen basado en ciertos objetivos instruccionales previamente presentados.

52. **Examen Posterior (post-test)** - Examen que se administra al final del curso para determinar el progreso del estudiante.

53. **Fonema (phoneme)** - Cada uno de los sonidos simples del lenguaje hablado.

54. **Fonética (phonetics)** - Conjunto de los sonidos de un idioma.

55. **Fonología (phonics)** - Estudio de los sonidos de un idioma.

56. **Idea Principal (main idea)** - Resumen del pensamiento principal (mensaje) expresado por el autor.

57. **Inductivo (inductive)** - Proceso de empezar con la comprensión total y luego derivar las partes o detalles.

58. **Inferencia (inference)** - La habilidad de sacar consecuencia o deducir una cosa usando la conexión lógica entre antecendente y consecuente.

59. **Interferencia (interference)** - Mezcla de dos idiomas al hablar o escribir.

60. **Interpretación (interpretation)** - Explicación con inferencia.

61. **Inventario Informal de Lectura (informal reading inventory - IRI)** - Un examen en el cual el individuo lee una serie de selecciones en escala ascendente (desde lo fácil a lo difícil), hasta llegar a su nivel de lectura. El maestro indica los errores en pronunciación, vocabulario y comprensión.

62. **Inversión o Reversión (reversals)** - Forma inadecuada de percibir los símbolos o las palabras, (i.e.: ele por elle, lavar por llevar.

63. **Láminas (prints)** - Dibujos o grabados usados en el salón de clases con el propósito de facilitar la comprensión.

64. **Lectura a Primera Vista (sight reading)** - Reconocimiento de frases u oraciones a primera vista.

65. **Lectura Correctiva (corrective reading)** - Programa de instrucción generalmente llevado a cabo por el maestro para corregir deficiencias de lectura.

66. **Lectura Dirigida (directed reading)** - Una lección de lectura con el uso de materiales que incluyen orientación, lectura silenciosa, el desarrollo de vocabulario y comprensión, lectura oral y actividad de refuerzo.

67. **Lectura Programada (programmed reading)** - Progrma de lectura que sigue un patrón de progreso en forma individualizada.

68. **Lectura Remediativa (remedial reading)** - Técnicas para ayudar al estudiante que no está leyendo al nivel de su capacidad mental.

69. **Letra Mayúscula (capital letter)** - Letra de mayor tamaño, distinta a la minúscula.

70. **Letras Mudas (silent consonants)** - Son las letras que no tienen sonido. (i.e. la *h*).

71. **Lexicología (lexicology)** - Relativo a la significación etimológica de los vocablos que han de entrar en un léxico o diccionario.

72. **Librería (bookstore)** - Establecimiento donde se venden libros.

73. **Libro de Trabajo (workbook)** - Texto diseñando para uso individual del estudiante con instrucciones y preguntas específicas para enseñar al estudiante cómo aprender una o varias destrezas.

74. **Libro Primario (primer)** - Libro que se usa en los grados primarios, especialmente en primer grado.

75. **Libros Básicos de Lectura (basal readers)** - Grupo de libros de lectura que siguen una secuencia en términos de dificultad y están escritos para ciertos grados y niveles.

76. **Lingüística (linguistic)** - La ciencia que estudia todo lo relacionado con el lenguaje.

77. **Lista de Cotejo (checklist)** - Lista de destrezas o actividades con espacio para marcar.

78. **Literal (literal)** - Información tomada dierectamente del texto.

79. **Método de Clausura (cloze)** - Técnica o tipo de examen que requiere que la persona que está siendo examinada use la palabra que ha sido sistemáticamente eliminada del texto.

80. **Método Global (whole language)** - Estrategia de enseñanza de lectura que parte de la comprensión general del texto.

81. **Método de Lectura a Base de Experiencias (Language experience approach, LEA)** - El uso del transfondo lingüístico y cultural del niño para iniciarlo en la lectura.

82. **Modalidad para Aprender (learning modality)** - La forma particualr que usa un individuo para aprender. Algunos estudiantes aprenden a través de la forma visual, otros por la forma auditiva.

83. **Morfema (morpheme)** - La forma lingüística más pequeña con significado propio.

84. **Morfología (morphology)** - Estudio de las formas de las palabras.

85. **Mudo (voiceless)** - Que no tiene sonido, i.e.: la letra *h*.

86. **Nivel de Dificultad (readability)** - La medida de un libro o pasaje escrito en terminos de sus grados de dificultad.

87. **Nivel de Frustración (frustration level)** - Nivel de lectura donde el estudiante pronuncia no más del 60 porciento de las palabras y comprende 50 porciento o menos del material.

88. **Nivel Independiente (independent level)** - Nivel de lectura en que el estudiante pronuncia no menos del 99 porciento de las palabras y comprende no menos del 90 porciento del material.

89. **Nivel Instruccional (instructional reading level)** - El nivel de lectura en que el estudiante pronuncia no menos del 95 porciento de las palabras y comprende no menos del 75 porciento del material.

90. **Objetivo del Autor (author's purpose)** - El mensaje o idea que intenta el autor al escribir su selección o texto.

91. **Objetivos Operacionales (behavioral objectives)** - Objetivos instruccionales que están redactados en términos de lo que el estudiante logrará adquirir al final de la lección.

92. **Oración (sentence)** - Conjunto de palabras con sentido ordenado y completo.

93. **Orden de Sucesión de los Hechos (sequence of events)** - Enumeración de los hechos en el orden en que ocurren.

94. **Ortología (orthology)** - Estudio de la pronunciación o arte de pronunciar correctamente.

95. **Parafrasear (paraphrase)** - Explicación o interpretación de un texto o un ensayo a fin de hacerlos más claros.

96. **Parónimos (paronyms)** - Palabras que suenan casi igual pero que cambian por una letra, el sonido y el significado. Ejemplos: asada y azada; casa y caza.

97. **Percepción Visual (visual discrimination)** - Habilidad para notar las semejanzas y diferencias y las incongruencias de todo lo que el estudiante ve.

98. **Prefijo (prefix)** - Sílaba que se antepone a una palabra para formar otra, (i.e.; *des*confiar, *re*poner).

99. **Proficiencia (proficiency)** - Aptitud o habilidad en una o varias destrezas del lenguaje.

100. **Reflexión Convergente (convergent thinking)** - Ideas que se dirigen a un mismo punto.

101. **Reflexión Divergente (divergent thinking)** - Ideas donde se ofrecen varias alternativas.

102. **Significado (meaning)** - Idea principal o sentido de una palabra; frase, oración o texto.

103. **Sílaba (syllable)** - Conjunto de letras que se pronuncian en una sola emisión de voz.

104. **Silábico (syllabication)** - Descomposición de las palabras en sílabas.

105. **Sintaxis (syntax)** - La combinación, el orden y la coordinación de palabras o grupos de palabras en secuencias gramaticales.

106. **Sufijo (suffix)** - Sílaba que se le añade al final a una palabra para formar una nueva. (i.e; morir*se*, dí*melo*).

107. **Tecnología Educativa (educational technology)** - La applicación de formas de comunicación electrónica tales como las computadoras y el "internet."

108. **Tema (theme)** - Proposición, texto o asunto sobre el que versa un discurso, una discusión o un escrito.

109. **Tiempo Verbal (tense)** - El tiempo de una acción, que puede ser presente, pasado o futuro.

110. **Tomar Nota (note taking)** - Apuntes para recordar o tratar un tema con más intensidad.

111. **Tone (pitch)** - Mayor o menor elevación del sonido.

112. **Transfondo Cultural (cultural background)** - Las experiencias del lenguaje, actividades y pensamientos que el estudiante trae como miembro de un grupo social o étnico.

113. **Trozos Literarios, Fragmento (selection)** - Una o varias partes (varios párrafos) de una obra literaria.

114. **Vocabulario (lexicon)** - Lista de palabras.

115. **Vocabulario a Primera Vista (sight vocabulary)** - Reconocer y entender palabras al verlas por primera vez.

116. **Vocal (vowel)** - Letra que se pronuncia con una sola emisión de voz (el español tiene cinco vocales: a, e, i, o, u).

Author Index

A

Ada, A. F. 161RES.
Aiken, L. R. 137, 143R
Allen, C. 59, 69R
Alonso, J. 51, 68R
Altwerger, B. 112, 122R
Alvarez Henao, L. E. 88, 100R
Ambert, A. N. 22, 27, 28, 39R
Anderson, T. 6, 8, 9, 15R, 19, 20, 21, 30, 39R
Andrews, J. F. 155, 160R
Armstrong, T. 160, 160R
Arnaldi de Olmeda, 105, 122R
Arreaga-Mayer, C. 149, 160R
Asenjo, C. 53, 68R

B

Badía, A. M. 88, 100R
Baecher, R. E. 147, 161R
Barnitz, J. G. 19, 21, 22, 27, 28, 32, 33, 37, 39R
Bartolome, L. 22, 40R
Bennhardt, E. B. 10, 15R, 39R
Bishop, R. 173, 183R
Braselton, S. 143R
Bridge, C. 187, 198R
Brown-Azavowitz, M. 30, 39R
Brown, D. L. 18, 20, 39R
Brown, P. 105, 122R
Burns, P. C. 130, 144R

C

Calfee, R. C. 185, 192, 193, 198R
Cantieni, G. 132, 138, 143, R
Capizzi-Snipper, G. 72, 74, 85R, 106, 123R
Carlson, L. M. 176, 183R
Carrasquillo, A. 1, 2, 7, 8, 9, 13, 15R, 19, 39R, 41, 43, 52, 68R, 69, 85R, 101, 147, 161R, 164, 165, 183R

Carrell, P. 53, 69R
Carta, J. 149, 160R
Cassany, D. 54, 69R
Castañeda, A. 8, 10, 16R, 23, 41R
Centuríon, C. E. 33, 39R
Chadwich, M. 149, 161R
Chall, J. S. 105, 106, 120, 122R
Chang, J. 150, 161R
Chiodo, J. J. 131, 132, 143R
Clark, C. 156, 161R
Cloud, N. 148, 161R
Cohen, A. D. 19, 39R
Cohen, B. 29, 32, 35, 36, 39R
Collier, V. P. 10, 15R, 19, 20, 41R, 106, 123R
Condemarin, M. 3, 9, 15R, 30, 69R, 73, 85R
Conner, V. 39R
Conroy, A. A. 189, 198R
Cooper, J. D. 128, 129, 134, 143R, 178, 183R
Cornell, C. 131, 143R, 194
Cox , J. M. 137, 143R
Crawford, A. N. 148, 153, 161R, 183LR
Crawford, J. 18, 33, 39R
Cullinan, B. 183LR
Culyer, R. C. 137, 143R
Cumnins, J. 2, 8, 10, 15R, 19, 20, 27, 28, 34, 36, 39R, 183R

D

Davison , D. M. 131, 143R
Deker, B. C. 143R
Delacre, L. 161RES
DeLain, M. T. 189, 192, 195, 198R
De Leon, J. 149, 161R
Deville, G. 155, 160R
Dickinson, D. C. 45, 69R
Dixon, C. N. 183LR
Dolch, E. W. 103, 122R
Downing, J. 19, 39R
Dubin, F. 34, 36, 39R
Dubois, M. E. 6, 8, 15R

Duffy, G. G. 176, 183R
Dunkel, P. 48, 69R
Durgonoglu, A. Y. 30, 41R
Durkin, D. 73, 74, 85R, 105, 112, 122R

E

Earp, N. W. 140, 143R
Edelsky, C. 21, 39R, 112, 122R, 183R, 183LR
Eisner, E. W. 187, 188, 189, 198R
Elliot, P. G. 129 144R
Engle, P. L. 2, 15R, 19, 39R
Escobedo, T. H. 183R
Eshey, D. E. 34, 36, 39R
Eslin, J. 19, 39R

F

Fabregat, A. M. 3, 4, 15R
Feldman, D. 32, 39R
Ferdman, B. M. 105, 106, 122R
Fernández, A. 54, 69R
Fernández de la Torriente., 54, 69R
Ferreiro, E. 183R
Figueroa, R. A. 151, 151, R
Filby, N. 185, 192, 193, 198R
FloRES, B. 5, 9, 15R, 112, 122R
Forgione, J. D. 112, 122R
Franklin, E. A. 20, 21, 39R
Fredericks, A. D. 194, 198R
Freeman, D. 8, 15R, 24, 40R, 46, 69R, 153
Freeman, Y. 8, 15R, 24, 40R, 46, 69R, 153,
        161R, 183R, 183LR
Freire de Matas, I. 48, 69R
Freire, P. 20, 40R
Fuentes, J. 22, 49R
Fung, G. 150, 161R

G

Gaarder, B. 8, 10, 13, 15R
Gagne, R. M. 105, 112, 122R
Gago, R. 4, 7, 9, 15R
Gairín , J. C. 54, 69R
Gamez, G. I. 24, 40R
Garcia, E. E. 32, 34, 40R, 72, 73, 74, 85R, 134,
        143R
Garcia, G. E. 19, 40R, 41R

Garcia, S. B. 150, 161R
Gersten, R. M. 74, 85R, 150, 155, 161R
Glynn, S. M. 137, 144R
Gomez del Manzano, M. 2, 5, 15R
Goldenberg, C. 72, 85R
Gonzalez, L. A. 129, 130, 143R
Goodman, K. 5, 9, 15R, 22, 24, 40R, 85R, 102,
        112, 122, R 153, 161R, 183R,
        183LR
Goodman, Y. 5, 9, 15R, 22, 24, 40R, 85R, 102,
        112, 122R, 153, 161R, 183R
Gould, L. S. 19, 40R
Grave, W. 34, 36, 39R
Graves, D. 54, 69R

H

Hakuta, K, . 19, 32, 40R
Hall, R. 24 , 40R
Hamilton, C. D., 89 100R
Hayes, C. W. 137, 143R
Henney, M., 137, 138, 141, 143R
Henry, R., 30, 40R
Hewlett-Gomez, M. R., 31, 40R
Hiebert, E. H., 185, 192, 193, 198R
Hudelson, S., 19, 27, 40R, 183R, 183LR
Hymes, D., 5, 15R

J

Jiménez, R. T., 19, 23, 27, 28, 31, 32, 33, 34,
        37, 40R, 72, 73, 74, 85R
Joels, R. W., 19, 20, 21, 30, 39R

K

Kaluger, G., 3, 15R
Kaminsky, S., 24, 28, 40R
Kane, R. B., 137, 143R
Kaplan, R. B., 39R
Kessler, C., 137, 143R
Kolers, P. A., 20, 40R
Kolson, C. J., 3, 15R
Krashen, S. D., 20, 40R
Kucer, S. B., 51, 69R

L

Langero, J. A., 22, 40R
Lessow-Hurley, J., 22, 40R
Leung, B. P., 190, 198R

M

MacMillan, B., 165, 183R
MacMillan/McGraw-Hill., 138, 139, 140, 143R
Maldonado, J. A., 148, 161R
Malkin, D. A., 150, 161R
Marsh, L., 28, 33, 40R
Martorell, A., 161RES
Mateos, M., 51, 68R
Mather, J. R. C., 131, 132, 143R
Mayo, W. J., 61, 69R
McGintie, W. H., 198R
McEvedy, R., 23, 40R
McInnes, M. M., 23, 40R
McLeod, A., 20, 21, 40R
Medina, C., 149, 161R
Melendez, S. E. 22, 28, 39R
Metz, M. L., 54, 69R
Miller, C. H., 23, 40R
Modiano, N., 2, 15, R, 19, 24, 38, 40R
Mohr, N., 151, 153, 154, 161R, 161RES
Monroy Casas, R., 88, 100R
Montevio, R. P., 27, 30, 31, 40R
Moya, S. S., 195, 198R
Mulhern, M., 179, 183, R
Munniz-Swicegood, M., 19, 20, 30, 31, 33, 36, 41R
Muth, D. K., 137, 143R, 144R

N

Nagy, W. E., 30, 41R
Navarro, T., 109, 122R
Nessel, O., 183LR
Nieto, S., 20, 41R
Nieves-Falcón, L., 34, 41R

O

O'Malley, J. M., 191, 192, 195, 198R
Ortiz, R., 149, 161R
Otheguy, R., 88, 100R
Ovando, C. J., 19, 20, 41R, 106, 123R

P

Pacheco, L. C., 24, 34, 41R
Padilla, R. V., 32, 34, 40R
Padron, Y. N., 22, 27, 29, 41R
Paris, S. G., 185, 187, 192, 193, 198R
Pearson, P. D., 19, 23, 27, 28, 31, 32, 33, 34, 37, 40R, 72, 73, 74, 85R, 185, 192, 193, 198R
Perez, B., 6, 8, 9, 10, 16R, 183R, 183LR
Perrone, V., 187, 198R
Piaget, J., 112, 123R
Pierce, D. L., 131, 143R
Poe, V. L., 137, 143R
Prado-Olmos, P., 27, 33, 36, 41R
Prince, C. D., 31, 32, 41R

Q

Quiles, A., 88, 100R
Quinn, M. E., 137, 143R
Quintana, H., 189, 198R

R

Ramey, D. R., 10, 16R
Ramirez, A. G., 8, 10, 16R, 23, 24, 28, 34, 41R, 105, 122R
Ramirez de Arellano, H., 58, 69R
Ramirez, J. D., 10, 16R, 33, 41R
Rasinski, T. V., 194, 198R
Reyes, D. J., 23, 41R
Rigg, P., 69R
Rio, P., 69R
Rivera Viera, D., 30, 41R
Rivers, J., 19, 24, 41R
Roberts, J., 27, 41R
Rodriquez, V., 52, 68R
Rodriquez-Brown, F., 179, 183R
Roe, B. D., 130, 144R
Roehler, L. R. 176, 183R
Romero, M., 28, 34, 41R
Routman, R., 61, 69R
Rueda, R., 151, 161R
Ruiz, N. T., 151, 161R

S

Saez, A., 74, 85R, 102, 106, 112, 123R
Santos, S. L., 18, 20, 39R
Sayers, D., 27, 39R, 41R
Scagliotti, J., 149, 161R
Scarcella, R., 133, 144R
Schifini, A., 148, 153, 161R
Schon, I., 16R
Scott-Enright, D., 19, 20, 21, 22, 24, 27, 28, 30, 40, 41R
Seco, M., 88, 100R
Segan, F., 19, 32, 39R, 41R, 125, 145, 155, 161R, 164, 183R, 185
Sena, G., 149, 161R
Serra, M. B., 153, 161R
Shavahan, T., 179, 183R
Smith, F., 3, 4, 5, 6, 7, 9, 16R, 27, 40R, 41R, 96, 100R, 129, 144R
Smith, C. B., 129, 144R
Smith, M. E., 27, 33, 36, 41R
Soler-Galiano, A., 31, 32, 41R
Solis, A., 30, 31, 40
Spiridakis, J. N., 36, 42R
St. John, K., 156, 161R
Stoodt, B. D., 130, 144R
Szymanski, M., 27 33, 36, 41R

T

Tapia, Y., 149, 160R
Tchaconas, T. N., 36, 41R, 42R
Teberosky, A., 183LR
Terrel, T. D., 20, 40R
Thelen, J., 128, 144R
Thorndike, E. L., 137, 144R
Tikunoff, W., 76, 85R

Torres, A. L., 161RES
Torres-Guzmán, M., 6, 8, 9, 10, 16R, 183R, 188LR
Tremblay, R., 132, 138, 143R

V

Valencia, S. W., 185, 192, 193, 198R
Van Allen, R., 59, 69R
Van Dusen, L. M., 134, 144R
Valdez-Pierce, L., 191, 192, 198
Vasquez, O. A., 22, 40R

W

Weaver, C., 5, 9, 16R, 51, 69R, 73, 74, 85R
Wells, G., 20, 42R
Williams, J. D., 72, 74, 85R, 106, 123R
Winograd, P., 155, 160R, 187, 198R
Wolf, K. P., 185, 192, 193, 198R
Woodward, J., 155, 161R
Worthen, B. R., 134, 144R, 197, 198R

Y

Yven, S. D., 10, 16R

Z

Zentella, A. C., 28, 42R

R-References
RES-Resources
LR-Lecturas Recomendadas
  Recommened Reading

Subject Index

A

Abilities, 190
Achievement levels, 191
Active processing hypothesis, 31
Analyzing, see cognitive strategies
Analytical area, see areas of comprehension
Applicative area, see areas of comprehension
Areas of comprehension, 76
    Analytical / interpretive, 77
    Applicative, 76, 78
    Evaluative, 78
    Literal, 77
Assessment, 186
    Authentic / Alternative, 192, 193
    Performance, 192
    Portfolio, 192, 193, 195
ASL, American Sign Language, 155
Attitude, 23
    Positive, 23
    Negative, 23
Autism, see Disability

B

Bilingual
    bicultural program, 34
    educator, 72
    immigrant, 142
    prevention intervention program, 147
    resource room, 148
    self contained special education class, 148
    speaking, 72
    special education, 146
Biliterary, 19, 20
    instruction, 21
Biliterate individual, 20
Blindness, see Disability

C

Cognitive strategies, 29
    Analyzing, 29
    Concluding, 29
    Evaluating, 29
    Generalizing, 29
    Interpreting, 29
    Locating information, 29
    Recalling, 29
    Remembering, 29
    Summarizing, 29
Communication skills, 19, 20, 36, 49
    BICS, Basic interpersonal communication skills, 36
    Listening, 19, 20, 49
    Speaking, 19, 20, 49
    Reading, 19, 20, 49
    Writing, 19, 20, 49
Community, see Support System
Computations, see Mathematics Problems
Concluding, see Cognitive Strategies
Constructing meaning, 51, 128
Content area, 56
    teacher, 130
Culture, 23

D

Deafness, see Disability
Decoding, 51
Differences, 190
Disability, 147
    Autism, 147
    Blindness 147
    Deafness, 147
    L. D, Learning, 146
    Severe, 147
Drafting, 54
    Pre, 54

E

Emotional Problem, 146, 152
Environment, 56

Atmosphere, 56
Collaborative, 64
Ideal condition, 188
L R E , Least Restricted Environment, 147
Epistemic Level, see literacy
Equal educational opportunity, 23
ESL, English as a Second Language, see language
Evaluating, see Cognitive Strategies
Evaluative area, see Areas of Comprehension

F

Functional level, see literacy

G

Gender, 29
Generalizing, see Cognitive Strategies
Graphophonic function, see Reading
grouping, 76

H

Holistic approach, 24
Conference-Centered, 24
Dialogue journal writing, 24, 25
Ethnographic teaching method, 24
Language experience, 24, 25
Home, see Support System
Human beings, 44
Hypothesizing , 58
Predicting, 58

I

Ideal conditions, see Environment
Inferiority, 190
Informational
Level, see Literacy
Text, 133
Instruction
Biliteracy, 21
Content area, 153
Structure, 24
Integrated experiences, 147
Interactive processes, 22
Interpreting, see Cognitive Strategies
Interpretive area- see Areas of Comprehension

L

Language, 23, 24
CALP, Cognitive Academic Language
Proficiency, 36
Delay, 148
Dominance, 76
ESL, English as a second language, 35
Experience approach, 60
Learner, 44
LEP, Limited English Proficient, 20, 21
Native, 24
Oral, 49
Printed, 51
SSL, Spanish as a second, 155
Whole, approach, 36
Learning,
Collaborative, 64
ILS , Integrated system, 136
LD, Disability, see disability
Modes of,
Field sensitive student, 23
Field independent student, 23
LEP, Limited English Proficient, see language
Listener, 47
Listening, see communication skills
Comprehension, 47
Literacy, 18
Integrated classroom, 60
Levels,
Epistemic, 21
Functional, 20
Informational, 21
Performative, 20
Native approach, 25, 34
Literal area, see Areas of Comprehension
Literature, 61
approach, 60

M

Mainstreaming, 147
Mathematics concepts, 137
Computation, 137
Word problems, 137
Metacognitive hypotheses, 31
Motivation, 129
Multicultural activities, 148
Multiple intelligence, 158
Multisensory activity, 148

O

Orthographic function, see Reading

P

Participatory activity, 156
Performative level, see Literacy
Portfolio, 191
Pragmatic function, see Reading
Predicting, 58
  Hypothesizing, 58

Q

Question
  Asking, 30
  Instructional, 58
  Monitoring, 58
  Summary / Recapitulation, 58

R

Read, aloud, 59
Reading, see also Communication Skills
  comprehension, 22, 51, 73
  content area, 128
  Remedial program, 148
Recalling, see Cognitive Strategies
Recording, 65
  Remembering, see Cognitive Strategies
Retelling, 61
Revising, 54, 55

S

Schema Theory, 31
School, see support system
Short attention span, 152
Self contained bilingual special education
      class- see Bilingual
Semantic
  function, see Reading
  mapping, 57
  webbing, 57

Speaking, 49, see also Communication Skills
      and Bilingual
  English, 82
Story maps, 62
Strategy, 56
Strengths, 190
Student
  Spanish Monolingual, 76
  Spanish surnamed, 80
Summarizing, see Cognitive Strategies
Support system
  community, 149
  Home, 149
  School, 149
Syntactic function, see Reading

T

Teaching
  In the mother tongue, 33
  Reactive, 24
  Reciprocal approach, 29
  Remedial instruction, 30
  Spanish language, 46
Teacher, 35
  Content areas, 130
Technology, 134
Test, 188
  Group administered, 189
  Norm-referenced, 188
  Standardized, 188
Thematic Units, 166
Transferring individuals skills, 33

W

Weakness, 190
Whole, Language approach, see Language
Word problem, see Mathematics Concept
Writer, 53
Writing, 53, see also Communication Skills
  Interactive, 65
  Instructive, 65
  Journal, 64
  Programmatic, 65

Índice de Palabras

A

Acentuación, 91
Adivinanza, 93, 95, 169
Areas De Comunicación, 3
    Escribir, 3
    Hablar, 3
    Leer, 3
    Oir, 3
Audiovisual, 171
    Cassette, 171
    C D-Roms, 172
    Computadora, 172
    Juego Electrónico, 171
    T.V., 171
    Video, 171
Autor, 181

C

Cassette, Ver Audiovisual
C D-ROM, Ver Audiovisual
Comprensión, 3
    Información Inmediata, 3
Computadora, Ver Audiovisual
Comunidad, 180
Consonante, 89
    Grupo Consonántico, 91
Cuento, 166
    Acumulativos, 167
    De Hadas, 166
    De La Naturaleza, 167
    De Nunca Acabar, 167
    Humorístico, 166
    Realista, 167
Currículo, 7, 13

D

Diptongo, 91

E

Enseñanza, 17
    Método Ecléctico, 117
    Método Fonético, 90
    Método Structuro, Global, 90
    Proceso Analítico, 106
    Método De Palabras Generadoras, 110
    Metodo Integral O Global, 111, 116
        Etapa De Aplicación, 112
        Comprobación, 112
        Descomposición, 112
        Elaboración, 112
        Iniciación, 112
Entender, 4
Escuela, 5
Escribir, Ver Areas De Comunicación
Evaluación, 3

F

Fábula, 167
Fonema, 89
Fonética, 88

G

Grupo Consonántico, Ver Consonante

H

Hablar, Ver Area De Comunicación

I

Interpretación, 3
    Razonamiento Abstracto, 3

J

Jitánfora, 94
Juego Electrónico, Ver Audiovisual

L

Lectura, 2, 97, 103
Leer, 3, 4, 102, Ver También Areas
      De Comunicación
Leyenda, 167
Literatura, 165

M

Maestro, 176
Material, 165
   De Referencia, 172
      Diccionario, 172
      Enciclopedia, 172
   Internet, 172
   Informativo, 165
   Narrativo, 165
   Persuasivo O Argumentativo, 165
   Textos, 165
Mecanismo Sensorial, 2
   Auditivo, 2
   Tacto, 2
   Visual, 2
Minoría Cultural, 10
Motivación, 177

O

Oir, Ver Areas De Comunicación

P

Padres, 179
Palabra, Ver Símbolo Escrito
Periódico, 173
Pluralismo Cultural, 12

Poesía, 95
Proceso Cerebral, 2
Proverbio, 168

R

Razonamiento Abstracto, Ver Interpretación
Refrán, 168
Regionalismo, 175
Retahila, 170
Revista, 174

S

Signo, Ver Símbolo Escrito
Sílaba, 90
Símbolo Escrito, 106
   Signo, 106
   Palabra, 106
Sistema Gráfico, 11
Sonido, 88
Spanglish, 99

T

Tex-Mex, 99
Trabalengua, 94, 169
Triptongo, 91
T.V., Ver Audiovisual

V

Video, Ver Audiovisual
Vocal, 89
   Abierta, 90
   Cerrada, 90